The American Short
Story Handbook

Wiley Blackwell Literature Handbooks

This new series offers the student thorough and lively introductions to literary periods, movements, and, in some instances, authors and genres, from Anglo-Saxon to the Postmodern. Each volume is written by a leading specialist to be invitingly accessible and informative. Chapters are devoted to the coverage of cultural context, the provision of brief but detailed biographical essays on the authors concerned, critical coverage of key works, and surveys of themes and topics, together with bibliographies of selected further reading. Students new to a period of study or to a genre will discover all they need to know to orientate and ground themselves in their studies, in volumes that are as stimulating to read as they are convenient to use.

Published

The Science Fiction Handbook
M. Keith Booker and Anne-Marie Thomas

The Seventeenth-Century Literature Handbook
Marshall Grossman

The Twentieth-Century American Fiction Handbook
Christopher MacGowan

The British and Irish Short Story Handbook
David Malcolm

The Crime Fiction Handbook
Peter Messent

The Literary Theory Handbook, second edition
Gregory Castle

The Anglo-Saxon Literature Handbook
Mark C. Amodio

The American Short Story Handbook
James Nagel

The American Short Story Handbook

James Nagel

WILEY Blackwell

This edition first published 2015
© 2015 James Nagel

Registered Office
John Wiley & Sons Ltd, The Atrium, Southern Gate, Chichester, West Sussex, PO19 8SQ, UK

Editorial Offices
350 Main Street, Malden, MA 02148-5020, USA
9600 Garsington Road, Oxford, OX4 2DQ, UK
The Atrium, Southern Gate, Chichester, West Sussex, PO19 8SQ, UK

For details of our global editorial offices, for customer services, and for information about how to apply for permission to reuse the copyright material in this book please see our website at www.wiley.com/wiley-blackwell.

The right of James Nagel to be identified as the author of this work has been asserted in accordance with the UK Copyright, Designs and Patents Act 1988.

Library of Congress Cataloging-in-Publication Data

Nagel, James, author.
  American short story handbook / James Nagel.—First edition.
    pages cm.—(Wiley Blackwell literature handbooks)
  Includes bibliographical references and index.
  ISBN 978-0-470-65541-2 (hardback)—ISBN 978-0-470-65542-9 (paper) 1. Short stories, American—History and criticism—Handbooks, manuals, etc. I. Title.
  PS374.S5N336 2015
  813'.0109—dc23

                                                                    2014032718

A catalogue record for this book is available from the British Library.

Cover image: Gwen Nagel, *Freedom, New Hampshire*, watercolor.
Part opening image: © duncan1890 / iStockphoto

Set in 10/13pt SabonLTStd by Laserwords Private Limited, Chennai, India

1 2015

Contents

Preface

In her capacity as an editor at Blackwell, Emma Bennett suggested to me that I do this volume in the Handbook series the company was developing, and I am grateful for her encouragement and support. The entire production staff at Blackwell assisted me with tasks large and small and did so with grace, courtesy, and professionalism, and it was a pleasure to work with them.

My work on the short story has been assisted beyond measure by my position as the J. O. Eidson Distinguished Professor of American Literature at the University of Georgia, an appointment I enjoyed for more than two decades until my retirement in 2013. Serving as the inaugural scholar in that professorship has been the greatest honor of my life, and I am deeply humbled by the generosity of the Eidson family and the University of Georgia.

My doctoral students at the University of Georgia, many of whom have gone on to fine positions, contributed in many ways to my work on American fiction, none more so than Katherine Barrow, who, as a graduate student, served for many years as my research assistant. Her skills as a determined scholar, able to explore the dark and remote regions of the university library, will serve her well throughout her career in the field. Among my colleagues in the department, Hugh Ruppersburg and Hubert McAlexander offered wise counsel over the many years we worked together, and they have my deepest respect and gratitude. Steven Florczyk, Nicole Camastra, Robert Clark, Jon Dawson, and Katherine Barrow all completed their Ph.D. programs with me during the research for this volume, and I have learned a great deal about American literature, and life, from them. At Dartmouth College, where I now enjoy the position of Visiting Scholar, Donald Pease has offered friendship, guidance, and a tour of the campus. William C. Scott was especially gracious in providing encouragement and introductions to people on the research staff of Dartmouth Library, and I am forever appreciative of his generous humanity.

Among my fellow scholars in the American Literature Association, and especially in the Society for the Study of the American Short Story, an organization I serve as president, I have my greatest debt for encouragement, informed advice, and warm fellowship over more than three decades, particularly from Alfred Bendixen, Oliver Scheiding, Jeanne Reesman, Gloria Cronin, Donald Pizer, Jerome Loving, and Gary Scharnhorst. My most profound gratitude goes, as always, to my wife, Gwen, who is a constant source of humane good counsel and meticulous proofreading, and the example of her dedication to her art is a source of inspiration every day, as it has been for the last five decades.

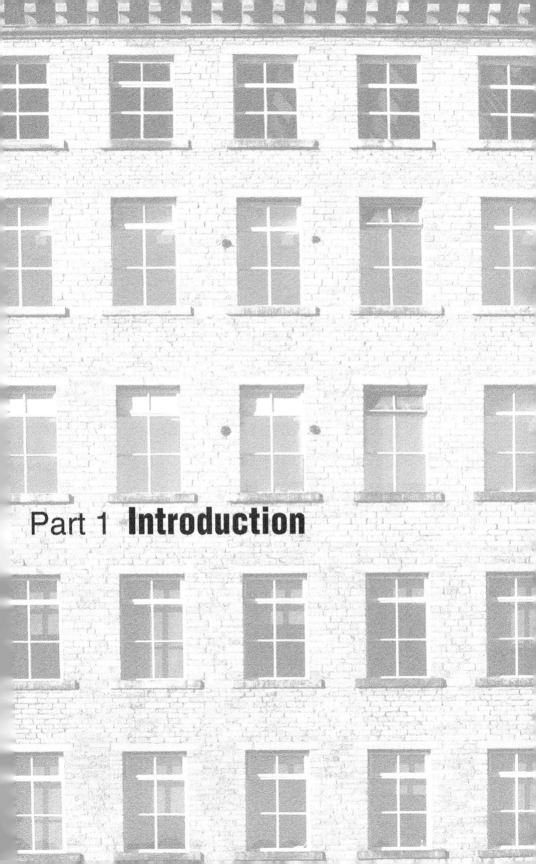

Part 1 **Introduction**

I am delighted that this book has appeared in the series of volumes published by Wiley- Blackwell covering the entire sweep of American letters, from
the earliest colonial period to the most recent contemporary literature. My
book can claim a special significance because although scores of studies of
the novel of the United States have appeared over the past century, many of
them distinguished works of serious scholarship, relatively few full-length
histories have been written about the short story since Fred Lewis Pattee published *The Development of the American Short Story: An Historical Survey*
in 1923. It is difficult to explain this curious lacuna in literary investigation,
but some of the neglect of the genre has been because of the general assumption that the story is a minor fictional partner in a field dominated by the
more important "novel."

Many recent developments have begun to challenge the validity of that
premise, including the establishment of the Society for the Study of the American Short Story, a vibrant organization of scholars that I am pleased to
serve as president. That group functions within the American Literature
Association, directed by the masterful leadership of Alfred Bendixen. The
professional students of literature within that society have produced an enormous body of serious scholarship on short fiction, and the genre has at last
begun to receive the attention it deserves. The form of the story is much
older than that of the novel, reaching back before the birth of Christ, and it
played an important role in cultural expression and preservation for centuries before the first "novel" appeared, and for that reason, and many
others, it deserves a seminal place in the study of American literature. This
book is also important in that it is the first study of the genre to take into
consideration the hundreds of examples of short fiction that appeared in

The American Short Story Handbook, First Edition. James Nagel.
© 2015 James Nagel. Published 2015 by John Wiley & Sons, Ltd.

America in the eighteenth century. These early stories addressed many of the most salient issues of the day, including the abolition of slavery, the status of Native Americans, the role of women in the formation of a new country, and the definition of an "American," what values and standards are to be associated with such a person. These vastly important matters in the early story have not received serious attention in any previous literary history.

From the beginning of human history, even the earliest records of emerging civilizations demonstrate the importance of narrative tales in charting the background of a given cultural group, presenting the myths that offer explanations for the origin of the universe, preserve fundamental values, and explain the meaning of life. A story is a window on a society, and before it pass the people of that culture, speaking in their own dialect, discussing the issues of the day, and struggling with the human conflicts central to that period of history. Looking through that window is entertaining and instructive, though it is not always easy to understand the meaning of what is going on. Cultures are complex entities, with assumptions deeply embedded below the surface. A story presents an opportunity to examine things more closely, to think about what values and traditions rest behind the actions of the characters, to weigh the wisdom of accepted standards of behavior and decorum.

The earliest forms of narrative seem to have been extremely important and reach as far back as to primitive societies. The "myth," for example, evolved as an important ancient convention because it could explain the ways of the gods and the reasons for natural events. Myths could also build cultural pride by recording the glorious accomplishments of ancestral figures, accounts that also emphasized central values exemplified in the life of the hero. A related narrative form is the "legend," which was less speculative and supernatural than the myth and more closely tied to cultural history. As a new country, America was free to establish a fresh catalog of legends based on historical personages who could plausibly be said to have exhibited some form of virtue or initiative. The account of George Washington, who, unable to tell a lie, once threw a coin across the Potomac River, is among the early national legends.

"Parables" are an ancient form of storytelling, reaching back to early Greek rhetoricians, that illustrated some religious virtue a society wished to preserve in the young. The Christian Bible contains many such narratives, the most famous being the parable of the prodigal son. This tradition is patently didactic in substance, teaching and sustaining modes of thought and behavior that a given society wishes to emphasize. They are thus closely related to the "fable," from which the parables were differentiated in that the former features anthropomorphic animals as characters. Told in either prose or verse, they entertained children and instructed them about the dangers of the world and the rewards of virtue. Aesop recorded his famous collection sometime around 600 B.C., and other fables were popular in medieval English literature as well, as the works of Geoffrey Chaucer make clear. The emphasis on animal characters links the fable to Native American tales, which animated and gave voice to nature in all of its forms.

Until the development of written languages, these early "stories" were not recorded in any precise manner but passed on from one generation to the next verbally, no doubt changing style and substance somewhat with each successive telling. These oral traditions are important in the formation of the genre of the "story" because they gave shape to how a tale could be told, how someone had to give voice to the account, how the events recited would be presented in a certain order and would somehow conclude in a satisfying way. Vocal recitations are perhaps a more important consideration in American literature than in most of the countries of the world because although some cultures established a means of written, or carved, recorded history several thousand years before the birth of Christ, Native American cultures were still essentially vocal when Europeans arrived in North America, and the indigenous spoken accounts quickly merged into the written languages the new settlers brought with them, especially Spanish, French, and British immigrants. What is unique about the history of the short story in English is that it constitutes a blending of narrative traditions from a broad spectrum of sources and languages and a means of presenting characters, action, and speech inherited from virtually every country of the world.

Perhaps for this reason, the story flourished in America as it had nowhere else in the world, and its earliest manifestations were linked to the oral tradition. A "yarn," even when it was written, implied that it was spoken by a narrator to an immediate audience that who could interact with the teller, sometimes interrupting with extraneous or even insulting remarks. The emphasis was not so much on the tale as on the person talking, on the personality of the speaker, who might be sincere or have tongue in cheek, who might not believe the truth of what he is saying. This manner of recitation is captured in American literary history as part of the early humor traditions and, at least for a few years, as part of the Local Color method of storytelling. Mark Twain's most famous tale, "The Celebrated Jumping Frog of Calaveras County," exemplifies how this early vocal method could be successfully adapted into a written literature. Yarns were generally told not by a learned Eastern sophisticate but by an old codger who spoke a regional dialect that was entertaining in itself. Most of them are essentially humorous in tone, and nearly all are brief and conclude with some kind of "snapper" that evokes laughter from the gathered folk.

Another early form was the "anecdote," which is a very brief narrative account of something that actually happened to a real person or, occasionally, an exchange of comments between two characters. Such presentations have the feel of being oral in origin and of capturing an action or a personality. Reaching back in history, perhaps the earliest published collection of anecdotes was Plutarch's *Lives of the Noble Greeks and Romans*, which schoolchildren were obliged to read for many generations. In America, local events provided more than sufficient material for the anecdotes that ran in the newspapers and magazines in virtually every issue in the eighteenth and nineteenth centuries. As part of the pre-story continuum, anecdotes contributed unified plots with a concentrated focus on one event, which perhaps led to the controlled structure of the American form after Edgar Allan Poe. They also captured the vernacular in print decades before tales in regional dialects became a popular fictional form.

In the mid-nineteenth century, the role of the yarn quickly gave way to the "tale," a longer narrative that retained the emphasis on the manner of telling. Tales were longer than yarns and put more stress on plots, on events that often seemed improbable but were thrilling to hear about, backwoods hunters killing huge grizzly bears, for example. Tales strain credulity, and the more tenuous the hold on reality, the better. By the middle of the nineteenth century, magazines ran them in virtually every issue, and the nation found them entertaining, although most often they were not instructive. By the end of the century, however, the popularity of the form had run its course.

All of these early fictional methods contributed to what became regarded as the modern "story," a form of literature more easily described than defined. It could be said that the most direct influence on the beginning of the formal story in America is Daniel Defoe's "A True Relation of the Apparition of One Mrs. Veal," which appeared in England in 1706 and was quickly followed by imitations appearing in the newly founded magazines that had become standard reading. It was four decades later that the earliest stories were published in America, beginning with Benjamin Franklin's "The Speech of Polly Baker" in 1747.

To facilitate the study of the complex history of the American story, this Handbook begins with a Historical Overview that examines the broad sweep of American short fiction from its earliest beginnings in the eighteenth century to the contemporary period. It traces the subjects of interest to the early reading public at the time of the Revolutionary War, especially the hundreds of works that concentrated on the key issues being considered in the formation of a constitution, a new set of values to guide the functioning of a liberal democracy, including the roles to be played by women and ethnic minorities. Beyond subject, the rudimentary nature of early storytelling yields a fascinating study of difficulties in melding action and dialogue, of telling a narrative from a comprehensible point of view, and of presenting characters who were interesting and believable. These concerns then merge into the more mature literary period of American Romanticism, with its attempts to capture in literature something of the grand Truth about human existence, the meaning of evil, the spiritual essence in Nature that gave rise to the movement of Transcendentalism. The language of the stories of this period tends to be formal, elevated beyond the discourse of common society, and the authors included references to events and figures in classical literature, assuming an educated audience. This era produced some monumental short stories that earned the United States a new respect in the international world of cultural expression, a period that has been described in literature history as the American Renaissance.

The Civil War changed the nature of American life, including the literary traditions that emerged from that cataclysmic event. If the conflict itself was monumental, the fiction that followed it was in some senses small: it was told in the everyday language of common people, not in the elevated lexicon of the elite, and it assumed that the audience was the general population of the country. It featured characters who seemed ordinary, "real" in the sense that they resembled the people who were encountered in the course of a routine day. These characters struggled not with the quest for eternal truth, no doubt a worthy subject to be explored, but with the ethical conflicts that arise from social and political life, struggles that have to do with doing what seems right, with acting from conscience, with fair dealings with others, in short with fundamental values about how to treat individual human beings.

Those kinds of issues in the short story merged into the Modern era following World War I, a period of disillusionment for soldiers returning from the war and of unparalleled prosperity at home until the Great Depression beginning in 1929. The 1930s, of course, were years of hardship, of widespread unemployment, dust storms, drought, and despair. Ironically, World War II, for all its vast destruction, nevertheless drew the country out of its economic doldrums as the production of equipment and ammunition for the war, new methods of agriculture and industrial mechanization paved the way for the resurgence of American society following the conclusion of hostilities in 1945. The contemporary period is perhaps too close to be described with any accuracy, but in the short story one of the outstanding features has been the inclusion of writers from a wide spectrum of ethnic groups within American society, dominated by women authors of the genre, and exploring a range of issues unique to a postmodern age. Nonetheless, one of the most outstanding features in the contemporary age has been the prevalence of the short story, a form that in two centuries of development

finally joined the novel as the most popular and important genre in literature. Collectively, however, writers of varying ethnic backgrounds, religious
orientation, and countries of national origin have combined to produce the
rich complexity of the American story, a tradition of tragedy, power, insight,
and sensitivity that has helped define American identity.

The next section of the book discusses many of the individual writers of
short stories whose work made a permanent contribution to literary history, authors drawn from the earliest years of the nineteenth century to the
most recent period. These writers are explored not only for their contributions of individual tales but also for a body of work in the genre that
advanced the parameters of what the form could do and how it could do it.
The most rudimentary efforts in the telling of stories, for example, were no
longer acceptable to the reading public once they had encountered Washington Irving's "Rip Van Winkle" in 1819. His method of narration, the ironic
and playful tone in which he describes the area around the Hudson River
in New York, his deft drawing of charming and yet humorous characters
forever changed the direction of fiction. The chapter on Irving thus begins
the consideration of American writers of the short story as a rich and vital
subject.

That chapter is followed by a similar, if somewhat more detailed, discussion of individual stories that have been of sufficient significance to earn
a place in literary history, beginning with Benjamin Franklin's remarkable
"The Speech of Polly Baker" in 1747 and continuing into the twenty-first
century. These stories demonstrate a range of greatness in that there is no
single subject that dominates the focus of them, no area of the country that
is more important than the rest, no method of telling that made traditional
styles outmoded. The United States is a heterogeneous society, to be sure,
and its literature reflects the vast spectrum of cultural traditions from which
its writers could draw inspiration.

The final parts of the book present a glossary defining the most common
terms used in literary history and in critical discussions of fiction. Here a
student beginning the study of the genre could come to understand the differences between a parable and a fable or the distinctions to be drawn between a
tale and a story. These terms are not presented to resolve intellectual contro-
versies within learned societies but rather to establish a baseline from which
students could begin their own consideration of literary history. The final
section offers a substantial list of books that are worthy of serious scrutiny
in an effort to fully understand the American short story. Such a list also
suggests that this volume is only a starting point for such an investigation,
one that can reward a lifetime of engaging study.

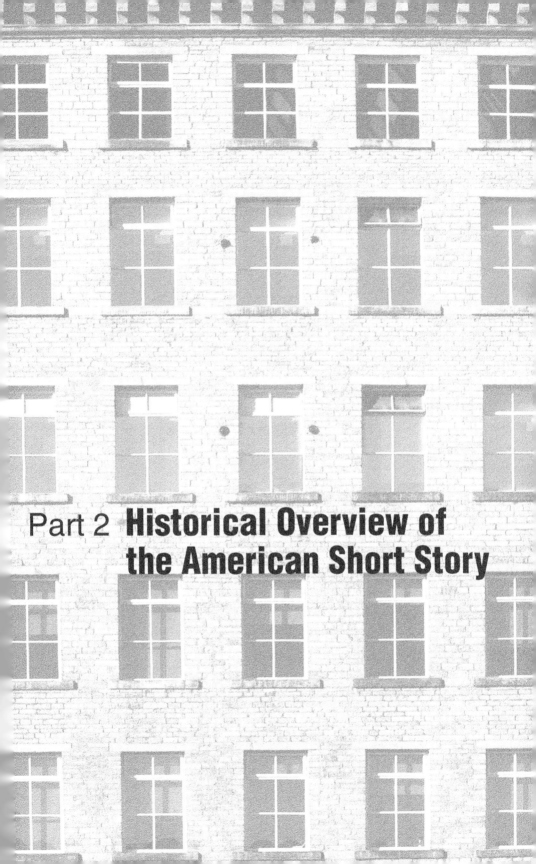

Part 2 **Historical Overview of
the American Short Story**

The development of the short story in the eighteenth century in America signaled the beginning of a long and vital literary tradition that reveals much about the basic ideas that energized the Revolutionary War and the founding of a new country. As a society of immigrants that had roots primarily in European countries that were monarchies, dictatorships, czarist states, or other forms of strongly centralized political power, the United States organized itself according to the principle of a weak federal government with primary authority in the individual states and in a free citizenry that elected officials who were sworn to serve the interests of the people, not of a ruling oligarchy. Even the most humble persons in this new country possessed powers unimaginable in most of the world: the right to own land and property; the right to bear arms; the right to keep the fruits of their own labor. Even more important than their rights, they had significant autonomy, beginning with the freedom from foreign domination, from taxation (the constitution did not give the federal government the power to tax the people), from conscription into military service, and from the intrusion of political officials into their private lives. The common individual was the prime entity of power in this new society, and from the first century or more of its existence, that point was made explicitly clear through the limitations placed on the reach of administrative control. In an important sense, even the most humble citizen mattered in this new political system. A culture that so values individuals is one that might very well endorse a type of literature that focuses on people and generates narratives that record the events and conflicts that they face in their everyday lives, and that form was the short story.

The American Short Story Handbook, First Edition. James Nagel.
© 2015 James Nagel. Published 2015 by John Wiley & Sons, Ltd.

The American Story
to Washington Irving

Of all the genres, the short story is the one that is most difficult to deal with in terms of origins. In part this is true because of the prevalence of oral traditions of anecdotes, personal accounts, biographical narratives, and raucous scatological humor. Families tell stories all the time, and so do societies. If the form is to be dealt with in its printed manifestation, it is easier to trace, although even then the influence of Europe makes its earliest appearances somewhat problematic. Stories appeared in European newspapers and magazines and were quickly reprinted in the colonies, sometimes with minor changes in place names and other details. But a few points of demarcation can be established. The first publication in English of what might be regarded as a short story was Daniel Defoe's "A True Relation of the Apparition of One Mrs. Veal," which appeared in Britain in 1706. It recounts how the ghost of a woman who has died earlier that day nevertheless acts in a perfectly ordinary way in coming to tea with a close friend who has not heard about her demise. They have a pleasant chat. Although it has decided Gothic elements, this tale has a strong narrative line, dialogue, and a shocking ending when the truth of the situation is revealed. Since England had established magazines during the reign of Queen Anne in the early eighteenth century, there were outlets for short fiction somewhat earlier than in America, although the *The Boston Gazette* appeared in 1719 and the *The New York Weekly Journal* in 1733. By mid-century there were fledgling magazines in all the major cities on the eastern seaboard, although none below what would later be known as the Mason-Dixon line until 1797 when the *South Carolina Weekly* emerged

The American Short Story Handbook, First Edition. James Nagel.
© 2015 James Nagel. Published 2015 by John Wiley & Sons, Ltd.

in Charleston. It could be said, however, that the early tradition in short fiction thus had an understandable northern and eastern bias that reflected the growth of a cultivated population along the Atlantic coast.

In any event, in 1747 Benjamin Franklin published what is regarded as the first story by an American author, although it appeared first in London prior to coming out in the New World a few weeks later. Although it is a humorous tale, largely in the form of a monologue before a judge by a woman who has had a child out of wedlock, it is a masterful piece of social satire aimed at the hypocrisy of a legal system that pretends to an elevated standard of conduct while even the magistrates who administer the law deviate from its rigid proscriptions. Appearing in the Age of Reason, it is also a masterful demonstration of the systematic use of logic and common sense in rational discourse, a presentation that is so persuasive that the woman not only wins her argument but is married the next day to one of the judges hearing the case. It also demonstrated that gender places no limitations on intellectual engagement, that a simple, uneducated woman from the lower classes might nevertheless be fully capable of intelligent disputation, and that such a woman may reveal herself to be an admirable mother who loves her children, works hard to support them, and proves worthy of the admiration of society. These themes were important in the foundation of a culture that was still a subservient colony in 1747, and Franklin would be instrumental in ensuring that these ideas were incorporated into the founding documents of the emerging United States a few decades later.

Another important early story in the colonial period is "Adventure of a Young English Officer among the Abenakee Savages," which came out in the *Royal American Magazine* in 1775, just before the outbreak of the Revolutionary War. As a work of literature, this tale featured a strong narrative line, a conflict and resolution, action and dialogue, and an important humanistic theme. In terms of subject, it dealt with an incident in the French and Indian War, which ranged from 1756 to 1764, and pitted the English against the French and their Native American allies, in this case the Abenakee, an indigenous tribe that ranged across Maine and southern Quebec. The situation is that the Indians have overwhelmed an English unit, killing all but a badly wounded officer, whom they are about to dispatch when the chief intervenes and not only saves the life of the young man but takes him home for convalescence. He teaches the young officer their language and much about their culture, and when, after many months, the officer is well enough to travel, he sends him home to England. In a moving speech, the chief explains that he has saved the life of the young man because his own son was killed by the British, and he has grieved for him ever since. When he saw the officer about to be killed, he realized that somewhere in England there was a father waiting for him to come home, and should the officer be killed, the father would never again enjoy the beauty of life, the rising of the sun, the feel of the gentle wind. It is significant that the protagonist is not the British officer but the Indian. He is the character who experiences the most dramatic internal growth, moving from intense grief to compassion, and it is he who makes the most important decisions. The officer is passive, with little character development. He is more the occasion for the story than the subject of it. Even before the Revolutionary War, the humanness of Native Americans had become a subject for fiction in the New World, and it would be difficult to find a more sterling character than this chief who exhibits empathy for a father in a distant country he wishes to save from the despair he himself has known himself.

After the Revolutionary War, the number of magazines increased at a rapid rate, although their success was hindered because initially the postal regulations would not allow them to be mailed, so they sold in bookstores and on street corners. In the eighteenth century, the interest in the role of the Native American in the new society continued to be a prime subject for fictional tales, many of them devoted not simply to events but to defining the moral character of the aboriginal peoples who had lived on the continent for roughly ten- thousand years. The portrait that emerges from scores of early stories is invariably laudatory, as it is in "Indian Fidelity," a tale about a brave who is asked to deliver a message from his chief to an American major. Unknown to the brave does not know that the major has become ill and has been moved to upstate New York. Undaunted, the indian sets out to walk for nearly a week in order to deliver the letter, which inspires the omniscient narrator to applaud the dedication the man has shown and his steadfast devotion to principle. A more typical account, because the captivity narrative was a popular form, is William Richardson's "The Indians: A Tale," which appeared in 1798. In it a young woman is taken captive and lives as a prisoner among the Hurons and comes to admire their culture. They are portrayed as being both correct in their social behavior and dignified in stature, precisely the kind of citizens who should be welcomed into mainstream society. Scores of such stories appeared in the early newspapers and magazines, educating the reading public about the native peoples who lived near them.

Another early topic of enormous importance was the abolition of slavery, a concept hotly debated even before the adopting of the Constitution of the United States. Indeed, Benjamin Franklin attempted to have abolition as one of the principles of the Articles of Confederation, which governed the country before the constitution was ratified. His attempt failed because of the opposition of the state of Virginia, which was dependent on slavery for its agricultural economy. Nonetheless, American writers of the time, most of them anonymous, continually pressed the issue in stories. One entitled "Anecdote" featured a black man arguing that his master had, in effect, purchased stolen property, that he had belonged to himself he was captured and forced into servitude. Since his children have also been enslaved, he argues that they represent appropriated assets that belong to their parents, not to the plantation owners. The logic was inescapable, and the case was won. Inherent in this simple narrative is the black man's intelligent and persuasive handling of an ethical and legal point, one with enormous significance for the newly formed country. This thinking quickly became widespread, and many of the New England states banned slavery in the late eighteenth century, as did New York and New Jersey. It should be remembered that some of the Southern states also harbored these sentiments, as represented by the fact that the original constitution of Georgia, written in 1730, forbade slavery in the colony.

Short fiction on the subject became popular, some of it introducing events that would be repeated in literature for more than two centuries. For example, a key plot point of "Intrepidity of a Negro Woman," published in the *Massachusetts Magazine* in 1791, included the birth of a baby during the middle passage, and rather than see the child live in slavery, the mother throws it overboard. This powerful incident was included in Harriet Beecher Stowe's abolitionist novel *Uncle Tom's Cabin* and, more than a century later, in Toni Morrison's *Beloved* in 1987. Another story in the same magazine, "The Wretched Taillah: An African Story," featured the situation of intelligent people of noble birth and high moral character who are captured by slave traders. In "The Negro," a white narrator becomes aware of a slave's longing for a woman left behind in Africa, and it inspires in the white man a reflection on how he would feel were he separated from his wife. This awareness of the parallel human emotions for people of different races is driven home through dialogue that ends with the narrator making a direct plea for the recognition of the human quality of African slaves. These early works of short fiction were obviously didactic in purpose and polemical in method, but they were a call for social improvement through a stinging indictment of people "who call themselves civilized." Indeed, the underlying concept behind the tradition of these stories was anti-racist, calling for a recognition of the intrinsic worth of people from all cultures and ethnicities, a principle fundamental to the founding values of the United States.

Many other subjects energized the early American short story, including the compelling drama of military conflict. Since the Revolutionary War was taking place during the inception of these narratives, it was inevitable that the rebellion should be covered by the new genre. Since war is not only a political conflict but disrupts and changes domestic life as well, these two issues were often linked in the plot structures at the center of the narratives. "The Calamities of War, and the Effects of Unbridled Passion," which was published in the *Boston Magazine* in 1784, is representative of these tales. Martius is a young husband devoted to his wife, but he nonetheless serves the revolutionary forces as an officer. As was common in that age, his wife, Sophia, joins him at the front, serving him meals and seeing to his needs. When he is mortally wounded, he lives long enough to tell her that her brother was the soldier who shot him, but he forgives him and understands that he was doing his duty. The brother is impressed with the nobility of this sentiment and swears to assist his sister in raising her infant son. The thematic center thus shifts from military conflict to domestic loyalties, issues pertinent to a conflict in which families were sometimes divided in their political allegiances.

As was the case with "Polly Baker," the early story was preoccupied with courtship and family issues, and it often dealt with sexual matters rather frankly. For example, in "Amelia; or, The Faithless Briton," which appeared in the *Columbian Magazine, or Monthly Miscellany* in 1787, an innocent American girl is seduced and abandoned by a British rogue who takes advantage of her trust. Although the plot became a standard one for novels and stories, this romantic tale demonstrates an advance in the art of narrative in that it features realistic dialogue that moves events forward rather rapidly. It also employs temporal shifts that show simultaneous events in two different locations, a device that did not become common for more than a century. In 1789, Thomas Bellamy's "The Fatal Effects of Seduction, Exemplified in a Letter from the Reformed Edmund, to His Friend" also depicted how vile sexual corruption leads to inevitable tragedy, although the death of a the young maiden brings about a transformation on the part of her seducer. However, "Three Days after Marriage: or, the History of Ned Easy and Mrs. Manlove. A Story Founded in Fact," introduces a twist in the standard account by introducing a woman who is the one obsessed with sex and her husband who is, in a sense, the victim. Mrs. Manlove, as her name implies, has an insatiable appetite for amorous adventures, and her husband begs for relief after three days of continuous romance. He arranges for a friend to substitute for him and plans to sue for divorce on the basis of adultery.

Perhaps the best of the early works of short fiction is Ruri Colla's "The Story of the Captain's Wife and an Aged Woman," which was published in 1789. It also deals with adultery but in an inventive and mythological way, placing the events in the realm of the supernatural. A first-person tale, told by someone who heard it from a clergyman some years earlier, giving the account a dubious authenticity, it features a young wife whose husband sails away on long voyages. When he returns from a journey of many months, he finds a pregnant wife waiting for him on the wharf. He accuses her of adultery and says he will never set eyes upon her again. She begs to explain what has happened, and her account constitutes the rest of the narrative.

She says that after he departed, each day she walked to the wharf to look out to sea, hoping to see the sails of his ship coming home. One day an aged woman, skilled in sorcery, and impressed with her continuous longing for her husband, offered to grant the young woman a favor. The wife says she wanted nothing so much as to spend a night in bed with her husband. That night, she returned to the wharf where the aged woman transformed a half-bushel into a sailboat, and in a short time they were in England. She showed the wife the door to a house and said that her husband was dining within. The wife, who had been somewhat altered so that she could not be recognized, seated herself at his table and in due course he proposed to spend the night with her. She demanded as payment the unique knife and fork he had been using. Later, after he had fallen asleep, she left the house and quickly returned home with the aged woman. The husband does not believe this explanation, and he denies any wrongdoing on his part until the wife produces the knife and fork he gave her that night in England. He is shocked by the evidence of his indiscretion, and he confesses that he is the guilty party who has wrongly accused his wife, and they are reconciled. The story ends with the didactic observation that people should not condemn others for crimes they themselves commit.

The wife's spirited narrative of these marvelous events constitutes a rather complex tale that suggests several possible interpretations. The simplest is that her account is literally true, and she lives in a world with magical dimensions. Another explanation is that the wife was simply unfaithful and has fabricated a lie to conceal her indiscretion, although the knife and fork inconvenience this approach. Yet another possibility is that she was indiscreet but she also knows that he is unfaithful on his many voyages. She calculates that he loves her nonetheless and, in the context of her pregnancy, he would be grateful for any contingency that would allow their marriage to continue. This outlandish story, from this point of view, convinces no one but establishes a pretext upon which he can sustain their relationship without loss of face. Everything about this strategy is false, and yet it saves a marriage from dissolution.

The great masterpiece of the early history of the story in America is Washington Irving's "Rip Van Winkle," which has been widely read ever since it first appeared in *The Sketch Book of Geoffrey Crayon* in 1819. It represents a transition in literary history in several senses. It skillfully wove an ironic narrative voice together with compelling action, granting gentle humor to a marvelous tale. Perhaps for this reason, it was the first story published in the United States to be heralded on the continent as well as within America. Although it featured a putative author, Geoffrey Crayon, who claims not to have written it but to have found the manuscript in the documents of Diedrich Knickerbocker, the true author was known from the beginning. Irving was living in Europe when he adapted the German tale of Peter Klaus, a legendary sleeper, to an upstate New York setting and placed it at the time of the Revolutionary War. Escaping a nagging wife and the possibility that he might be asked to do some actual labor, Rip ambles into the mountains for a day of squirrel hunting where he encounters some small men in strange clothing carrying a keg of ale. He follows them to a celebration at which he drinks deeply, falls asleep, and awakens twenty years later. When he returns to his village, everything has changed. The portrait of King George has been replaced by one of George Washington; Rip's wife is dead and his children have grown into adulthood; and there is a new spirit to the local society, which has been energized by the transformation into a democracy, resulting in a lively citizenry engaged in the affairs of their village. What is most stunning about this marvelous account, however, is the skill of its telling, the satire and wry comedy of the portrait of Rip, the swift pace of the plot, and the refined style, all of which set the narrative apart from any short fiction that had appeared before. Irving was similarly successful in *The Sketch Book* with "The Legend of Sleepy Hollow," which rivals "Rip" as his most popular tale, and with "The Specter Bridegroom," which also contains supernatural elements in an entertaining narrative. In other volumes, his European stories, such as "The Adventure of a German Student" or "The Legend of the Moors," did not attract a wide audience in the United States.

As these few examples illustrate, from the very beginning short stories addressed subjects that were central to the issues of the day, a significant concept in a period that saw a major war against a colonial power, the formation of a new government based on principles that empowered common people rather than the aristocracy, enormous transitions in the conduct of social and domestic life, and a consideration for the character and rights of people of color, who were part of the conversation even before the constitution had been ratified. Other stories addressed a wide range of issues, the evils of gambling, for example, and relationships among agrarian neighbors, a matter more important now that the property belonged to the farmers and not to the lords. There was plenty of adventure in the fiction of the time, with captivity narratives, naval escapades, duels over issues of honor, and struggles, religious as well as moral, with matters of conscience.

The subjects of these early stories were vitally important to the forming of a new society, but the artistry expressing the basic ideas was slower to develop than the basic themes. Writing fiction was still not entirely a respectable enterprise, so the vast majority of early stories were anonymous. The point of view was, for the most part, handled crudely, with expository intrusions and didactic conclusions. Many writers found it difficult to integrate dialogue with narrative description, and some tales were entirely one or the other. As plots became more complex, with conflicts and resolutions, some stories featured flashbacks, simultaneous action, or duplicative time, devices that would not become standard fare until the twentieth century. In style, this period clung to the British idea that literature needed to be written in an elevated dialect, although there were a few experiments with rendering the vernacular, normally when rustics or ethnic minority characters were speaking. What is crucial in literary history, however, is the point that by the early nineteenth century, the short story had become a vibrant form, with hundreds of them appearing in scores of new magazines and newspapers, and they set the stage for the development of more sophisticated methods of storytelling in the decades to follow.

The Age of Romanticism

The Romantic period in American letters, which is generally regarded as covering the era from roughly 1820 to the end of the Civil War in 1865, reflected both broad intellectual changes in the assumptions about the nature of the universe and more local developments in the geographic and population growth of the United States, which tripled during these decades. In contravention of the Age of Reason, which assumed that a creator had withdrawn from the world once it was formed, the new feeling, inspired by European Pantheism as well as mystical ideas drawn from East Indian theology, was that the deity made the universe out of himself and therefore he was in it, spiritually present in every aspect of Nature. Codified in the new movement of Transcendentalism, this idea placed the emphasis not on logical processes but on intuition, which was a form of communication with the divine. Anyone was capable of sensing the sacred within Nature, and all were equal in this most important aspect of their lives, a point that underscored once again the democratic basis for the formation of a new country. The call for the abolition of slavery swelled decade after decade, and the result was the Civil War, fought from 1861 to 1865, beginning with the Confederate attack on Fort Sumter in Charleston Harbor.

At the beginning of the Romantic period, however, short stories were becoming ever more popular, and the growth of the magazine industry made them accessible. Although, in the early years, there was no formal definition of short fiction, the general trend was for plots with a single major character and a narrative line that moved forward to some kind of conclusion. Edgar Allan Poe finally provided the genre with a formal definition, stressing, above all, the concept of thematic, stylistic, and narrative unity toward a single effect, and his early stories illustrated the principle. Inspired by the

The American Short Story Handbook, First Edition. James Nagel.
© 2015 James Nagel. Published 2015 by John Wiley & Sons, Ltd.

French *novella*, some stories ran to impressive length, with greater character development and secondary plots, as did Herman Melville's "Benito Cereno," but the general trend remained aimed at control and concision.

Some writers, following in the tradition of "Rip Van Winkle," introduced mythic figures, as did the attorney William Austin in his tale "Peter Rugg, the Missing Man" in 1824. Both entertaining and instructive, this story focused on a man who swears an oath that he will get to Boston that very night or may he never get there. As he begins the journey with his daughter, a squall intensifies and he is unable to find his way. As a consequence, given his oath, he and his daughter become perpetual travelers, never stopping, forever attempting to find their way to Boston on a stormy night. They are spotted by numerous people over the decades, always asking which way to go and hurrying on their way, their black horse never seeming to tire. Austin's intriguing tale thus created an American legend of a mythic quester, a figure that reaches back to the Wandering Jew, the Flying Dutchman, and other perpetual seekers. His account was so compelling that it was repeated in other works throughout the century, including Nathaniel Hawthorne's "A Virtuoso's Collection," Stephen Vincent Benet's "John Brown's Body," Louise Imogen Guiney's "Peter Rugg, the Bostonian," and Edward Everett Hale's "Man without a Country." There was evidently something powerful about this entertaining tale based on the didactic admonition against tempting fate by making hasty vows for it became the most popular story of its period.

The regional humor traditions emerged during these years, becoming popular with a rapidly growing reading public and introducing some new character types such as the confidence man who sold snake oil or traded horses, the ring-tailed roarer who bragged about impossible conquests, and the hunter who killed giant bears with his hands. Beyond entertainment, such tall tales presented local dialects and personalities and captured the folkways of parts of the country that had not appeared in literature earlier. Although these attributes would later inspire the development of Realism, even before that movement such works as Thomas Bangs Thorpe's "The Big Bear of Arkansas," Augustus Baldwin Longstreet's "The Horse Swap," Davy Crockett's "Bear Hunting in Tennessee," and James Kirke Paulding's "Nimrod's Wildfire Tall Talk" became wildly popular in their portrayal of common folk.

The increase of interest in the story brought into the mainstream of American literature many female and minority authors who became more prominent than they had ever been before. For example, Francis Harper's "The Two Offers" appeared in 1859 as the first African American short story, and the eloquence of its language, the graceful interplay of exposition and dialogue, and the gentle introduction of racial themes were all widely admired. Since many of the early magazines were aimed at a female audience, stories dealing with issues pertinent to women began appearing on a regular basis, and Harriet Spofford's "Circumstance" and Elizabeth Stoddard's "The Prescription," along with many stories from Harriet Beecher Stowe, were part of the new emphasis.

Perhaps the most important writer of the period was Edgar Allan Poe in that he contributed not only scores of brilliant stories but a new theory to define the genre as well. His postulations that a well-crafted tale should exhibit both thematic coherence and aesthetic congruence established a new standard for assessing the form, and his own work demonstrated that even within such rigorous standards fiction could be both entertaining and instructive. Within those confines, Poe originated several sub-forms that became permanent fixtures within the form, including the detective story. His "The Murders in the Rue Morgue" and "The Purloined Letter," for example, established the tale of ratiocination in which the investigator captures the criminal not by brute force or superior weapons but through the exercise of perceptive reasoning. In the first story, C. Auguste Dupin never even sees the perpetrator, yet he cleverly uses induction to piece together clues that lead to the eventual identity of the murderer. In the second, he comes to the understanding that the document must be hidden in the most obvious place, in plain sight, rather than in the most obscure recesses of the room. "The Tell-Tale Heart," on the other hand, relies on a profound grasp of psychology to understand that guilt would haunt the murderer until he finally confessed. Similar motivation would seem to explain the detailed review of a crime committed decades ago by the narrator in "The Cask of Amontillado," which recounts in genteel language how he obtained revenge for a slight by walling in the offending party during a celebration in Venice. "The Fall of the House of Usher" drew on both European Gothic traditions and on an interest in psychological aberrations to form a haunting tale of mental illness. Poe's fiction retains all of its power and fascinating artistry nearly two centuries after it was written.

Nathaniel Hawthorne plays an important role in literary history not so much for the introduction of new forms of literature but for his introduction of original thematic material, much of it based on astonishing psychological insight. In an era suspicious of the heavy emphasis on science in the Age of Reason, in Hawthorne's stories scientists and physicians are portrayed as having pried into the sacred mysteries of life, attempting to discover, or alter, matters reserved for the deity. For example, in "The Birthmark," a scientist attempts to remove the only defect he can discover in his wife, a small birthmark. His manipulations seem born of excess pride and a single focus on physical features rather than on her inner qualities, her love and sensitivity and regard for others. This quest for perfection, driven by the obsession of the researcher, ultimately brings about her death. Similarly, in "Rappaccini's Daughter," a scientist has a daughter who seems to be a hybrid of human traits and those of a poisonous plant, and she is ultimately deadly to other persons. She becomes intrigued by a suitor, a young medical student, but that plot ends in death as well. Dr. Rappaccini has reached too far in his quest to improve human life through science and has had too little regard for the original beauty of creation. "Young Goodman Brown" introduces a theme presented in various formulations throughout Hawthorne's fiction, the concept of the "fortunate fall," the idea that being aware of one's own failings, a propensity for temptation and sin, can actually be beneficial in that it teaches one to be more accepting of the weaknesses of others, allows people to forgive themselves for common failures, and provides insight into the dual nature of humanity. The protagonist of this story, on a midnight journey through the forest during which he discovers a witches' Sabbath, becomes aware that his wife has her own weaknesses and is capable of sin, and it destroys him. He has no joy in life again, and he dies in misery. "My Kinsman, Major Molineux" is an allegory of an innocent young man starting out in the world who encounters temptation for the first time, much of it sexual. In a rare positive conclusion, however, he learns that he must accept the complexities of the world and make his own way in it. His encounter with evil has strengthened him for life in the city, for an engagement with the full range of humanity.

If the stature of Hawthorne and Poe is enormous for their numerous contributions to the development of the short story, Herman Melville's reputation rests on a few brilliant tales that are well-crafted and deal with monumental issues of the day. Perhaps the most important of those is "Benito Cereno," which is renowned both for its strong anti-slavery theme and for the deft utilization of historical context in what is essentially a psychological narrative. For his plot Melville drew on an account of a slave rebellion aboard ship by Captain Amasa Delano, entitled *Narrative of Voyages and Travels in the Northern and Southern Hemispheres Comprising Three Voyages Round the World: Together with a Voyage of Survey and Discovery*, which appeared in Boston in 1817. Using one detailed chapter recounting the facts of the insurrection, Melville placed the point of view of his narrative in Delano's mind, allowing the truth of a confusing situation to unwind slowly as the narrator comprehends the meaning of the events. Finally, the story illuminates the grotesque human damage wrought by slavery and the moral and psychological destruction it brings to all involved. In 1855, these were dramatically pertinent issues being discussed continuously in American society, and "Benito Cereno" quickly became part of that national discussion.

One of the most frequently taught works of short fiction in American literature is "Bartleby, the Scrivener," which Melville published in 1853. He knew a good deal about the practice of law in New York City because his brother Allan was an attorney with an office on Wall Street, and Herman would visit him there. In essence, the story recounts how a scrivener, a copier of legal records, progressively withdrew from his duties and from all activities of normal life, starring out the window at a brick wall, and eventually starved to death in a prison. What gives the narrative substance is that it is told, in retrospect, by the lawyer who employed Bartleby, and although he needs the services of all of his employees, he finds something deeply intriguing in the sense of emptiness, pointlessness, and resignation that the scrivener exhibits. An intelligent man, the lawyer is capable of searching his own mind and recognizing the degree to which Bartleby is but an exaggeration of the impulses that seem to invest his own life and, perhaps, that of all mankind. That interest in the tale has remained strong over all of the decades since it was originally published, the lawyer would seem to have been right: there is a universal appeal in Bartleby's strange and yet touching hopelessness.

If Hawthorne, Melville, and Poe occupy positions as the major writers of the short story in the Romantic period, there were other authors who made important contributions, sometimes anticipating developments to come after the Civil War. For example, although Harriet Beecher Stowe is often studied as part of the Local Color movement initiated by Mark Twain and Bret Harte, in fact her regional tales began appearing in the 1830s, well ahead of the stirrings of Realism and Naturalism. The first short fiction that carried her name as author was "A New England Sketch," published in *Western Monthly Magazine* in April of 1834, and even this early effort defined the geographic focus of her best work. A decade later, "The Yankee Girl" further developed this interest with a protagonist who is a New England woman who refuses the proposal of a wealthy Canadian gentleman because she does not wish to become his decorative ornament. Many of her best stories appeared in volumes with nostalgic titles such as *Oldtown Folks*, *Oldtown Fireside Stories*, or *The Minister's Wooing*, which recounts the courtship of a man of the cloth and his housekeeper. Many of these tales are narrated by Sam Lawson, a continuing figure whose use of language, knowledge of localized customs, and mastery of the oral tradition made him a popular fictional personality in the nineteenth century. Although Stowe's work suffered from didactic intrusions, moral lessons, and sentimental religious instruction, it also captured the humor of New England, the dialects of the area, the character of village folk, and the central values that invest their lives.

Frances Ellen Watkins Harper's "The Two Offers," first published in 1859, is widely believed to have been the first short story written by an African

American, although her tale is remarkably free of racial indicators. That fact is even more strange in that the state of Maine sponsored her lecture tour on the abolition of slavery, the temperance movement, the rights of women, and the virtue of marriage as an equal partnership, all of which were central to the founding of the Republican Party, the political home for African Americans in this period. Although she would go on to a distinguished career covering all of these matters, especially in her volume *Sketches of Southern Life*, her first story is focused almost exclusively on courtship and marriage. The central conflicts of the plot are not developed dramatically but are handled in exposition, with the narrator summarizing the stress placed on young women to marry and have children, the danger that drinking poses for a happy home, and the obligation that men assume to provide for their families. Some writers of the period gave the domestic scene a more threatening representation, as did Harriet Spofford in "Circumstance," in which there is a threat to a woman's life. Elizabeth Stoddard dealt with mental pathology in marriage in "The Prescription" resulting from a domineering husband, an issue that would be more directly explored during the period of Realism.

The decades of American Romanticism were vitally important in the growth of the short story in that the number of magazines, gift books, newspapers, and other outlets not only increased but became more stable. Very few of the earliest periodicals survived more than two years, having exhausted their initial funding. More established venues for short fiction allowed authors to focus on them as part of their long-range creative plans, and scores of stories appeared that became a permanent part of American literature. Indeed, it was fiction that lead to the realization that the United States had established a cultural center, joining the European nations in the world of letters, as testified to by the fact that an English writer, Mary Russell Mitford, published a three-volume edition of American stories. These were the last great works of short fiction to rely on allegory as a literary mode, to concentrate on Gothic elements as part of the setting, to use symbolism and personification to universalize characters and conflicts, and to develop themes that dealt with revealing the secrets of humanity or the universe. Nothing quite so grand would appear in the years after the Civil War. But the Romantics also addressed more earthly matters, including slavery and the rights of women, the status of Native Americans, and the vagaries of human psychology.

Realism and Naturalism

The period of Realism and Naturalism in America was the most important era in the history of the short story, for it was during the decades from 1865, the end of the Civil War, to 1918, the end of World War I, that the genre became the dominant force in literature. To some extent, this development was the result of changes in science and technology. The establishment of the telephone and telegraph made possible the publishing syndicate, so that scores of magazines and newspapers could run the same story on the same day. The royalties for stories suddenly became many times what they had been just a few years earlier. Advances in public education, the swelling of the population as a result of immigration, and a new era of economic prosperity all contributed to a much larger reading public, and the form of choice was short fiction. Even the novels of the day appeared chapter by chapter, in sections designed to be read at a single sitting, a hallmark of the tale, and story cycles, volumes in which the individual stories derived unity with the others through continuing characters, a common setting, a unifying narrator, or developing themes, became a popular form for the first time.

Intellectual changes helped bring the Realistic story to the fore as well. In the wake of the horrible destruction of the war, it was difficult for people to believe in a benevolent deity who watched over humanity and protected everyone from harm. A new skepticism swept the country, as reason once again replaced faith as a guide to a good life, and the mysterious spiritual inquiries of the Romantics gave way to the reality that the folk lived in throughout their lives, the world "in the light of common day." One particular concern was for the reunification of the regions of the country because the United States had become one nation again, legally if not in spirit. The westward migration, which stretched all the way from the Alleghenies to

The American Short Story Handbook, First Edition. James Nagel.
© 2015 James Nagel. Published 2015 by John Wiley & Sons, Ltd.

the Pacific Ocean, gave settlers from virtually all of the European nations an opportunity to make a promising life for themselves and enjoy the prosperity that hard work and personal discipline was bringing to millions of new citizens. Even on the prairie, one-room schoolhouses, normal schools, quickly appeared in the midst of homestead farms, and rural children became readers and consumers of literature.

To serve this population, new magazines began publication following the war, beginning with *Galaxy* in 1866. Soon, periodicals that would become household names found their place on the newsstands: *Overland Monthly, Scribner's Monthly*, the *The Atlantic Monthly*, the *The Ladies Home Journal, Harper's Monthly*, and scores of other monthlies flooded the bookstores. The first wave of short fiction to find its place in these new periodicals was Local Colorism. Growing out of the humor traditions, particularly those devoted to the Southwest and the Northeast, regional fiction used the vernacular, the everyday language of common folk, for the purposes of literary art, rejecting the elevated lexicon of Romanticism. Although early in the movement the standard narrative method was to present a sophisticated frame narrator who turned over the telling to a old codger speaking in his regional dialect, that frame narrator quickly disappeared, leaving local characters to tell their own stories from beginning to end. The tendency for these tales was either humor, reaching back to the earlier tradition, or sentimentality, although the gradual progression was to address more serious subjects until, finally, it engaged the most serious issues of the day: racism, the suppression of women, various forms of social prejudice.

Local Color fiction is generally regarded as having begun with the publication of "The Celebrated Jumping Frog of Calaveras County," a shaggy-dog story in which the frame narrator is tricked into listening to Simon Wheeler deliver an interminable, digressive tale filled with improbable events and irrelevant characters. The frame narrator asked Wheeler if he knew the whereabouts of the Rev. Leonidas W. Smiley, and Wheeler backs him into a corner and delivers a monologue about Jim Smiley, who used to make the most outlandish wagers on just about anything, even on whether the parson's wife would die. The joke is that the narrator is trapped by Wheeler and cannot escape his ridiculous recitation. Twain did a great deal with this form, especially in such early tales as "Jim Baker's Blue-Jay Yarn," "The Petrified Man," and "A Bloody Massacre Near Carson" and later in challenging the normative ethics of the day with such works as "The Story of a Bad Little Boy Who Didn't Come to Grief."

Twain was joined in these early Local Color stories by Bret Harte, who became successful in turning out such tales as "The Luck of Roaring Camp" and "The Outcasts of Poker Flat," both of which end with the death of the sentimental favorite. Although Harte often used stock characters such as the righteous gambler or the innocent young man, he invented some figures who proved to have enormous appeal, including the whore with a heart of gold and the tender tough guy. Twain and Harte both captured the dialect, personalities, and folkways of the far West, especially Nevada and California, but the regional movement in literature soon spread to virtually every section of the country.

In New England, building on the work of Stowe before the war, Rose Terry Cooke, Sarah Orne Jewett, and Mary E. Wilkins used localized material for scores of important stories. Jewett focused on Maine for "A White Heron," "Miss Tempy's Watchers," and "The Dulham Ladies," depicting not only surface features such as dialect but the values underlying the interactions of her characters. Freeman did the same, although her region expanded to include New Hampshire and Massachusetts, and her work involves feminist issues in such stories as "Louisa," "The Revolt of Mother," and "A Church Mouse." Cooke's stories sometimes stressed women's issues, as in "Freedom Wheeler's Controversy with Providence: A Story of Old New England," but humor is the hallmark of most of her most famous work, including "Cal Culver and the Devil" and "Clary's Trial."

Perhaps the most active regional literature emerged from the South, especially from Louisiana, a subject covered by stories from George Washington Cable, Alice Dunbar-Nelson, Grace King, and Kate Chopin. Although many of their tales went beyond the limitations of a purely Local Color tradition, all of their work featured detailed descriptions of the unique settings of New Orleans and the surrounding bayous, the complex mixed-race populations presided over by aristocratic Creoles, and a dialect that featured English with an amalgam of French, Spanish, and Caribbean influences. Especially important was a fascinating complex of cultural traditions that established a highly stratified social spectrum, a *plaçage* tradition of gentlemen and their mistresses, a code of honor that erupted in dueling and feuds, and a heritage of high regard for the arts, one that resulted in the construction of the largest opera venue in the world, the French Opera House. Cable's "Belles Demoiselles Plantation" demonstrated how intricate the local familial customs can be when two relatives with the same first and last names, one white and one of mixed race, live in close proximity. Blood lines, family connections, meant much more in this part of the country than they did anywhere else, even among the members of a mixed-race minority who nonetheless, under the *Code Noir*, enjoyed inheritance rights and the pride of descent from nobility. Chopin's "Désirée's Baby" demonstrated the destructive ignorance of deep-seated racial prejudice in a powerful story that is among the finest works of short fiction America ever produced. Dunbar-Nelson's "The Goodness of St. Rocque" captured the mythos of the mixed-race population of the Crescent City and the melding of Roman Catholic beliefs with those of the voodoo traditions practiced in the Caribbean. Grace King's "La Grande Demoiselle" drew on her personal experiences living in New Orleans during and after the Civil War and seeing the decline of the "best" families of the city when their currency suddenly became valueless and their slaves were freed, leaving them with no way to farm their plantations. The psychological impact of such a social disruption provided her with a wealth of material as people from all races struggled to reconfigure their lives and their sense of themselves in a vastly changed social structure.

In the central part of the country, many writers emerged to capture the language and folkways of the region, including Octave Thanet, Ruth Suckow, and Zona Gale, but often their stories developed plot elements that were more serious than was customary in regional literature. Indeed, the general transformation was for writers to use many of the techniques of Local Colorism, the characterizations and dialects, as central elements in their fiction. Although the early tales of Twain are largely humorous, and those of Harte sentimental, within little more than a decade of their first stories other writers had expanded the themes of such work to address the most salient issues of the day, including questions of race, gender, religion, and morality.

The literary movement that resulted was Realism. Influenced by the important books in this vein in European literature, and by the Local Color tradition in the United States, it quickly came to be the dominant cultural expression for more than a century. Unlike the spiritual underpinnings of Romanticism, and its quest for the knowledge of lofty matters, the nature of good and evil, for example, Realism dealt with the physical world people saw every day, the common vision of reality. The characters of fiction were no longer personifications of abstract qualities but representations of ordinary people, the kind who could be observed in daily life. The conflicts were real matters that confronted American society constantly. For example, in *The Rise of Silas Lapham*, a novel by William Dean Howells, the protagonist must choose between his sense of moral integrity and the opportunity to become wealthy by selling a company he knows to be worthless. These kinds of questions meant a great deal to an economy based on free enterprise, and America was beginning to consider questions of greed and social welfare. Similarly, in Twain's *Adventures of Huckleberry Finn*, a young boy must choose between doing what he has been taught was "right," turning in a runaway slave, and his loyalty to a black man who has become a surrogate father to him. These were profoundly important matters, and they were presented to the reading public in the form of novels and stories.

The ideological assumption in both novels was that the central characters have moral sovereignty, that the choices they make provide a dramatic climax for the developing action.

In a sense, Realism helped humanize American literature, dealing with the struggles of common people in the language of everyday life. The narrators were intellectually congruent with the characters they described, and they spoke in the vernacular. The stance was often first-person or third-person limited, identified with the mind of the protagonist and limited to what that character could know or perceive. God-like omniscient narrators were rare. Nature was no longer a transcendent spiritual entity, although a vestigial subtheme persisted throughout the period that being alone in the quiet of Nature was morally uplifting, an idea that informed much of American Modernism as well. Realism took its subjects from genuine events or situations, and the most significant single activity of the nineteenth century was the Civil War.

Stephen Crane emerged as the most important writer to capture that dramatic conflict, even though he had not been born until 1871, when it was well over. What is unique about his fiction is that it focused on the psychology of the common soldier in war, not on the strategy or grand purpose of it. His "An Episode of War" dealt with a young officer who loses an arm while dividing coffee into equal piles for the men, a decidedly anti-heroic action, and his return home with an empty sleeve is underplayed with his insistence that it is not terribly important. In "The Veteran," an old Henry Fleming, the protagonist of *The Red Badge of Courage*, recalls for his grandson how frightened he was in his first battle and how he ran from the front lines when the Confederates charged. He loses his life in a burning barn attempting to save his grandson's ponies. "A Mystery of Heroism" presents the simple task of getting a bucket of water during a battle, and the lingering thematic issue is whether it was brave or stupid for a soldier to risk himself on such a commonplace endeavor. All of Crane's tales have the power of seeming real, true to life, and the verisimilitude of his work, its direct style, its artistic grace, built his reputation as one of America's great writers, even though he was only twenty-eight when he died of tuberculosis.

Other authors brought their own approaches to the subject of war, sometimes with powerful effect. Perhaps the most famous such story is Ambrose Bierce's "An Occurrence at Owl Creek Bridge," a brilliant evocation of a Southern farmer about to be hanged for espionage. By following the working of his mind against a backdrop of the military proceedings, Bierce was able to underscore the significance of everyday domestic life, since the protagonist desperately wishes to return home to his wife and children. Part of the power of "Chickamauga" is in the point of view, for this devastating battle is portrayed as seen by a child who is deaf and mute and thinks it is all a game. Hamlin Garland, drawing on memories of his father's arrival home from combat, portrayed a simple Wisconsin farmer's sacrifice for his ideals in the war. In "The Return of a Private," he comes back to his family ill and emaciated, not fully recovered from his wounds, and barely capable of resuming the hard work required to sustain the farm he had homesteaded. William Dean Howells, better known for his novels, also wrote some important short stories, "Editha" among them. Here the focus is not on the action of combat but on the domestic scene that supported American intervention in the Spanish- American War. Basically an anti-war story, it depicts the false patriotism that allows a woman to glory in the sacrifice her intended is willing to make for his country, only to discover he has been killed in the first engagement. Her trip to express her condolences to his mother is one of the most powerful confrontations in literature.

Another crucial subject for the fiction of the late nineteenth century was the role of women in American society, a matter of special interest because an intriguing character type was introduced in the 1890s, the New Woman. This figure, an outgrowth of the suffragist movement sweeping the country, represented a strong woman capable of not only voting intelligently but of acquiring an education equal to that of men, of supporting herself economically, and of insisting on the same social and sexual freedoms that only men had traditionally enjoyed. The archetypal literary representation of such a person was Edna Pontellier in Kate Chopin's novel *The Awakening*, although there were soon many such figures in American fiction, including Rose in Hamlin Garland's *Rose of Dutcher's Coolly*, Nellie in Stephen Crane's *Maggie: A Girl of the Streets*, and scores of characters in the short stories of the period, as in Willa Cather's "The Bohemian Girl," Edith Wharton's "The Other Two," and Freeman's "The Revolt of Mother." Wharton's story also introduced the concept of divorce, a controversial issue in American social life at the time. A related thematic structure featured women who were subservient to men and suffered because of it, as in Charlotte Perkins Gilman's "The Yellow Wallpaper," Willa Cather's "A Wagner Matinee," or Theodore Dreiser's "The Second Choice."

The expanding opportunities for publishing fiction allowed a wide variety of ethnic writers to contribute to the growing legacy of the national literature. Following Frances Harper, Charles Chesnutt was the first African American writer to become popular with a largely white audience. His dialect stories in *The Conjure Woman* seemed closely patterned after those in the work of Joel Chandler Harris, but those in *The Wife of His Youth and Other Stories* were entirely original. "The Sheriff's Children" blended the issue of race with the thematic structure of Realism so that in the climax the protagonist, a Southern marshal, must make a complex moral decision regarding his responsibilities to his mixed-race son. The titular story "The Wife of His Youth" follows this pattern, although the choice to be made involving race is made by an African American, not a white man, and he gives up wealth and a wedding to a beautiful young widow to affirm his slave marriage to the elderly woman who stands before him. Alice Dunbar-Nelson also wrote about racial issues, although her stories are set in her home state of Louisiana, which had laws and customs that were unique among the other states. The ethnic and religious complexity of the tales in *The Goodness of St. Rocque and Other Stories* presented a rich tapestry of values and mores that confused readers unfamiliar in the New Orleans and the surrounding bayous. The title story involves Manuela, a young woman of Spanish descent, and her desire to marry Theophile, who has a French name. Manuela seeks the powers of both a voodoo practitioner and that of St. Roch, who was said to aid young women in their quest for marriage. Many people did not remember that French Louisiana had been sold to Spain in 1762, and the Spanish ruled the territory for forty years before selling it back to the French, who promptly relinquished it to the United States in 1803. The complex amalgam of laws, languages, currency, religions, and customs created the most multifarious city in America, the subject of hundreds of intriguing stories and novels. Dunbar-Nelson made good use of the diversity of the population in "Little Miss Sophie," which draws on the long tradition of white Creole gentlemen having a quadroon mistress and on the intense emotional ties that many such relationships engendered. They could not marry because of the restrictions of the *Code Noir*, which forbade mixed-race unions. In "Tony's Wife" the issue is a domineering Italian husband who makes life miserable for his German wife, even disinheriting her when he dies. "M'sieu Fortier's Violin" deals with an impoverished French musician who is forced by poverty to sell his instrument only to discover he cannot live without his music. The fortunate conclusion is that the wealthy American who returns it to him allows him to keep both it and the money. All of this is even more powerful for those who remember that the Americans brought business and the free enterprise system to New Orleans, including many thriving entrepreneurs, but the French had built the largest opera house in the world and treasured their cultural traditions more than the acquisition of wealth. "Sister Josepha" deals with the poignant case of a young orphaned woman of uncertain racial identity who is unsure of what role she could play in the highly stratified and rigid ethnic codes of the Crescent City, so she chooses to remain behind the walls of the convent even though she longs for the excitement of urban life.

Writers from other ethnic groups made important contributions as well, including Abraham Cahan, whose "A Providential Match" demonstrated that the lives of Jewish immigrants provided a rich background for urban fiction. Sui Sin Far wrote the first Chinese American stories in her volume *Mrs. Spring Fragrance*, which explored the cultural duality of Asians living on the west Coast. John M. Oskison, a Cherokee writer who had grown up on a reservation, graduated from Stanford, and had gone on to write sophisticated stories with an anthropological insight. In "The Problem of Old Harjo," the issue is polygamy, which was common among the protagonist's people, and the old man cannot understand why becoming a Christian means he must reject one of his wives. Paul Lawrence Dunbar further enriched African American literature not only with his poetry but also with a series of stories, the most powerful of which was "The Lynching of Jube Benson," the account of a wrongful hanging of a faithful retainer based on racist assumptions. Jessie Fauset dealt with race delicately in "Emmy," a story of courtship in a racially sensitive society, the subject of many of her tales.

No one hit the issue of race, and the fate of the quadroon, more directly than did George Washington Cable in his stories in *Old Creole Days*. Two of them dealt with the regional practice of *plaçage*, an outgrowth of the *Code Noir*, which forbade marriage between races. As a result, many white gentlemen established families with young quadroon women, who were protected by a legal contract giving them a small house and a monthly income. Their children carried the name of their father, and they were entitled to inherit a portion of his estate. No other culture so protected the offspring of children born out of wedlock. "'Tite Poulette" dealt with the issue by having a young Dutch gentleman fall in love with the daughter of a *plaçage* mistress whose "husband" had died. They were forbidden to marry under these legal provisions, but the mother claims that her daughter was adopted and that the true parents were a Spanish couple who died of yellow fever. After the quadroon community in New Orleans objected, Cable wrote a longer version of a similar story entitled "Madame Delphine" in which the same situation develops, the mother claims not to be the parent, the couple are wed, and then the mother confesses that she lied, that she is the mother and her daughter is of mixed race. Although it became an obscure piece of short fiction, it is one of the great stories in American literature. Maria Cristina Mena wrote the first Mexican American fiction in the period, showing the complex cultural interactions along the Southern border of the United States. Finally, Zitkala-Sa wrote from a Lakota perspective, and "The Soft-Hearted Sioux" made clear that Native American writers had much to contribute to the development of a national literature that covered the spectrum of ethnic groups within the country.

Beyond the focus on the diversity of the population, and the contributions that various cultural and religious groups could make to the growing literary legacy of a still fledgling country, the artistic quality of the fiction produced was impressive. No other country in the world had ever produced so many important short stories as now poured forth from a host of writers. The tales of Henry James, for example, emphasized not so much dramatic events as significant psychological and moral growth. In fact, his "The Real Thing" developed three levels of thematic movement: the issue of what is "real" in art; the social inversion in England with a collapsing gentry and a rising lower class; and the moral growth of an artist who feels compassion for the faded aristocrats who attempt to pose for him as models. His famous "The Beast in the Jungle" also rests on psychological growth as a Narcissistic man finally realizes that the momentous event he has been waiting for has been right before him all the time, the love of the woman who has been his faithful companion but has now died. Stephen Crane wrote some of the most entertaining and yet powerful stories of the period, including the racially charged "The Monster," the sensational "The Open Boat," based on the actual sinking of a ship, and "The Bride Comes to Yellow Sky," a satiric portrait of the fading wild west. When Fred Lewis Pattee wrote *The Development of the American Short Story* in 1923, he proclaimed that the great genius of the form was Kate Chopin, a claim based almost entirely on two volumes of tales, *Bayou Folk* and *A Night in Acadie*. Her "Désirée's Baby," often described as the most perfect American story, emerged as a social powerful statement against racial prejudice, as did the equally compelling "La Belle Zoraïde," in which ethnic insensitivity on the part of a white woman drives a slave mother insane. "A No-Account Creole" revealed some of the cultural differences between the white Creoles and the Acadian immigrants who lived in the bayou country of Louisiana. Her "Athénaïse" was based on a plot that ran counter to that of her famous novel *The Awakening*, in which a woman escapes a marriage through suicide. Athénaïse, on the other hand, is thrilled to learn she is pregnant and rushes to rejoin the husband she had left for life in the city. Chopin was a sophisticated writer who did not create stories to fit the politics of the moment but rather explored the full complexity of the issues that confronted her, none more compelling than the role of a woman in what was becoming a modern society.

Realism was a literary movement of transformative significance for American life for it presented a way of representing the experience of common humanity, including the difficult moral issues that they inevitably encountered. There was, however, a counter set of ideas with a correspondingly different set of aesthetic principles that arose in the midst of this period, the movement that became known as Naturalism. This mode had originated in Europe, and it derived largely from the sciences, whereas Realism had its earliest manifestations in painting. One stream of thinking in Naturalism derived from a book by a French physician, Claude Bernard, entitled *An Introduction to the Study of Experimental Medicine*, the thesis of which was that the practice of medicine should begin with an assessment of the origin of a given condition and by understanding the causal history the doctor could devise an intervention that would cure the patient. This was a startling theory at a time when most people believed human illness was a matter of divine will, that faith and prayer would cure everyone. Bernard took the supernatural out of science and replaced it with reason and experimentation. The objective was to improve the patient. Emile Zola read this book and, for a stream of novels he was about to write, he concocted a parallel literary objective: that the novel should explore social pathologies, showing their cause, and by suggesting interventions that solve those problems improve society. Zola presented this thinking in a book entitled *The Experimental Novel*, and it was to have enormous influence on American fiction.

The result of Zola's postulations was the tendency in fiction to concentrate on social problems: poverty, violence, exploitation, and unfair labor practices. The characters were nearly always from the lower classes, uneducated, and vulnerable, as were the destitute in the major cities or impoverished farmers on the frozen plains. Such figures did not possess enough knowledge to narrate their stories because, for the most part, they did not understand the situation. Even if they did, as is the case in a few instances, they lacked the money or the power to change things. Characters in Naturalism lack moral agency and are driven by forces beyond their control; those in Realism have free will, and they must take full responsibility for the choices they make. The narrators in Naturalism thus tend to be omniscient, disembodied entities that know everything and can relate what multiple people are thinking, their backgrounds, what motivates them. In Realism the point of view is normally limited to what one character would know in that situation. Realism tends to be carefully structured, often with a symmetrical design or with numbered sections that signify a shift in setting or circumstances. Naturalism tends to be loose and baggy, often with little or no concern for structural design. The imagery of Naturalism tends toward the violence of the natural world, with wild animals preying on one another, or tropes conveying the power of storms on the sea or the cold of winter. The central themes of Realism stress moral responsibility for the ethical choices the character is forced to make to resolve a conflict. In Naturalism, the central characters most often lack the power or understanding to make choices, but their decisions would be moot in any event. They are up against implacable powers of such overwhelming proportions that their small musing would have no effect. Impoverished people lack the resources to fight a railroad company that takes advantage of them by paying unfairly low prices for wheat, for example. Farmers lack the means to fight Nature, to end a drought, to push back a flood, to disperse the millions of grasshoppers eating their fields. Naturalism most often depicts characters trapped by economics, natural forces, the greed of the wealthy, or by psychological illness. Only massive, national changes would have any effect on their condition, the objective of the Populist Movement, which rose in the 1890s in America.

In literature, the Naturalist movement is generally thought to have been initiated in 1890 with the publication of Jacob Riis's photographic book *How the Other Half Lives*, a study of poor immigrants living in squalor in New York City. At about the same time, the short stories of Hamlin Garland began appearing, depicting the lives of poor farmers in the Midwest. His classic story "Under the Lion's Paw" is often used to illustrate the standard scenario. It deals with the plight of a farmer named Haskins whose crops in Kansas were are destroyed by grasshoppers, an example of a hostile Nature, so he attempts to move his wife and children north to start over. He rents a farm from Jim Butler with an option to buy it after three years if he gets established. Another farmer, Council, helps Haskins at first, putting the family up for the winter and supplying him with seed for his first year of farming. Haskins works desperately hard and succeeds, bringing in a good harvest and making many improvements on the farm, greatly increasing its value. However, after three years, when he decides to buy the farm, Butler has now doubled the price on the logic that it is now more valuable than it was before. Haskins is enraged and seems about to kill Butler when he realizes that he cannot, that his family needs him to produce an income. He is caught, having to pay an unfair price for the property, in effect paying twice for the improvements he has made. The story ends with Haskins sunk down with his head in his hands, powerless to resist being cheated by Butler.

The world is not fair in Naturalism, nor is it merciful. Frank Norris published a similar story, "A Deal in Wheat," in 1902, in which Lewiston, a farmer in Kansas, is forced to sell his land because the price of wheat has been driven down so low. He does not understand the manipulation of commodity prices, nor could he do anything about it, but he suffers the consequences of this speculation and moves to Chicago, looking for work. The scene then shifts to two wealthy commodities investors who are trying to outwit one another. One of them drives up the prices and makes a fortune from the other, but he simply manipulates supply to elevate the price even higher. Meanwhile, Lewiston is forced to stand in the bread line every night to have anything at all to eat, but when the higher prices take effect, the baker cannot afford to give away bread even at the end of the day. Lewiston is about to starve when he finds employment cleaning the street, and he is able to survive. Norris ends the tale with an intrusive polemical statement, representative of the Naturalistic tendency for expository comment, in which he observes that both the poor farmer who grew the wheat and the impoverished in the city suffered while the rich speculators made millions in what was merely a game for them. Clearly, such an economic system would have to be seen as unjust.

These two stories illustrate the extent to which Naturalism was a reformist literature that lamented the tragedies caused by natural forces that could not be changed and protested against those powerful economic and legal regulations that could be revised to afford protections against exploitation. No one wrote better stories about the urban poor than did Stephen Crane in his "Bowery Tales," stories set in the section of New York dominated by Irish immigrants. The focus of his urban tales is not only on the injustice done to the poor but also on the cruelty and violence they inflict upon themselves. In "A Dark-Brown Dog," for example, a little boy brings a puppy to his home in a tenement. The tenor of the household is chaotic, and the parents treat one another with threats and violence, a mode of behavior the children soon emulate. When the drunken father comes home, he grabs the small dog and flings it out the window, where it falls to its death. The plot concludes with the small boy sitting beside the body of his dead dog. It was not outside forces that caused the tragedy but the internalization of the worst kinds of instincts that led to the shocking end. "The Men in the Storm" deals with a soup kitchen that serves the destitute a free meal in the evening. While the men wait for the door to open, a snow storm reveals the hostility of Nature as the snow stings the men around their collars and on their hands and seems to be deliberately causing as much damage as it can. "An Experiment in Misery" involves a newspaper reporter who wants to understand such men, so he dresses as a derelict and joins a line on the street, finally sleeping in a flop house amid a host of ragged men, who seem grateful to have a bed for the night. In the morning, however, before they have dressed, he views their magnificent naked bodies that look dignified and noble, suggesting that these derelicts could have had fine lives given the opportunity, that they had an innate worth that a social construct had taken from them, as signified by their tattered clothing.

Jack London's stories emphasize a different Naturalistic theme, the savagery of Nature and its hostile intent toward human life. In "The Law of Life", an old Inuit, who can no longer contribute to the welfare of his people, and facing the moving of the village, resigns himself to being torn apart and eaten by wolves, just as he had seen them do to a moose many years earlier. His son asks him if all is well, and he replies that it is, accepting the law of life as he knows it. For countless generations the Inuit elderly had ended their lives this way. In "To Build a Fire" a man in the Yukon ignores the warnings not to go out in the bitter cold, which is more than fifty degrees below zero, and where he trudges along with his dog. When he falls through the ice covering a stream, he needs a fire to get warm and dry his clothing. But his hands freeze when he takes off his gloves, and the snow falling from a branch extinguishes the small fire he was able to start, and he is finally unable to save himself. His dog has instincts for survival that the man lacks, however, and he is able to not only withstand the temperature but trots off to find someone else who will feed him. In Naturalism, there are times when animal instincts are better than the human capacity for reason.

Many other writers in the 1890s and the early years of the twentieth century contributed to the growing interest in Naturalism. Theodore Dreiser, for example, not only wrote major novels in this tradition but a series of stories as well. "The Second Choice" shows a young woman trapped in the squalor of the lower class, and she hopes for a better life, one promised to her by a new suitor. When he suddenly leaves and writes to her about his new opportunities in Fiji, she realizes he was exploiting her sexually, and she resigns herself to marriage to her old beau, who will subject her to the very world she finds so oppressive. Her capitulation is indicated when, at the end, she puts on an apron and sets the table. Resignation of this kind is also at the center of Ruth Suckow's "A Start in Life," which portrays a young woman from a poor family who is sent to be a servant in another household. At first she thinks that she will be one of the family and entitled to all of the privileges she sees the children enjoying, but on the day of a picnic, when she is expecting a splendid outing, she is given instructions to sweep the house and start the fire. She weeps as she begins to understand that she is now out on her own, that no one cares about her happiness, and that there is nothing to be done but to accept the limitations that lie ahead of her. This is also the case in John Steinbeck's "The Chrysanthemums," in which a ranch housewife longing for greater adventure and comfort is forced to resign herself to the humdrum world she has known. In Sherwood Anderson's "Death in the Woods," however, a woman who has devoted herself to feeding her family dies in the woods and is eaten by wild animals, thus feeding others to the very end. Human beings occupy no special place in Nature in Naturalistic philosophy.

American Modernism

Because of the tendency for exposition to explore at great length the causal history of sociological pathologies, the novel and not the short story became the natural outlet. Nearly all of the great Naturalists produced blockbuster novels, Steinbeck's *The Grapes of Wrath* and Richard Wright's *Native Son* being perhaps the greatest of the lot, but their impact on the tradition of the story persisted into Modernism as well. The period is normally dated from the end of World War I in 1918, which, although it was not a literary event, so dramatically altered the psychological landscape that the tenor of Western civilization was permanently transformed. Part of that change derived from a new sense of depersonalization. In the Civil War, there were clear instances of bravery, nobility, and, sometimes, common sense, as when in Mississippi the fighting was called off for a day so that both sides could clear their dead and wounded from the field. Soldiers from both sides were intermingled without incident as they pursued their gruesome duties. But even under normal circumstances, many men, from North and South, risked their lives in an attempt to save their comrades, perhaps the best definition of heroism. But personal behavior of that sort means little if a cloud of deadly gas is floating over, killing thousands of men in the process, or if Big Bertha, a German artillery piece, is firing a shell from more than fifty miles and obliterating everything for hundreds of yards when it finally hits the ground. Metal dog tags were are invented in an attempt to identify the soldiers who had been blown to bits. The men in the trenches on both sides suffered from the cold, from infection, from diseases such as the flu pandemic that spread rapidly among the ranks. There was little evidence of a benevolent deity protecting anyone or spreading its grace among the combatants, and confidence in conventional religious values was sorely shaken.

The American Short Story Handbook, First Edition. James Nagel.
© 2015 James Nagel. Published 2015 by John Wiley & Sons, Ltd.

When the men returned home from the war, they came back to a country that was rapidly being transformed by technology, industry, and mechanization. The Eighteenth Amendment brought a new era of prohibition in 1919, and drinking very much increased in popularity, especially among young people. The traffic in illegal alcohol instituted a criminal element to even casual consumption, and the mobs ruled the inner cities, supplying speakeasies nightclubs, and backdoor sales operations. The Nineteenth Amendment gave women the right to vote and a claim on full participation in American commercial, political, and social life. The Jazz Age had begun, and flappers drank with the boys, had sex in the back seats of automobiles, and danced on table tops in the nightclubs that ringed towns all across the country. People flocked to the major cities, and America became a predominantly urban society for the first time, and with that development came other changes as well. In New York City, a Bohemian movement in Greenwich Village issued a manifesto that advocated free love, unfettered artistic license, and an almost total rejection of traditional middle-class life.

Such gigantic cultural transformations were certain to have manifestations in literature as well, and one of the most obvious new developments was that the short story became even more established as a dominant form. New periodicals were established to join the *Atlantic Monthly* and *Harper's Magazine*, still flourishing from the previous century, and among these were the *The Saturday Evening Post*, *Cosmopolitan*, the *The Ladies Home Journal*, and scores of what were called "little magazines" housed on college campuses, such as the *The Kenyon Review*. Two annual collections of short fiction suddenly appeared to celebrate noteworthy contributions, *The Best American Short Stories* and the *O. Henry Memorial Award Prize Stories*, both published by leading houses on the eastern seaboard. The story paid better than ever, and many novelists used the income from short fiction to support themselves as they worked on novels, as did F. Scott Fitzgerald and Katherine Anne Porter. The form had become big business, and stories flooded the market in collections, magazines, and even newspapers.

The writer who gave the decade its most popular title was Fitzgerald, whose *Tales of the Jazz Age* not only presented a term that caught the fancy of teenagers but characters their own age who drank and danced and rebelled against the restrictions of their parents. His *Flappers and Philosophers* lent another term to the culture of the day, and his third collection of stories, *All the Sad Young Men*, revealed that amid the hectic pace of modern life there was an inherent loneliness, a longing for an unattainable love object, a desire to be accepted into society. Indeed, Fitzgerald's standard protagonist is a young man from modest means who comes into contact with members of the upper crust and who not only wishes to be one of them but falls in love with a young lady from a wealthy family. The autobiographical origin of this narrative line is perhaps too obvious to discuss, but he made it into an enduring American mythology, especially in his celebrated novel *The Great Gatsby*. Before that, however, he had presented very much the same basic plot in "Winter Dreams," which is about a young man who caddies at a golf course, where he meets the girl who will haunt him the rest of his life. Later, he discovers that over the years she has lost her beauty, married badly, and aged poorly, and he was better off without her. The intense romantic desire that he feels for her, however, is characteristic of the new emphasis on love Fitzgerald brought to fiction.

His dazzling stylistic flourishes used to describe the daring flappers and athletic youths also impressed a generation of readers. His tales of the young, such as "Absolution," seemed to tell the truth about the post-war generation and their difficulties achieving the American Dream, adjusting to adult sexuality, and dealing with disillusionment. His later stories, written in the 1930s, gave a more mature consideration to the consequences of a hedonistic lifestyle, as did "Crazy Sunday" and the brilliant "Babylon Revisited," in which marriage and parenting problems have replaced the turmoil of courtship.

If Fitzgerald was the literary icon of the Jazz Age, Ernest Hemingway assumed that role for the Lost Generation, that cohort of young Americans drawn into World War I who came home disillusioned with middle-class life and eager to find a new direction for themselves in Europe, especially in Paris, the moveable feast for intellectuals and expatriates of the 1920s. Hemingway's fiction has little time for the social climbing and intense romanticism that is at the center of Fitzgerald's work, for he dealt with tougher issues: pain, death, and psychological wounding, even among the very young. In "Indian Camp," for example, a young boy witnesses his father perform a Caesarian section on an Indian woman without the benefit of anesthesia, and he is shaken by the procedure and by her screaming. When the baby is born, his father discovers that the woman's husband has committed suicide by slitting his own throat, and young Nick Adams sees that as well. Amid the bloody beginning of life he has also seen the end, a matter he is still struggling to understand in the conclusion. In both "Now I Lay Me" and "A Way You'll Never Be" his mental instability is more directly evident, but the psychological effects of violence are nearly always at the center of a Hemingway story. In other stories, Nick goes off to war and sees the destruction and suffering all around him, and he has difficulty hanging on to sanity, an issue even when he eventually comes home, as in "Big Two-Hearted River."

Unlike Fitzgerald's stylistic elegance, Hemingway's prose is stripped down to its minimalistic essence, presenting the sensory nature of experience so that the reader feels part of an actual event, seeing and hearing the action. This approach produced some of the greatest stories of the twentieth century, including "A Clean, Well-Lighted Place," a tale about an old man who has lost everything and an old waiter who sympathizes with his plight, having himself felt the same sense of emptiness, and "The Snows of Kilimanjaro," in which a writer on safari, dying of an infection, reviews his life and the events he always meant to translate into fiction. Meanwhile, he plays out the drama of an unhappy marriage to a wealthy woman. Hemingway's "marriage group" of stories invariably show courtship and family life to end badly either with the tragic loss of one of the people involved or with betrayal and bitterness. "Hills Like White Elephants" is often used to illustrate one of the techniques he contributed to modern fiction, the "iceberg principle" of showing only one-eighth of the meaning on the surface. In that case, a man and a woman, waiting for a train in Spain, argue over whether she should have an abortion, but that central conflict is available only through implication since her pregnancy and his desire that she terminate it medically are never mentioned directly. Hemingway presented a new figure to fiction, the vulnerable man in a tough and destructive world, a person who finds it difficult to live with the pain and tragedy he has witnessed and is trying to find some code, some meaning to give his life stability. Very few of them ever find it.

William Faulkner is something of an anomaly as a Modernist in that throughout his career he used many of the techniques and subjects of the Local Color movement, albeit in innovative and often startling ways. Virtually the entire corpus of his work is set in a single fictional county in Mississippi, and the same families and individual characters appear repeatedly, as do the central themes concerning them. Essentially, his vast output of important novels and stories tells three interrelated narratives about the area: the decline of the aristocratic class after the Civil War; the rise of the poor white trash after they come down out of the hill country and become tenant farmers and merchants; and the plight of African Americans who had been slaves and now seek to find a role for themselves in society. The collapsing upper class is represented by Emily Grierson in "A Rose for Emily," who still lives on family money but has degenerated to the extent that she now practices necrophilia, which is shockingly revealed to the community in the conclusion. The archetypal poor family in Faulkner's work is the Snopes clan, which appears in multiple stories. In "Spotted Horses" the focus is on their skill, their stealth, in horse trading, a subject traditionally treated with humor in American literature, as it is in this case. In "Barn Burning," young

Sarty breaks from the values of his family when he observes his father about to burn the barn of the wealthy Major De Spain. "That Evening Sun" depicts the wealthy Compson children in association with the black servants who have assisted the family for many generations, and they became the protagonists of some of Faulkner's best stories about race.

All of these families and themes come together, in a sense, in Faulkner's greatest work of short fiction, "The Bear," in which traditional social stratifications are stripped away along with all racial divisions in favor of a new structure based on a knowledge of the woods and skill at hunting. Here, in a primitive wilderness, young Ike McCaslin learns what he needs to know to really become a man, following an ancient Chickasaw ritual of initiation. As a result, he later renounces all wealth derived from slavery and moves into the county seat to become a carpenter. In terms of aesthetics, Faulkner was the most inventive of the Modernists, dealing with stream of consciousness, narrative simultaneity, multiple points of view, unreliable narrators, and forbidden subjects, including aberrant sexual practices. His insight into a the Southern population adjusting to the dramatic changes wrought by the Civil War constitutes the single richest subject utilized by any writer of the twentieth century, and his brilliant and sensitive treatment of the psychological conflicts brought by this transformation make him the greatest author the United States has ever produced.

The early phase of American Modernism contributed a host of new stories that approached life from innovative perspectives. Although ethnic issues had emerged as a popular topic even in the 1890s, in the post-war era they carried a vitality and complexity that encouraged a wide range of racial and religious writers. Abraham Cahan wrote about Jewish immigrants in the 1890s, and Anzia Yezierska was the first Jewish American woman to develop a reputation for her short stories. Beginning with "The Fat of the Land" in 1919, her fiction demonstrated the conflict inherent in belonging to two cultures, of being suspended between two worlds. In this case, a mother finds that her successful children, fully assimilated, are embarrassed by her backward ways and awkward English, and they move her uptown to a better apartment. But she misses the sense of community she had known in the years she was striving, and her new wealth does not compensate for her lost friends.

One of the richest ethnic literatures in America has been African American, and in Modernism the short story was a major form in both art and substance. Jean Toomer's composite novel *Cane* contained several important tales, foremost among them "Blood-Burning Moon," an example of his ability to use poetic techniques in writing fiction. That story, built on the classic love triangle, although multi-racial in this case, depicts a murder and a lynching, to be sure, but it does so in lyrical language, lending a haunting tone to the description of events. Arna Bontemp's award-winning "A Summer Tragedy" from 1933 conveys the hopelessness of sharecroppers during the Depression, when their annual income was less than their expenses. That an elderly couple decides to end their lives with dignity rather than persist in their forlorn labors gives beauty to their mutual affection and poignancy to their suicides. Zora Neale Hurston, Richard Wright, and James Baldwin contributed to this wave of stories from the black community, a major force in literature as well as in social impact. Baldwin's "Sonny's Blues" was a tour de force of point of view, with as much emphasis on the narrator as on the protagonist. In fact, the most significant psychological transformation is in the mind of the speaker, who undergoes an epiphany that reveals to him the meaning of the events he describes in reverse chronological order. The richness of his lexicon also underscores the sophistication of his supple mind and the depth of his insights.

Another thematic strain that dominated Modernism dealt with gender issues, especially the complex role of women in a vibrant and difficult age, and sexuality, courtship, marriage, and parenting provided abundant material for female writers from a broad spectrum of society. The stories in Hisaye Yamamoto's story cycle *Seventeen Syllables* provided a brilliant look at Japanese Americans forced into internment camps after the bombing of Pearl Harbor. Rather than belabor the obvious, the injustice of imprisoning families who were loyal to the United States, and in many instances had sons serving in the armed services, she focused on the psychology of the people in the camp, on their personal, religious, and sexual conflicts and intellectual transformations. One story deals with a father, a devout Buddhist, who is delighted to have the time for prolonged meditation, seeking the divine spiritual state at the center of his devotions. In another tale, "The Legend of Miss Sasagawara," his daughter struggles with her burgeoning erotic impulses, feelings that, given the restrictions of their situation, manifest in voyeurism and emotional pathology. Eudora Welty's "Petrified Man" lends a comic touch to gender issues, in this case the revealing conversations of women in a hairdresser shop, which reveals the extent to which they dominate their husbands. In particular, their insensitive observations about a deformed man on exhibit in a circus demonstrate their lack of humane compassion, and these Southern women are ultimately revealed to be the true monsters of the story, not the petrified man. Katherine Anne Porter's "Maria Concepción" also deals with marriage but in a far more anthropological sense than Welty's story. Set in Mexico, the plot rests on marriage and a child in a culture that values both but in ways different from standard American society. In this tale, a betrayed wife murders the woman her husband now loves and takes custody of her child, whom she raises as her own. All of this is well known to the surrounding community, which seems to condone the situation and finds it just. Maria Christina Mena, the first Mexican American author of stature, explored courtship rituals of the two societies in a fascinating story titled "The Education of Popo."

Perhaps the most celebrated of feminist short fiction of this period was Tillie Olsen's "Help Her to Believe," which later became known as "I Stand Here Ironing." It depicts a single mother, seeing to the mundane tasks of everyday life, who reflects on her poverty and the limitations of her ability to help her young daughter, and in her despondency she resolves to do nothing. The ultimate theme is not so much an indictment of society in general, as some readers have assumed, as an intimate portrait of the mind and personality of an individual mother, preoccupied with her own problems, who has failed to comfort her child. It does not take a fortune to put an arm around another person, to offer words of guidance, to lend emotional support. In some measure, the method of the telling inspired interest in the story, for its temporal and tonal shifts, the revelations of domestic failures, and the sympathetic portrayal of a mother reviewing her responsibilities have all made it the subject of enormous controversy.

The form of the short story matured during Modernism, and many of the innovations these writers brought to fiction, especially to the methods of narration, gave renewed interest to the genre. The subjects of the age—the new stress on ethnicity, cultural duality, and poverty—spoke to the social concerns of the moment, while the emphasis on the formation of a sense of identity revealed the growing psychological insight in society at large. American culture had begun to question its own standards, particularly with regard to civil rights for people of color and equal opportunities and freedoms for women, and these subjects were starting to move beyond the fascinations of literary entertainment toward the intense cultural concern that was about to change American society in the 1960s.

The Contemporary American Short Story

The contemporary period in American literature is generally dated from the early 1960s, although there is no specific event that denotes its inception. Rather, that decade saw a dramatic shift in the tenor of society, and after a postwar scene that was relatively placid, this era brought social unrest fueled by racial tensions in the major cities and by a rapidly spreading opposition to the war in Vietnam. There were urban riots throughout the country, and the demonstrations on college campuses changed forever the relationship between faculty and students at the university level. A new spirit was abroad in the land, and it brought with it fresh opportunities for minorities in education and employment, a greater participation for women in all levels of the economy, and a new feeling that a culture was being reborn, formed by a vitality behind the quest for free speech and the confidence that the voices of a new generation were now being heard.

The era brought historic events at a dizzying pace. A man walked on the moon; Thurgood Marshall became the first African American member of the Supreme Court; the Soviet Union tore down the wall that had kept an unwilling population trapped inside a communist nation; and Congress passed the Civil Rights Act in 1964. There was now an awareness that more immigrants had come to the United States than had ever moved into any other country in the history of the world, and the diversity of the nation was a cause to be celebrated as part of the strength of a multicultural society. The passage of Title IX in 1972 opened new opportunities for women to participate in athletics, and in 1977 a National Women's Conference was held in Houston. Sandra Day O'Connor became the first woman to serve on the Supreme

The American Short Story Handbook, First Edition. James Nagel.
© 2015 James Nagel. Published 2015 by John Wiley & Sons, Ltd.

Court, and other breakthroughs soon followed: Geraldine Ferraro ran for vice president; Janet Reno assumed the role of the head of the Department of Justice; Condoleezza Rice succeeded another African American, Colin Powell, as secretary of state. The country had grown in ways that would have been unimaginable only a decade earlier, and those alterations very quickly brought changes to the national literature as well.

But not all of the writers of this period used innovative methods. Andre Dubus wrote stories that were aesthetically rather traditional, although his ideas were highly original and innovative. His central focus was on domestic issues, conflicts within a family group, an emphasis some people found uncomfortable. His basic plots, as in "Killings," often involve cruelty and death, and his fundamental themes, reaching back to Realism, are centered on moral questions including whether what is legal is necessarily what is morally "correct." John Cheever's six volumes of stories received nearly unmatched acclaim, winning not only a Pulitzer Prize but the National Book Award and the American Book Award, but in a sense his short fiction recapitulates the emphasis in Realism of the crisis of ethical choice and internal growth. He wrote out of the New England heritage his family embraced, with its established codes of conduct and traditional moral decorum, although he often did so using innovative narrative methods and dealing with new subjects. For example, in "Clancy in the Tower of Babel" an apartment superintendent is outraged by a tenant's open homosexuality and decides to say hurtful things to him at every opportunity. However, on reflection, he thinks about his wife and son, their beauty and their weaknesses, and he decides to simply pass the man by in silence, having moved to a heightened level of moral awareness. In "The Housebreaker of Shady Hill," a man desperate for money burglarizes his neighbors' homes only to find that he is disgusted by his own behavior and returns the items he has stolen. "The Country Husband" features a protagonist who survives an emergency landing of his airplane and is hurt by the indifference of his immediate family. He contemplates an affair with the babysitter but realizes that ultimately it would cause pain and damage to many people. In all of these cases the conflicts are internal, in the traditional mode of Realism, and the transformations are in personal self-respect and ethical stature.

Raymond Carver's tales often explore some of the same issues but with conclusions that are less certain and often unsettling. Much of his reputation as a Minimalist, however, rests on his spare and yet powerful prose, resembling the work of Ernest Hemingway, and the meaningful small touches he could bring to a charged situation. In "Fat," for example, a waitress tells a friend about a fat man who consumed an enormous meal, one so astounding that it has left her confused and depressed. Her telling of the incident seems an exercise in realization, as though by sharing the incident she will come to understand the meaning of it, why it so disconcerted her, but she never achieves a full comprehension of it. Rather than arriving at an epiphany, a revelation of clarity, she finds only a further sense of qualified understanding. In Carver's most famous story, "Cathedral," the narrator, a husband, accompanies his wife to see a blind friend, a man the husband does not like and who inspires suspicion. In the course of the evening, however, the blind man shares some of the salient events of his life, how his wife died of cancer, for instance, and the narrator begins to develop compassion for him, a feeling that grows as he attempts to explain to the man who cannot see what a cathedral looks like. As together they attempt to draw the structure on paper, the narrator feels a sense of intimacy and kinship that he has not expected, and the revelation of that awareness invests the poignant conclusion.

Bobbie Ann Mason also focuses on psychological dramas within a family, as does "Shiloh," told in a restrained narrative voice, in an envelope structure, and with a highly controlled plot. Susan Minot, a brilliant Minimalist in the style of Ernest Hemingway, began her career with *Monkeys*, a short-story cycle of grace, impressive subtlety, and psychological power. The opening tale, "Hiding," establishes issues that resonate throughout the volume: an emotionally remote father; a sensitive and needy mother; and emotionally damaged children who are intelligently perceptive and understand the family drama playing out before them. Minot also draws on her knowledge of the highly stratified society of Boston in bringing together a wealthy, Harvard- educated, protestant Dad and an Irish, Roman Catholic Mum, a Southie who went to Boston College, a mixture fraught with disastrous potential.

Some of contemporary fiction dealt with the most dramatic event of the period, the Vietnam War, although in general, writers tended to avoid a subject that was so politically controversial. The two best authors who did cover it are Tim O'Brien and Robert Olen Butler, both of whom actually served in country and wrote from personal experience. O'Brien's "The Things They Carried" conveyed much of the psychological nature of the conflict, showing how in the midst of horrible events, and terrifying destruction, the soldiers still carried the enormous weight of fear, doubt, guilt, love, and the life they left back home. "On the Rainy River" deals with the courage it would have taken for the protagonist to have fled to Canada when he was drafted, but he did not dare because he would have had to face his father. "The Sweetheart of the Song Tra Bong" is about a grunt whose girlfriend, an innocent young thing in culottes and a pink sweater, comes to Vietnam to see him, becomes fascinated with the green berets, and finally disappears into the bush with them. She has become morally corrupted by the brutality of war. The theme suggests that if someone so supremely pure can be drawn to the dark side by the ghastly inhumanity of the conflict, an ordinary person will surely be debased by it. These kinds of anti-war themes run throughout O'Brien's short fiction.

The same themes are at the heart of Robert Olen Butler's stories as well, but with a twist. Whereas O'Brien wrote about Americans in Vietnam and the psychological impact that the war has had on them, Butler portrays Vietnamese in America dealing with the same issues, the horror and guilt and sense of loss they carry with them. His best tales are in *A Good Scent from a Strange Mountain*, which won the Pulitzer Prize for in 1993, and virtually all of them contain innovative plot twists that are entirely original. For example, in "Open Arms" a narrator struggling to understand his own commentary tells about a communist defector who was is a deeply sensitive man dedicated to personal purity in thought as well as action. He was a sincere soldier fighting against the United States, but when the communists killed his wife and children he fled and aligned himself with the Americans. To his horror, he finds the common soldiers morally objectionable, viewing a pornographic film and speaking about women in a grossly sexual manner. He commits suicide. The ultimate emphasis is on the narrator's attempt to understand this unusual man and his impressively complex values about family life, war, and humane society. Butler is also notable for his later experimentation with extremely short tales of a single paragraph, brief fictions that he manages to make compelling in their pointed situations. In *Severance*, for example, he portrays the final thoughts of people who have had their heads cut off. *Intercourse* reveals the thoughts of notable people engaged in sex, and the result is both hilarious and insightful, trademarks of Butler's often startling fiction.

Native American writers have played a progressively more important role in the contemporary period than ever before, and their work has ushered in new ideas and techniques to recent fiction. For example, Leslie Marmon Silko's "Storyteller" is closely related to the oral tradition of her ancestors in many ways, including using a speaker who seems to represent the community rather than an individual. Her use of poetic images and mythic allusions invest her prose with spiritual values as well as psychological insights. In this tale she presents the thoughts of a Yupik woman in Alaska who is awaiting trial for murder, and thus there is no physical action other than in her memories, which are emotionally wrenching. Louise Erdrich writes about the Native Americans in North Dakota and Minnesota who are struggling to find a place for themselves in society. Their culture has been largely destroyed, and they are ill suited and unwilling to commit themselves to conventional middle-class life in the general community. "The Red Convertible" demonstrates some of the conflicts that inform her work. In it Lyman

Lamartine tells about the death of his brother, Henry Jr., who is home from the Vietnam War and is suffering from post-traumatic stress disorder, among other pathologies. Unpredictably violent, haunted by what he has seen, frustrated by the restrictions on his life, he drowns himself in the flooded Red River of the North. Erdrich's stories create a world parallel to Faulkner's Yoknapatawpha County in that in more than a hundred tales she weaves the lives of a small number of families through the last century, tracing the complex of issues that have shaped their lives for multiple generations.

Nearly a score of other Native American writers have worked in the short story, including Sherman Alexie, a proponent of "reservation fiction" dealing with people trapped by government dependency, their dignity and self-respect stripped away, their sense of identity diminished by racism, poverty, and alcoholism. His most famous tale is "The Lone Ranger and Tonto Fistfight in Heaven," which has a simple plot but is technically complex, with multiple points of view and chronologies, and presenting incremental thematic development. At the center is the aimless life of the narrator, obsessed with his broken romance and the history of his people, and unable to adapt to the life around him. Less angry, but just as powerful, are the stories of Susan Power, who writes about Lakota characters who live in the present but are always aware of the past. Perhaps that is why the time schemes of her tales shift forward and back, switching from one character to another, as in "Morse Code," which traces two generations of the Thunder family. It was incorporated into *The Grass Dancer*, an award-winning collection of inter-related works of short fiction.

African American stories continue to be a major force in the genre, with scores of writers contributing to a rapidly growing body of work. Jamaica Kincaid published eight stories about the John family in Antigua before she brought them together in *Annie John*. Together they recount the life of young Annie from age ten to seventeen, when she leaves the island to begin a new adventure. Along the way, she faces the classic conflicts of adolescence as she strives for individual sovereignty, adjusts to puberty, becomes aware of love, and discovers the opposite gender. Particularly important is "Columbus in Chains," in which a young schoolgirl, Annie, first realizes that the voyages of Columbus resulted in her ancestors being brought to the islands as slaves. Her education is dominated by British concerns, even though she lives in the Caribbean, and her rebellion seeks freedom from that domination, from the control of her mother, and from the restricted life of a small island.

Toni Morrison, a Nobel Prize winner, may be the most famous living writer in America, especially for a string of novels beginning with *The Bluest Eye* and *Sula* and continuing through the Pulitzer Prize– winning *Beloved*. But her short stories are also notable for their thematic subtlety and artistic grace, as is "Recitatif," which portrays the friendship of two girls from differing races who first meet in an orphanage but now come together for an awkward reunion as adults. Their precise racial identity is never as clear as their class identifications: one works in a restaurant while the other is obviously wealthy, with a chauffeur and a limousine. They have drifted apart, but they share memories of their important early friendship.

Much of the legacy of the American story is the result of the vast linguistic, religious, national, and ethnic diversity of the United States. The reading public obviously has an insatiable fascination for fiction that reveals unique cultural traditions that deviate from normative standards, even if they ultimately are based on fundamental relationships within a family or social group. Early in the twentieth century, Sui Sin Far's story cycle *Mrs. Spring Fragrance* depicted an immigrant Chinese family learning English and adjusting to American culture, sometimes with tragic outcomes. In contemporary literature, Amy Tan's *The Joy Luck Club* plays a similar role although for four families that have been in San Francisco for less than a generation. It is a carefully constructed volume, with four stories about each of four families, with each mother and each daughter telling two with one exception, when one mother in "A Pair of Tickets" dies and her daughter tells her tale for her. She tells the story of the abandoned babies and how, more than two decades later, her father arranged for her to go to China to meet them. These are themes that cut across the sixteen tales: the mothers all want their daughters to retain a knowledge of the language and customs of China; the daughters are intent on assimilation. The conflicts of the volume are nearly always within these families, not with a hostile or indifferent white society. "Rules of the Game," for instance, is about a mother's pride in her daughter's chess prowess and the young girl's rebellion by refusing to play. In all of the cases there are flashbacks to the struggles of the mother in China set against the conflicts their daughters face in a multicultural California. A brilliant volume, it quickly established Tan as a major force in American letters. Frank Chin also writes about immigrant Chinese families in such stories as "Railroad Standard Time," which shows a young man driving from Seattle to San Francisco to attend his mother's funeral. On the way his mind wanders to dwell on the many years his grandfather worked on the railroad and carried the very watch he now wears, and it provides a point of departure for him to engage the direction and meaning of his own life. Yiyun Li offers impressively innovative fiction from this tradition in both artistic methodology and subject matter. In "The Princess of Nebraska," for example, she presents the complicated tale of Boshen, a gay physician who emigrated from China by virtue of a token marriage, although he still longs for his male lover on the mainland, Yang. Also a recent arrival, Sasha, a Mongolian with a Russian name, is carrying Yang's child, but he has remained in China. Now, she is contemplating an abortion as she make drives to Chicago. The conflicts thus involve ethnicity, to be sure, but also international homosexuality in two vastly different cultures that results in a strange love triangle that is bisexual and based on multiple dimensions of the concept of love.

These cultural themes are equally as intense in Julia Alvarez's *How the Garcia Girls Lost Their Accents*, in which the stories are told in inverse chronological order from the present to the childhood of the Garcia daughters in the Dominican Republic. The issues throughout are not only ethnic but generational and personal, with a linguistic charm, as they are in "The Blood of the Conquistadors" and "Floor Show," and both of which offer a penetrating psychological insight into the struggles of an immigrant family in contemporary America. That is also true of Sandra Cisneros's volume *The House on Mango Street*, in which her poetic touches in prose can be humorous, poignant, or dramatic. A complicated collection of interrelated episodes, it develops several dominant thematic strands: the desire of the continuing protagonist, Esperanza Cordero, for a respectable home in a safe neighborhood, runs throughout, as does the progressively dominant threat of sexual assault by the boys in her Latino society. There is little conflict of this family with the white community in Chicago, although there is a mix of nationality types in the inner city. In "The First Job," for example, she is kissed by an Asian man at work, the first physical assault she has experienced. By the end of the volume, in "Red Clowns," she is raped at a carnival, and her first sexual experience is threatening, painful, and disillusioning. She knows that she could end up like many of the older women in the area, trapped in an unhappy marriage with a house full of children, no money, and a husband who beats her. She sees these women every day, leaning out of a window, longing to be part of a wider world.

Among the unique strengths of the contemporary American short story is the wide range of nationalities of the authors, a spectrum that includes nearly every ethnic and religious group in the world. Judith Ortiz Cofer writes out of her Puerto Rican background with impressive artistic skill and insight into the issues that dominate that immigrant society. Her "Nada," for example, offers a rich evocation of life in the barrio of Newark, New Jersey, during the Vietnam War. Using rather traditional methods of narration, she presents an innovative cast of characters and thematic subjects throughout her fiction. In this story, a woman loses her entire family when her son is killed in the war, and she sheds all of her worldly possessions, ending naked, dead, and alone in her apartment in "el building." Her neighbors in the tenement clothe her, and one of them relates her story in retrospect, revealing the depth of her understanding and sympathy for this decent woman.

Writing from yet another ethnic background, Bharati Mukherjee has emerged as the most visible writer with a South Asian heritage. Born in Calcutta, and educated in India, she lived in Canada for many years before moving to the United States. Her characters often share a similar biographical trajectory. In "The World According to Hsu," an immigrant couple from Canada becomes involved in a coup on an island off the coast of Africa. In "A Father," a man realizes he has lost control of his life, and he withdraws into religion and mental illness. Unlike the other members of his family, who successfully assimilated into the American society, he seems a patriarch from a forgotten world, wedded to tradition, unable to adapt or adjust to modern life.

Along with Bharati Mukherjee, a host of productive writers of short fiction continue to enrich the national literature, among them Gish Jen, whose "Birthmates" won her wide acclaim and whose collection of stories, *Who's Irish*, established her as among the foremost American authors. Tobias Wolff began his impressive career with "Smokers" in 1976 and quickly became an important figure with his first collection of stories, *In the Garden of the North American Martyrs*, in 1981, and his fiction has won a long list of significant prizes, including the PEN/Faulkner Award. Writing about love, loss of faith, and family issues, Joy Williams, in stories such as "The Lover" and "Shepherd," covers some of the same concerns that epitomized the career of Andre Dubus. Williams' volumes *Taking Care* and *Escapes* solidified the standing of her work in the genre. Sylvia A. Watanabe follows in the footsteps of Hisaye Yamamoto in providing stories about Japanese Americans, although those born in Hawaii. Her most famous tale is "Talking to the Dead," which deals with the threat posed by industrialism and commercialism to the traditional values of living in harmony with Nature. Writing out of a different set of cultural values, Melena María Viramontes made her mark among Latina writers with her first book, *The Moths and Other Stories*, about immigrants on the West coast. The title story, "The Moths," along with "The Cariboo Café," are often anthologized. Leslie Marmon Silko made the art of telling Native American narratives a key theme in her work, especially in *Storytellers*, which also emphasizes individual and community identity. Annie Proulx also used her personal background in New England and, later, Wyoming, for her short fiction, as collected in *Heart Songs and Other Stories* and *Close Range*, enriched in part because of the French-Canadian heritage of her father. Lorrie Moore's stories deal predominantly with mothers and their daughters, who are usually thoughtful and unhappy young women, as in the collection *Self-Help*.

Although David Wong Louie is perhaps best known for his editing of the popular collection *The Big Aiiieeeee!: An Anthology of Chinese American and Japanese American Literature*, his own ethnic tales have appeared to impressive acclaim, as did "Displacement" and "Birthday." His themes typically grow from the tensions between the pressure for assimilation of Asian protagonists and the indifference of mainstream America to this minority population. In fact, the conflicts inherent in the cultural duality of immigrant groups is one of the things that unites writers from a broad spectrum of countries of origin, since virtually all of them deal with the isolation and identity crisis faced by recent arrivals and yet the desire to sustain the traditions, language, and religions of their birth. The United States is the only country to present a rich literary legacy of short stories on this theme, one that begins with European settlers in the 1850s and continues into the twenty-first century.

The short story grew in popularity in America as it had nowhere else, in part because of the continuous wave of immigrant authors with a unique and dramatic adventure to tell. These writers brought a vitality of narrative methods to their new world, adding to what was already a rich legacy of tales from every section of the country. In the new century, the genre continues to dramatize the most salient issues of a heterogeneous population with writers from contrasting racial, religious, and linguistic cultures. A literary tradition in fiction that originally was almost exclusively devoted to the novel evolved over the centuries to one that celebrates the form of the story, and nearly every important living writer has made important contributions to this rich legacy. The short story has become the genre of choice within the Creative Writing programs at colleges and universities throughout the country, and many of the authors now widely celebrated had their beginnings in such programs, as did John Steinbeck, the first important American writer to derive from such academic instruction. From the wonderful tales that are published every month in the United States, to the rich stories that form the literary history of the genre, reaching back to the middle of the eighteenth century, there is much to celebrate in the history of short fiction in America, a precious legacy filled with human greatness, national identity, and promise.

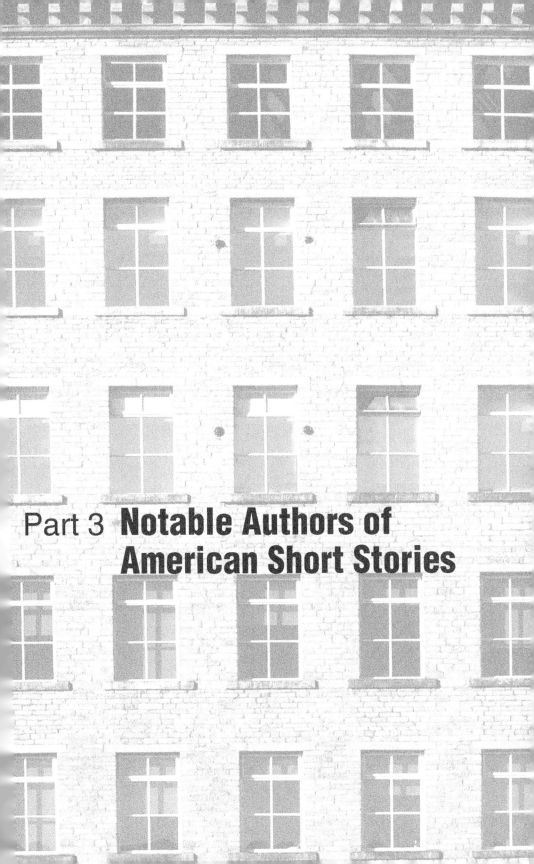

Part 3 Notable Authors of American Short Stories

Washington Irving (1783–1859)

Although it is not literally accurate to claim that the American short story began with Washington Irving's "Rip Van Winkle" in 1819, as is often claimed, he is nevertheless a monumental figure in the literary history of the form. He was the first writer of fiction in the New World to establish a sustained international reputation, a status that has not diminished in the nearly two centuries since his career began. Although hundreds of pieces of prose narrative had appeared in the newspapers and magazines in earlier decades, Irving's best work brought a new artistic standard to the genre, blending narrative voice, action, dialogue, and vivid descriptions. As Fred Lewis Pattee pointed out in *The Development of the American Short Story* in 1923, these stories were enormously popular, providing entertainment to vast audiences in fiction set in recognizable American settings, even when adapting European myths to a new region. He offered both humor and charm, an elegance of style and presentation, and a delicacy of character development that made his work acceptable even to the people being satirized. On the other hand, his literary proclivities were more suitable to the sketch than to narrative fiction, and he produced no novels and only a small number of genuine short stories, a handful of them set in America.

His best stories come out of only a few of his many books, most importantly *The Sketch Book*, which included "Rip Van Winkle," "The Spectre Bridegroom," and "The Legend of Sleepy Hollow." These works are presented in the customary guise of putative authorship at some remove from Irving himself. The writing of fiction was not yet a respectable endeavor for proper gentlemen, and he followed the established practice of claiming that the tale was the work of someone else. Actually, he presents himself as being two removes from authorship: *The Sketch* Book is said to be the work of

The American Short Story Handbook, First Edition. James Nagel.
© 2015 James Nagel. Published 2015 by John Wiley & Sons, Ltd.

Geoffrey Crayon, Gent., but "Rip Van Winkle," he says, was found among the recently discovered papers of Diedrich Knickerbocker, a man known for "scrupulous accuracy" that lends to the events related the certainty of "unquestionable authority." Irving is thus playful with the reliability of his narrator and with the fundamental truthfulness of what is told, issues that give his work a humorous surface and a more philosophic edge. It suggests that what is accurate historically may not be "morally" true, whereas fabricated events can sometimes present the deepest truth of the human situation, issues that Tim O'Brien resurrected in his celebrated volume of stories *The Things They Carried* at the end of the twentieth century.

Essentially an Americanization of the German myth of Peter Klaus, the story is set in the Catskill mountains of New York and the strange characters Rip meets on his strange journey recall the Dutch settlers of the region. As in the original tale, Rip leaves behind a shrewish wife, a son and a daughter, and his native village, and he sets out with his dog on a hunting trip through the forest above the Hudson River. Resting from his climb on a green knoll, he thinks he hears his name called, and looking about he spies a strange figure, small and stout, and dressed in the Dutch manner of the previous century, carrying a keg of ale. The man does not speak but gestures that Rip should help with the burden. Together, they carry the keg into a glen where there are other small men, similarly dressed, playing at nine pins, the sound of which echoes like thunder down the mountainside. No one speaks, but Rip joins the group in drinking of the brew and, somewhat befumed, falls asleep.

He awakens on the green knoll and finds his gun rusted, his dog vanished, and his beard a foot long. Despite the stiffness in his joints, he makes the long walk back to his village only to discover it is larger than when he had left and many of the buildings changed. His own house has collapsed of neglect, his wife has died, and there is a strange flag with stars and strips flying above the village. During his slumber of twenty years, the American Revolution has taken place, and he mistakes the portrait of George Washington for one of George III of England. His son has replaced him as the lazy wastrel of the community, and his daughter has married and has a child of her own. When he tells the tale of his long sleep in the Catskills, the villagers regard him as a harmless old fool with an entertaining story to tell, and he resumes his earlier life of fishing and lounging about free from the labors of ordinary life. Diedrich Knickerbocker returns at the conclusion to testify to the veracity of Rip's account, one that is true without the possibility of doubt.

"Rip Van Winkle" lends itself to a wide variety of speculative interpretations, from the philosophical, a look into the world of the dead, to the psychoanalytic, a character's journey into his unconscious, but it can also be read on the simplest level as an entertainment featuring a marvelous event or as the playful invention of a man who escaped his nagging wife, ran away for twenty years, and returned after she had died. He has managed to enjoy the freedom of childhood pursuits and the restful privileges of old age without ever having to assume adult responsibilities. In the humorous context of verifying the accuracy of Rip's tale of his long sleep, Irving has also focused on the enormous political change that has taken place, with the voting of the villagers and the vibrant new economy free of the King's taxes, making the events an expression of the ethos of the New World. Although the plot lacks the central conflict and resolution upon which most stories are built, it nonetheless presents an entertaining tale with a charming narrator, gentle satire, and the absolute assurance that it is all true.

In many ways "The Legend of Sleepy Hollow" is a companion piece to the account of the Good Rip Van Winkle in that they are both set in the Dutch regions of the Hudson River Valley and purport to be written by Diedrich Knickerbocker. They are both based on well-known Germanic tales, "Sleepy Hollow" on G. A. Büger's tale "Der wilde Jäger" in the late eighteenth century. Both of Irving's stories capture important elements that are uniquely American, in this case the conflict between the country ruffian who knows the folkways and mythos of the region and the city slicker from the outside, a Connecticut Yankee in the person of a schoolmaster, Ichabod Crane. The central conflict of the plot is a love triangle in which the schoolmaster and a local farmer, Brom Bones, vie for the affections of a comely lass, Katrina Van Tassel. But Brom knows the local legend of the Headless Horseman, said to be a Hessian left over from the Revolutionary War, a German conscript from Hesse who fought for the British. Ichabod is purely a comic figure, with his knees above his hands as he rides a horse named "Gunpowder" who is too much for him. When he presses his suit for Katrina, lusting after her father's wealthy estate, Brom plays on his imagination by staging an appearance of the Headless Horseman in the neighboring woods on a dark night, and poor Crane is never heard from again. This comic tale is set in the rich agrarian lands along the Hudson that Rip observed on his journey into the mountains, and the two stories have entered American mythology as unforgettable early legends.

The rest of *The Sketch Book* contains tales and sketches set in various European countries and rely on picturesque or Gothic elements for interest. One exception is "Traits of Indian Character," an essay that reflects on a popular subject of the day, the Native American and the role that an indigenous population might play in the formation of a new society. The only story is "The Spectre Bridegroom," a German tale that rests on the fascination of the local population on ghost accounts and reports of marvelous events. In this brief plot one Baron Von Landshort, a devotee of the supernatural, arranges a marriage of his comely daughter to Count Von Altenburg, even though the two young people have never met. On his passage to his wedding, Altenburg encounters Herman Von Starkenfaust, a stout fellow well met, and they agree to journey together. They are set upon by thieves in a dark forest, and Altenburg is killed in the confrontation, but before he dies he asks his companion to explain his absence to his intended, not wishing to insult her on what was to have been her wedding day. When he sees her, young Starkenfaust is smitten and pretends to be the bridegroom, but before the marriage ceremony, he claims to be a spectre called back to the grave, and he makes his escape. Soon after, however, he returns of an evening and runs off with the fair maiden, confessing to her father his deep devotion to his daughter, and everyone is happy at the conclusion. It is not as compelling a situation as in the two best stories, but it draws on some of Irving's standard elements: the Gothic setting, the swirl of darkly mysterious legends that the local population embraces, a kind of courtship triangle that is resolved and leads to an appropriate marriage. Told with grace by a narrator with an ironic edge, the tale presents entertainment, a sketch of local color in the German wilderness, and a cast of characters who each embody some aspect of the regional European population.

After *The Sketch Book*, Irving wrote scores of additional prose narratives, none of them set in America and all of them strong on description and character but somewhat weak on plot and tension. *Bracebridge Hall* is an entertaining volume of sketches and tales, all of them set in Europe. Of these, "The Stout Gentleman" has the grace and charm of his best work but nothing of consequence comes of the central issues. "Annette Delarbe" returns to the subject of courtship and its complexity but without the humor of "Sleepy Hollow." *Tales of a Traveller* is intriguing in narrative terms and for the theme of veracity in telling, especially in the opening ghost stories. The most famous of these tales is "Adventure of the German Student," which presents young Gottfried Wolfgang in Paris during the French Revolution. His love for a young woman he believes to have been beheaded drives him mad. Indeed, the narrator heard the account from Gottfied in an institution for the insane. The fiction in *The Alhambra* is all set in Spain, as the title implies, and it contains such entertaining pieces as the "Legend of the Moor's Legacy," a tale about the lust for the wealth a dying Moor left behind. "The Legend of the Enchanted Soldier" returns to marvelous events and the supernatural. Of his other short pieces, "The Adalantado of the Seven Cities" is of greatest interest in that it presents yet another legendary sleeper, Don Fernando de Ulmo, who slumbers for more than a century, but the account lacks the artistic grace of "Rip Van Winkle."

Indeed, Irving was never again to surpass the aesthetic virtues of his two most famous early stories, "Rip Van Winkle" and "The Legend of Sleepy Hollow," which continue to buttress his reputation as the first American writer of short stories to gain an international following. This point is historically significant because in the early years of the young nation, Americans in a broad variety of fields were eager to promote the fledgling country as a source of serious cultural expression. Irving contributed significantly to that effort, especially in *The Sketch Book*, and the literary movement that followed in his wake became known as the American Renaissance, a movement in the arts of mid-nineteenth century that established the United States as a genuine center of important literary creativity.

Suggestions for Further Reading

Aderman, Ralph M. *Critical Essays on Washington Irving*. Boston: G. K. Hall, 1990.

Bowden, Mary. *Washington Irving*. Boston: Twayne, 1981.

Jones, Brian Jay. *Washington Irving: An American Original*. New York: Arcade, 2008.

Reichart, Walter A. *Washington Irving and Germany*. Ann Arbor: University of Michigan Press, 1957.

Rubin-Dorsky, Jeffrey. *Adrift in the Old World: The Psychological Pilgrimage of Washington Irving*. Chicago: University of Chicago Press, 1988.

Wagenknecht, Edward. *Irving: Moderation Displayed*. New York: Oxford University Press, 1962.

Edgar Allan Poe

Edgar Allan Poe is in many ways the most impressive figure in the history of the American short story. Known not only for his brilliant tales in a wide variety of fictional modes but also for his poetry and insightful essays on creativity and form, his commentaries on the artistic nature of a "story" and the intellectual process by which short fiction is composed remain the most compelling treatment of the subject more than a century and a half after they were published. In his review of Nathaniel Hawthorne's *Mosses from an Old Manse* and in "The Philosophy of Composition" he gave his best explanations of his approach to planning and executing works of short fiction meant to be read at a single setting. This stress on brevity was related to the idea that the author should begin a story with a consideration of the "effect" it will have on the reader and then proceed to relate all aspects of fiction, especially tone, plot, and character, to contribute to that end. Poe thus established a standard for the evaluation of the modern short story in terms of its coherence and congruence, the extent to which all aspects contribute to its aesthetic unity and psychological impact.

One of the areas in which Poe contributed a new sub-genre is the detective story, what became known as his tales of ratiocination, in which a crime is solved not through superior physical process or skill with weapons but through the power of rational thought. In "The Murders in the Rue Morgue," for example, C. Auguste Dupin uses the empirical process to unravel a seemingly impossible crime without ever seeing the perpetrator, merely by investigating the scene of the action, selecting clues, and reasoning *inductively* (not *deductively*, as many readers mistakenly assume), gathering pieces of evidence and drawing a conclusion from them. Using this method, he determines that an Ourang-Outang climbed up the outside

The American Short Story Handbook, First Edition. James Nagel.
© 2015 James Nagel. Published 2015 by John Wiley & Sons, Ltd.

of the building, entered through the window, and committed the murder, and the mystery is solved. Narrated by a somewhat ineffectual friend of the detective, who marvels at the mental processes of Dupin, Poe established a pattern that was followed by countless other writers in the detective vein, including, most famously, Arthur Conan Doyle, whose Sherlock Holmes tales are told by his friend Dr. Watson.

Poe used this precise method again in what he regarded as the best of his tales of ratiocination, "The Purloined Letter." Part of what makes this mode so intriguing is that all of the details available to the protagonist are also presented to the reader, who can attempt to reason through the evidence and arrive at the conclusion ahead of Dupin. Set again in Paris, the plot involves the request of Monsieur G_____, the Prefect of the Parisian Police, for the assistance of C. Auguste Dupin in solving an unusual crime, one in which the criminal, the date and moment of the incident, and the motivation are known but the location of the incriminating purloined letter seems impossible to ascertain. The Prefect outlines how his men have searched every corner of the rooms in which the document must be hidden, but not a trace of it has been uncovered. Dupin immediately suggests that the location of it must be self-evident, so much in plain view that no one has even thought to look at it, a comment that elicits laughter from his guest. Dupin then visits the apartment in question and immediately finds the letter, which he replicates at home in advance of his second visit, when he secrets a replica in place of the authentic envelope. Thus, when the Prefect next visits, Dupin is able to provide him with the purloined letter along with a logical explanation of how it was found. The method is an understanding of the habits of thought of the perpetrator, who has reasoned that the most obvious location will be the least suspected, and so he has left it in plain view the entire time. Dupin solved the crime by understanding the mind of the minister D_____, not by force or direct confrontation. Poe had set a high standard for future practitioners of detective fiction, one rarely even approached in subsequent decades.

Another sub-genre for which Poe became famous is the horror story, often a situation in which the protagonist finds himself trapped with no discernable method of escape, no motivation for the fiendish means of his impending demise, and no opponent he might convince of his right to freedom. The fictional epitome of that circumstance is "The Pit and the Pendulum," in which the protagonist also serves as first-person narrator, a necessary stratagem in that no one else appears in the narrative. Set in Spain in the city of Toledo, the location of the horrors of the Inquisition, the protagonist finds himself confined to a room in a dungeon obviously used for the most ghastly of executions, since the outlines of skeletons are evident as are the implements for inflicting agony and death. In the dank and totally dark confines of his cell, he discovers, in crawling about the room, a deep pit filled with rats into which he could easily have fallen. When he later sleeps, he awakens to find bread and water placed beside him, and he eats and drinks of it, immediately falling again into a prolonged slumber. Regaining consciousness, he finds himself tied to a low table over which there swings a large pendulum with a razor-sharp edge, slowly descending to slice him in half. He again sleeps and finds pungent meat and water placed next to him and, as the blade draws near, cleverly rubs some of the meat onto the bands that confine him, and the rats chew him free. Finally, in his last threatening situation, he finds the room constricting, designed ultimately to force him into death in the pit. Just as it is about to do so, the Count de La Salle appears with the French army and frees him. Napoleon's forces have taken northern Spain and ended his maddening proximity to a painful demise. The portrait of a horrible circumstance that threatens a nearly helpless victim is a standard Poe stratagem, as is the suggestion that life can end without reason or justification, without meaning, without compassion or concern.

"The Fall of the House of Usher" is another Gothic tale of horror of a rather different sort for in this instance the narrator is an observer and not directly threatened in any way. The story opens with his arrival at the ancient home of a childhood friend, Roderick Usher, summoned by a letter requesting his presence. From the beginning the narrator feels as sense of "insufferable gloom" and a "depression of soul" that establish the tone and underlying mood of the narrative. Roderick offers a cordial welcome, but there is something troubling him, a portent that seems to involve his twin sister, Madeline, who appears so weak that the narrator fears he will never see her again, at least not alive. She appears only briefly, and she never speaks, functioning more as a familial externalization than as a character in her own right. In any event, it is clear that whatever malady has afflicted her awaits her brother since they are so closely identified. When he learns that she has died, the two men prepare the body and care for the funeral arrangements, but later, when they are relaxing in the sitting rooms, they hear strange noises from the tombs below, and, in a scene of shock and horror, Madeline appears at the door with blood on her robes and falls dead into her brother's arms, and he immediately dies as well. The family had a history of some kind of cataleptic seizure that might cause a premature burial, an idea that has haunted Roderick. The horrified narrator flees the huge house only to look back and see it collapsing into the tarn, the building and the Usher family gone forever. The Gothic suggestions of an ancient house resembling a castle, with turrets above and submerged family tombs below, gives a decidedly European setting to a scene of shocking action, of madness in Roderick and catatonia in his sister, both of which are profoundly disturbing to the narrator.

Poe drew on many standard Gothic elements in the construction of "The Fall of the House of Usher," and he added several dimensions common to his own work, including being buried alive. Poe also used this idea of a form of catalepsy that so resembled death that people were interred while still alive in "The Premature Burial." Quintessentially Gothic in "Usher" is the open-ing arrival at a castle-like ancient house anthropomorphized into a vaguely threatening and depressing being, with empty windows that seem to be eyes, a structure so identified with its inhabitants that they all die together. The home and family are doomed from the beginning, a supernatural twinning of substance and spirit that strike the narrator from the moment he enters the building. The tone throughout is one of gloom and decay, of pathologi-cal aberration, of impending decline and death. There is little to relieve this atmosphere, which heightens with the announcement of Madeline's demise and reaches its apex with her emergence from the tomb, covered with her own blood, when she collapses dead into her brother's arms. None of this is a direct threat to the narrator except psychologically, and he seems on the edge of insanity himself as he flees the house immediately prior to its collapse into the tarn. He has entered into the realm of madness and death; he has seen much, and he will never be the same.

Poe's work in the short story extends to many other areas as well, some-time with brilliant effect, as in the use of Gothic elements for a confessional narrative such as "The Cask of Amontillado," in which a revenge murder many decades past still haunts the narrator. The intriguing suggestion of a psychological double in Madeline and Roderick Usher is more directly addressed in "William Wilson," a Doppelgänger story. The death of the beautiful Madeline is echoed in many stories, including "Ligeia" and "The Oval Portrait." The destructive power of hidden sin, a powerful theme in Hawthorne's work, invests much of Poe's fiction, as it does in "The Tell-Tale Heart" and "The Black Cat." In these works, as in scores of others, Poe demonstrated his fundamental theories of the art of short fiction as demand-ing concision, coherence, and congruence with a central effect that con-trolled all other elements. Very few writers over the last century and a half could even approach his demanding level of aesthetic control, one reason he continues to be a vital presence in the twenty-first century.

Suggestions for Further Reading

Carlson, Eric. *Critical Essays on Edgar Allan Poe*. Boston: G. K. Hall, 1987.

Davidson, Edward H. *Poe: A Critical Study*. Cambridge: Harvard University Press, 1957.

Fisher, Benjamin Franklin. *The Cambridge Introduction to Edgar Allan Poe*. Cambridge: Cambridge University Press, 2008.

Halliburton, David. *Edgar Allan Poe: A Phenomenological View*. Princeton: Princeton University Press, 1973.

Thompson, G. R. *Poe's Fiction: Romantic Irony in the Gothic Tales*. Madison: University of Wisconsin Press, 1973.

Nathaniel Hawthorne

Nathaniel Hawthorne is a monumental figure in the historical development of the short story in America. In essentially two decades of literary production, he altered the course of fiction by shifting its focus from the reconfiguration of European mythological tales to the introduction of an entirely new American series of legendary figures and ideas rendered with unprecedented psychological depth, moral insight, and stylistic integrity. His reputation rests primarily on the works brought together in three important collections, *Twice-Told Tales* (1837), *Moses from an Old Manse* (1846), and *The Snow Image, and Other Twice-Told Tales* (1852), all of which went through multiple editions that added stories and made significant alterations. These volumes helped establish the fiction of American Romanticism as a serious form of artistic expression with an intellectual depth and aesthetic rigor that demanded international attention.

The finest of Hawthorne's stories helped to establish the stature of the American Renaissance, the fruition of a burgeoning cultural production that had come to rival the output of the finest writers in England and the continent. Following Washington Irving, Hawthorne sometimes transformed a standard European plot structure into a tale with local applications, as he did with "My Kinsman, Major Molineux," in which the "young man from the provinces" theme is retold using a local political struggle in the city. A country youth, Robin Molineux, nearing his eighteenth birthday, sets off for an unban center that closely resembles Boston to find his relative, who has been appointed governor by the King of England, overturning the established right of the citizenry to elect their own leaders. In response, the people of the city rise up in rebellion, predicting the fervor that led to the American Revolution. A handsome innocent, and the son of a clergyman, Robin is unaware

The American Short Story Handbook, First Edition. James Nagel.
© 2015 James Nagel. Published 2015 by John Wiley & Sons, Ltd.

of the machinations of social drama and thinks only of his relative's promise to help him get a start in life.

As is standard in the European version of this myth, the innocent country lad is introduced to the temptations of urban life, all of which threaten and confuse him, especially a young woman with a scarlet petticoat who stirs his sexual interests and a strange man with a bulging forehead and a face both black and red who seems the very embodiment of temptation. As he wanders the city, searching for his kinsman, Robin has a fantasy of his family gathered about in warm communion, but as he approaches his house, the door is closed to him. There is no going back. He finally enlists the assistance of a kindly gentleman who tells him that if they will wait at the side of the street, Major Molineux will shortly pass by. He does so, but not in a position of honor as Robin expected but in utter humiliation: he is being tarred and feathered and ridden out of town in a political uprising. The young man asks his friend the way to the ferry so that he can return home, and the older man suggests that he remain in the city with him for a few days. He is certain that Robin can rise in the world on his own resources without the assistance of his kinsman, Major Molineux. The concluding theme is thus the necessity of independence, of carving a path in life based on one's own initiative and capability, an idea fundamental to American social life.

If Robin Molineux's tale has universal overtones for the maturation process in Western life, so does "Young Goodman Brown," although in the form of an allegory. Here the young man carries the name of "Goodman," a term for an innocent young man. His wife's name is "Faith," which has obvious religious implications, especially when he leaves his wife for a midnight journey through the dark woods guided by a devilish figure who personifies the evil in human nature. On his long walk, Goodman sees many of the leading citizens of the village, all of whom have clearly confronted the sin within themselves, making them annual celebrants at the gathering, a kind of Sabbath of evil. Goodman is shaken as he sees all the people he has admired for their virtue joining the festivities, but he is devastated when he sees his wife fly over on a broom to become part of the unholy group, and he never recovers from the shock and, as the narrator reports, "his dying hour was gloom." He cannot accept human weakness, not even his own. This idea, that recognition of personal sin is a positive and humanizing awareness, is part of a larger theme of the "fortunate fall" that runs throughout Hawthorne's fiction. An admission that the human spirit is inconstant, prone to moments of temptation by the seven deadly sins, allows one to forgive the weakness in others, to reserve harsh judgment, to embrace a loving generosity rather than a harshly stern moral superiority.

The theme of sin and its psychological implications is a central issue in several of Hawthorne's major stories, but in "The Minister's Black Veil" it is played out is an especially intriguing way. One morning the good Parson Hooper appears before his congregation wearing a veil over his face, the motivation for which he never explains, nor does he ever remove it. It is a shocking sight for his people, who interpret it with a spectrum of responses from assuming their minister has gone mad to the suspicion that he had committed some secret sin for which he was paying penance. The narrator universalizes this idea by observing that the veil "had reference to secret sin and those sad mysteries which we hide from our nearest and dearest, and would fain conceal from our own consciousness . . . ." The members of the congregation all feel as though the minister had found them out, had peered into their minds and discovered "their hoarded iniquity of deed or thought." Hooper explains to his intended, Elizabeth, that the veil is a "type and a symbol" of the dark sorrows that people do not wish to expose, and it must never be removed, not even before her. Filled with remorse, she breaks off their engagement.

One irony of the situation is that the veil gives Hooper a strange power over his congregation, as though his veil indicated an intimacy with their inner lives and allowed him to sympathize with their inmost feelings. But even on his deathbed, many years later, he refuses to have the veil withdrawn, hiding forever the secret of his sin, the dark mystery he wishes to conceal. He is buried, and lies forever, beneath the Black Veil. The concept of the secret sin, that weakness of spirit that all mankind seems to wish to remain hidden, is countered in some of Hawthorne's fiction by the public exposure of wrongdoing, as in *The Scarlet Letter* in which Hester is forced to stand before the people of her village wearing a scarlet A on her breast acknowledging her adultery. Her humiliation seems to provide expiation of guilt, however, whereas the good Reverend Dimmesdale, the father of her child, hides his complicity and lives in torment the rest of his life. His hidden sin burns within him, eventually killing him at an early age.

Another subject that Hawthorne explored on numerous occasions was the attempt of an artist or a scientist to improve nature, to manipulate through empirical reasoning the very essence of human existence, attempts that always end tragically. In "The Birthmark," the artist Aylmer attempts to remove a small blemish from the cheek of his wife, Georgianna, thus making her perfect. When he succeeds in removing the birthmark, she dies giving Nature a "triumph over the immortal essence." "Rappaccini's Daughter" similarly ends with the death of the young woman at the hands of her father, in this case a scientist who has somehow produced a child who partakes of both animal and plant natures. An emblem of purity and beauty, Beatrice is nevertheless poisonous to human beings as is the deadly plant she regards as a sister. Her beauty attracts a university student, Giovanni, who falls in love with her. She is deadly to all natural living things, but the young man, spending time with her in the garden, gradually absorbs the poisonous atmosphere himself. Rappaccini's rival at the university, Baglioni, gives Giovanni an antidote to the poison, but Beatrice insists on drinking it first. She does so, and she dies, the victim of her father's quest for forbidden knowledge, the competition among scientists, and the vulnerability of a divided nature. Among other stories, "Dr. Heidegger's Experiment" also features a scientist who searches for forbidden knowledge, whereas "Ethan Brand" deals with the unpardonable sin, the intellectual emphasis on reason at the expense of faith in God and love of humanity.

Hawthorne's stories thus expanded the range of subjects that had been addressed in the early decades of American short fiction and deepened the themes that could derive from them. The introduction of "Romantic ambiguity" in these stories allowed the narrators to present possible explanations for certain events without precluding other answers, a device that enriched the spectrum of readings and confounded scholars who searched for final conclusions. The richness of language in Hawthorne's prose is unmatched in his time, rivaled only by the work of Herman Melville, and it continues to impress readers more than a century and a half after initial publication. In total, Hawthorne's work made an enormous contribution to the growth of indigenous short fiction at a time when it needed a major figure to establish it in the world of serious letters, and his reputation and artistic legacy continue to enrich American literature.

Suggestions for Further Reading

Becker, Isidore H. *The Ironic Dimension in Hawthorne's Short Fiction*. New York: Carlton Press, 1971.

Colacurcio, Michael J. *The Province of Piety: Moral History in Hawthorne's Early Tales*. Cambridge: Harvard University Press, 1984.

Doubleday, Neal F. *Hawthorne's Early Tales: A Critical Study*. Durham: Duke University Press, 1972.

Matthiessen, F. O. *American Renaissance: Art and Expression in the Age of Emerson and Whitman*. New York: Oxford University Press, 1941.

Newman, Lea Bertani Vozar. *A Reader's Guide to the Short Stories of Nathaniel Hawthorne*. Boston: G. K. Hall, 1979.

von Frank, Albert J., ed. *Critical Essays on Hawthorne's Short Stories*. Boston: G. K. Hall, 1991.

Herman Melville

Herman Melville is known primarily for his great novels, especially for *Moby Dick*, *Redburn*, *Billy Budd*, and his early travel accounts, *Typee* and *Omoo*, which made him famous. But he was also the author of some of the most substantial short stories in American literature, including "Bartleby, the Scrivener" and "Benito Cereno," to mention only two. What is remarkable is that virtually all of his important short fiction was written in a very brief period, from 1853 to 1856, during which he composed sixteen tales, placing nearly all of them in the leading magazines of the day and later collecting them into a volume entitled *The Piazza Tales*. These stories are notable for both the substance of their central ideas, generating themes as pertinent a century and a half later as they were upon original publication, and the consummate skill of their artistry, qualities that are tributes to Melville's creative genius.

Perhaps the most widely known of the great stories of this period is "Bartleby, the Scrivener," his portrait of a document copier who takes a position in the office of a Wall Street lawyer. A complex narrative, it has been given a broad spectrum of interpretations, from the philosophical to the psychological, and it is still widely controversial. The best approach to it is to concentrate on fundamentals. It is essentially a first-person retrospective narrative told by the lawyer, who speaks many years after the events. What he relates is how he had a quiet but remunerative practice copying legal documents, an office of human Xerox machines, and he hired Bartleby to perform such a function. At first, the young man did so with great diligence while surrounded with somewhat comic figures, other copyists who are good in the morning and worthless in the afternoon, and vice versa. Then one day Bartleby announces that he would prefer not to do any copying, nor anything else, although he lives in the office day and night,

The American Short Story Handbook, First Edition. James Nagel.
© 2015 James Nagel. Published 2015 by John Wiley & Sons, Ltd.

never going out. In due course, the lawyer attempts to have him removed, but it does not work, so he moves his office. The new tenant has Bartleby arrested and taken to the Tombs, a prison in New York, and there, despite efforts by the lawyer to see that he is well cared for, he dies. The lawyer finds his body. In concluding his narrative, and reflecting on it, he says "Ah Bartleby! Ah humanity!"

Most readers of the story take Bartleby to be the main character, but the protagonist of a work of fiction is generally taken to be the one with the internal conflict, the one who is transformed by the experience related. Bartleby is essentially the same throughout and seems not to have grown in any way. It is the lawyer who has witnessed a man who seems to have concluded that human life is pointless, an empty charade he does not wish to pursue any further, a feeling that may very well have derived from his dreary duties at work. In any event, the lawyer who attempted to evade all forms of conflict and complications is drawn to reflect on the meaning of his copier's withdrawal from life, and he seems nearly obsessed with it. Somewhere in Bartleby's strange behavior there was the suggestion of something that touched the lawyer, that made him endure his refusal to work far beyond reasonable limits. The lawyer has been changed by the experience, deepened by a man who choose to starve himself to death, and the narrator's sense of humanity has been enriched by it. He does not finally understand Bartleby, but he knows that life can be empty and complex far beyond the workaday world he has lived in all these years, and he will never be quite the same.

This basic structure is employed in "Benito Cereno," one of the truly great stories in English, rivaled in American literature only by William Faulkner's "The Bear." It is a brilliant artistic achievement in the same mode as "Bartleby," a first-person retrospective narrative and a profound commentary on issues of race, slavery, morality, cruelty, justice, and the value of a single human life. A long story, it involves many complex events that were difficult to interpret even at the time they happened, but its central plot involves an American ship captain, Amasa Delano, aboard the *Bachelor's Delight* off the coast of Chile, who comes upon the *San Dominick*, which appears to be in distress. Captain Delano decides to board the ship to see if he can offer assistance, and his visit provides the major part of the narrative. There he meets the Spanish Benito Cereno, who seems to be ill. He is attended by an African servant, Babo, who sees to his every need and refuses to be away from his master for even a moment. When Delano is preparing to return to his own ship, Cereno leaps into the small boat with him and declares that Babo is the leader of a deadly slave rebellion and that he has been held prisoner, threatened at every turn by his servant. Babo also leaps into the boat, but Delano overcomes him and takes him prisoner. In due course, he frees the *San Dominick* from African control, and the rebels, including Babo, are tried for murder and executed. The tale concludes with depositions from the trial, written in typically legal prose style, and giving the facts of the case once again.

The suspense of this dramatic action is heightened by its narrative technique. The emphasis is on Delano's mind, on his somewhat obtuse inability to understand the meaning of the strange behavior he is witnessing. In his pervading innocence, he seems unwilling to imagine the depth of evil that is parading before him, both the cruel practice of slavery and the horrendous middle passages that Africans were subjected to, and the equally barbaric actions of the rebellious slaves, who kill the original captain and mount his body on the front of the ship as a masthead. Delano's good nature is so deeply ingrained that he seems unable to detect the façade of kindly behavior behind Babo's conduct, for example, and he crushes any suspicions he might have that there is something sinister going on. When he does finally see through the mask of civility, he acts decisively, freeing Cereno and rescuing the ship. For his part, Benito Cereno has been psychologically damaged by his experience, by the constant threats of imminent death, by the cruelty he has observed, by what he has realized human beings are capable of doing to one another, and he dies haunted by the image of Babo. The African proves to be a man of complex parts, capable of presenting the most benevolent of exteriors while contemplating the cruelest actions toward the white men about him. On the other hand, his rebellion seems a justifiable retort to the cruelty shown to men forcibly taken from their native land, men about to be bound into a lifetime of slavery. Virtually any act that holds even the slightest promise of freedom would seem justified under the circumstances. The story thus ends with some of the most important issues of the nineteenth century introduced but not resolved, including the distinction between good and evil, the limits of cruelty and civil conduct, and the rights of individual human beings of all races. Melville does not suggest simplistic solutions to the most vexing of these problems, but he has turned the eye of American civilization on a set of ideas that within a decade would erupt into the most violent conflict ever to occur in the New World, the Civil War.

In "The Bell Tower," Melville develops a theme borrowed from his friend Nathaniel Hawthorne, that of the artist who reaches too far in his quest for perfection, who seeks to outstrip even God in his creative abilities. A celebrated designer and builder, Bannadonna is commissioned to construct a huge tower that will house both a bell and a clock, something that has not been done before. Beyond simply building the structure, however, he seeks to invest his mechanical device with something close to human life, especially with respect to Tolus, a figure that has the function of ringing the bell. Indeed, to those who have observed it, this creature seems sentient and animated, as though its creator had gone beyond Nature in his abilities. But he has made a mistake in the construction, a flaw that resulted from his violent outburst in striking a workman, causing a small fragment to fall into the molten metal being cast. This defect is ultimately responsible for the collapse of the entire structure, the figure of Tolus striking and killing its designer. This conclusion suggests both a distrust of the burgeoning emphasis on technology in the mid-nineteenth century and a caution about uncontrolled pride. In one sense, Bannadonna's life of artistic achievement has gone unappreciated by the masses, a matter he seeks to overcome with a single masterful work, his bell tower. In his unbounded faith in his own abilities, however, he builds a marvelous structure but is ultimately destroyed by his own creation, his pride bringing about his inevitable fall.

"The Lightning-Rod Man" deals not only with technological development but with an underlying distrust of the primacy of reason and empirical science. The narrator, snugly at home in a cottage in the mountains, is interrupted by the arrival of a traveling salesman lining up orders for lightning rods. He does so in the midst of a storm, with bolts of lightning crashing down and the mountains trembling with thunder echoing down the valleys. The story is nearly entirely the conversation between the two men, and in it the narrator reveals his own distrust of science and his desire to determine his own course of action despite the perfectly reasonable arguments of the salesman. Indeed, everything his guest says about the nature of lightning, the probabilities of where it will strike, the efficacy of his copper rod in conducting a bolt into the ground without damage, and the dangers inherent in the narrator's disregard of all he has said, all of this is backed by scientific observation, experience, and experiment. But the narrator insists on his independence of such reasoning, and he is defiant even of the will of natural law, choosing to preserve his dignity in defiance rather than capitulate to the carefully crafted argument of the salesman. It is clear from the beginning, that he will never, under any circumstances, purchase a lightning rod.

Melville's other contributions to American short fiction are generally of lesser moment, although all of them contain elements of significant intellectual interest. Although an unusual form of narrative, "The Encantadas" is essentially a series of ten sketches of the island group that became known as The Galapagos, the subject of Charles Darwin's studies of evolution. Essentially volcanic uprisings, these structures are portrayed as a fallen world, a kind of hell on earth, with strange creatures found nowhere else. Melville's accounts of the people who have attempted to live on these islands invariably end tragically, revealing the worst elements of human nature. "Cock-A-Doodle-Doo!" is a more standard tale about a cynical narrator temporarily freed from despair by the crowing of a cock, who unfortunately soon dies. The narrator is left to contemplate the complexity of a world with both good and evil dimensions, a standard situation in Romantic fiction. There are many other stories, "Jimmy Rose" and "The Happy Failure" among them, but none of the other brief tales approach the artistic excellence and intellectual substance of "Benito Cereno" and "Bartleby, the Scrivener," both classic stories from the mid-nineteenth century.

Suggestions for Further Reading

Burkholder, Robert E. *Critical Essays on Herman Melville's "Benito Cereno."* New York: G. K. Hall, 1992.

Dillingham, William B. *Melville's Short Fiction, 1853-1856.* Athens: University of Georgia Press, 1977.

Fisher, Marvin. *Going Under: Melville's Short Fiction and the American 1850s.* Baton Rouge: Louisiana State University Press, 1977.

Fogle, Richard Harter. *Melville's Shorter Tales.* Norman: University of Oklahoma Press, 1960.

Gunn, Giles, ed. *A Historical Guide to Herman Melville.* Oxford: Oxford University Press, 2005.

Miller, James E. Jr., *A Reader's Guide to Herman Melville.* New York: Farrar, Straus and Giroux, 1962.

Newman, Lea B. *A Reader's Guide to the Short Stories of Herman Melville.* Boston: G. K. Hall, 1986.

Widmer, Kingsley. *The Ways of Nihilism: Herman Melville's Short Novels.* Los Angeles: California State Colleges, 1970.

Mark Twain

What is unique about much of Twain's short fiction is that it was not published separately in magazines, as was the norm, but instead he inserted his stories into his travel narratives and other long works. What differentiates him from the standard literary tradition of the day is the fact that his tales evolve out of the legacy of American humor, particularly the oral tradition, not out of the more respectable formal aesthetic enunciated by Poe and other writers of the early part of the century. His stories are not highly unified, for example, nor do they utilize every detail for a single effect. They are not concise, pointed narratives, written in a "proper" lexicon that parents wanted emulated by young people. Twain wrote in the regional vernacular of his various settings, using the language and formulations of the folk, not the learned elite. His digressive plots wander about in the manner of spoken yarns, taking new directions whenever they occur to the narrator, who is in no hurry to get to the point. As a result, these works have multiple effects, working in many directions at once, so that a tale can have satiric social or political elements, humor, and grim realism, all in the same story. Often Twain used a frame technique common to Southwestern humor, that of a genteel narrator who speaks in standard English at the beginning and end but gives the internal narrative over to a local character who tells a rambling story in authentic dialect. Twain does not condescend to such speakers, using their linguistic habits to reveal their rustic origins, making them cornpone buffoons; rather, he humanizes them, allowing them to reveal themselves in the stories they tell.

Simon Wheeler is such a figure in Twain's first immensely popular piece of short fiction, "The Celebrated Jumping Frog of Calaveras County," widely regarded as the archetypal example of Southwestern Humor. The key to such

The American Short Story Handbook, First Edition. James Nagel.
© 2015 James Nagel. Published 2015 by John Wiley & Sons, Ltd.

a story is the personality of the internal narrator, the manner and language of the telling, for in the oral tradition this deadpan speaker would show no indication that he was aware that there was anything funny about the absurd elements of what he was saying. The tale begins with Mark Twain arriving in a California mining camp, where a friend of his from the East has suggested he look up Simon Wheeler and ask him about the Reverend Leonidas W. Smiley. Wheeler backs Twain into a corner of the saloon and begins his wandering recitation, never smiling, changing expression, or altering the dawdling speed of his delivery. In effect, Twain has just been "sold," in the language of the West; he has become the butt of the joke.

Wheeler's tale is a masterpiece of folk narrative in that from the first moment it is pointless: he reveals he knows nothing of the good reverend but substitutes his rendition of the exploits of a notorious local gambler by the name of Jim Smiley, who would bet on virtually anything: a horse race, a dog fight, or which bird will fly off a fence first. The culmination of those examples comes in the illness of Parson Walker's wife, who was near death but now seems to be recovering. When the good parson tells Smiley this, Smiley offers to bet him that she will not survive. Wheeler then moves on to other exploits of Smiley's betting, the fifteen-minute nag, who runs with flailing legs but somehow manages to win every race; the fighting dog named Andrew Jackson who grabs its opponent by the hind leg and will not let go but loses in a contest with a dog that has no hind legs. The culmination of these absurd events is his tale of the jumping frog, Smiley's greatest accomplishment: he has trained a frog he names Dan'l Webster to jump better than any other in the county, and he is eager to bet on such a contest. A stranger comes to town, and Smiley is eager to take his money, but the man says he has no frog. Smiley offers to catch one for him. While he is gone, the stranger fills Smiley's frog with lead shot so that it weighs several pounds. When Smiley returns, his frog is too heavy to leave the ground and only "hysted up his shoulders—so—like a Frenchman." Paying off the bet, Smiley tips his frog over, and it belches out the heavy shot. At this juncture, Wheeler is called away, and when he departs, Twain makes his exit, having heard enough meandering tales even though Wheeler returns and offers to tell him about a cow that had no tail, "only a stump like a bannanner." Twain has been hoodwinked by his friend in the East into becoming the innocent victim of Wheeler's endless narrations, suffering through the most ridiculous accounts of a local gambler. This story turned Twain into a celebrity, and it was widely reprinted in America and abroad.

"The Story of the Old Ram" employs a nearly identical method but uses Jim Blaine as the internal narrator rather than Wheeler. Once again Twain is the butt of the joke as the local wags get him to listen to Blaine tell about his grandfather's old ram, a story that wanders about through a series of disconnected, absurd events. Blaine's digressive intelligence, especially when he is "tranquilly, serenely, symmetrically drunk," allows him to get no further than his first sentence before he leaves the topic of the ram to free associate from person to person beginning with who sold his grandfather the ram in the first place. Soon, he is ram-less, so far adrift that there is no getting back once he has lit on the hilarious, although, like Wheeler, he never lets on that there is anything funny in his tale. He tells about Miss Wagner, who used to borrow a glass eye from Miss Jefferson, one that was a bit too small and used to turn about at odd angles, making the children cry. She also borrowed Miss Higgins's wooden leg and Miss Jacop's wig, especially when she entertained company. Blaine rambles about throughout such characters, the best of which is a man named Wheeler who gets caught by the machinery in a carpet factory and is wound into fourteen yards of three-ply carpet. His widow buys the entire piece. At this juncture, Blaine falls asleep in the middle of his own story. The scallywags gathered about are convulsive with laughter, and Twain has once again been sold, a tenderfoot taken in by the local rustics. There is no real point to Blaine's tale, no conflict, no resolution, a perfect example of the Southwestern tall tale.

Twain explains the methodology of such fiction in an essay entitled "How to Tell a Story," one of his few commentaries on his artistic philosophy. He differentiates the American "humorous" tale from the English "comic" style and the French "witty" tradition. In the comic method, the teller states at the beginning that what he has to say is funny, and he laughs at it himself. His joke ends with a punch line, and everyone laughs, including the speaker. Twain finds such a method "pathetic" and a disgrace. Wit is largely a matter of clever language. Humor, he maintains, is an art form that depends upon the manner of the telling, a uniquely American tradition perfected by Artemus Ward and James Whitcomb Riley. The key to it is a deadpan narrator who portrays no hint that he thinks the tale is funny. His mind is digressive, and he cannot stick to the subject but wanders about in the telling, sticking in all kinds of absurd elements while remaining innocently earnest about the subject. The most subtle devise is the pause before the snapper, the capping absurdity, and the speaker must maintain a grave sincerity even at this point. Most of Twain's humorous stories follow this method precisely, and they are better heard than read because of the effect of the pause.

But Twain was also capable of writing short fiction in a very different vein. Although "Cannibalism in the Cars" has inspired very little formal criticism, it is actually a fairly complex utilization of the basic techniques of Twain's "Jumping Frog." It again employs a narrative frame in which a normative voice, speaking in standard American English, establishes the scene and circumstance of the internal recitation by another character, in this case not a garrulous drunk but rather a cultured, "mild, benevolent-looking gentleman" who proves to be a member of congress. Mark Twain meets this genteel figure aboard a train from Terre Haute to Chicago, and the stranger appeals to him to listen to his account of another such trip, one taken some years ago in December, when a violent snow storm stopped them in a huge drift and they were stranded, without food, for more than a week. Everyone on board seems to be a member of congress, and in due course they begin to discuss the most practical way for the majority of them to survive: eating some of the others. This situation is perfect for the political satire of the language of government, the false decorum of the proceedings, and the total lack of humanistic concerns in their deliberations. These aspects are clear from the moment the discussions begin: "Mr. John J. Williams of Illinois rose and said: 'Gentlemen—I nominate the Rev. James Sawyer of Tennessee." Other candidates are presented and discussed, and three of them are "elected" and eaten. In the following days other distinguished gentlemen are presented for consideration, amid hilarious conversation of their merits: "It may be urged by gentlemen that the hardships and privations of a frontier life have rendered Mr. Davis tough, but, gentlemen, is this a time to cavil at toughness?" A Mr. Morgan observes that Davis might be suitable only for soup. Then follows the narrator's comments on the experience of feasting on various of the men: Mr. Harris was good but might have been better done; Mr. Walker, from Detroit, was good, as the narrator later wrote to his widow. Mr. Morgan, from Alabama, a refined man who spoke several languages, was served for breakfast, and he proved to be "juicy." At one point, Twain barges in to ask a question, but he is told not to interrupt, a standard technique in this kind of dramatized narration. When the kindly internal narrator arrives at his station and departs, Twain again assumes control of the story. The conductor comes by and urges him not to be concerned, that the gentleman has once been a member of congress and had been briefly stuck in a snowstorm and had lost his mind.

There is much here that rewards analysis. In formal terms, the account is another example of Twain's frequent implementation of the frame technique. This time, however, there is no parallel shift in the dialect of the internal narrator. Members of congress are presented as having no real moral sense at all, responding to a crisis only in utilitarian terms. The fusing of the most macabre of decisions being made in the inflated language of parliamentary deliberations provides the underlying humor, supported by the commentaries assessing the virtues of the gentlemen just eaten. Members of congress are shown to be as barbaric as any cannibalistic savages, a point that is essentially egalitarian: they are no better than anyone else.

Perhaps Twain's most famous social satire is "The Man That Corrupted Hadleyburg," first published in 1899. A rather long story, it rests solidly on the theme of moral weakness, on the potential for selfishness and deception within everyone given the opportunity for the sudden acquisition of unearned wealth. Hadleyburg has long prided itself on an incorruptible virtue, but members of the community offended a visitor one day, and the plot rests on his meticulous means of obtaining revenge, revenge prolonged in a public arena that touches all of the most prominent people in town. To deflate the self-righteousness of the community, he sends a letter promising a great deal of money to anyone who can recite what someone told a stranger when he gave him twenty dollars, thus transforming his life. The letter, along with a sack said to contain $40,000, first goes to Edward and Mary Richards, a member of the prominent "Nineteen" group of leading citizens, each of whom receives such a document. What follows is a predictable pattern of initial personal pride on the part of the virtuous followed by hesitation, temptation, and complete deception in pretending to be the person who helped the outsider. The culmination of the humor comes in a crowded town meeting in which, one by one, the member of the Nineteen are exposed as frauds and liars, and they are humiliated. Only the Richards are spared, but they are haunted by hidden sin and soon die. The pariahs of the village are spared, for they never pretended to any superior morality. Nonetheless, the stranger has exacted a devastating price for his initial insult. For its part, the town changes its town motto from the Biblical "Lead us not into Temptation" to "Lead us into Temptation," the thought being that temptation prompts a sense of common humility, a self-knowledge of the limitations of human virtue. Told by an omniscient narrator, of substantial length, exhibiting no localized settings or dialects, and generating the most misanthropic of Twain's basic themes, the story is unusual among his short fiction, despite being his most anthologized work.

Twain wrote scores of tales over the years, many of which were incorporated into larger travel books, but his keen sense of humor, his deft handling of regional dialects, his brisk sense of character, are evident throughout his long career. He raised the humor traditions, long considered a minor form of American letters, to the level of serious art while at the same time addressing some of the most salient aspects of human strength and weakness, an achievement that makes his work timeless.

Suggestions for Further Reading

McMahan, Elizabeth, ed. *Critical Approaches to Mark Twain's Short Stories*. Port Washington: Kennikat Press, 1981.

Lynn, Kenneth S. *Mark Twain and the Southwestern Humorists*. Boston: Little, Brown, 1959.

Quirk, Tom. *Mark Twain: A Study of the Short Fiction*. New York: Twayne, 1997.

Sloane, David E. *Mark Twain as a Literary Comedian*. Baton Rouge: Louisiana State University Press, 1979.

Wilson, James D. *A Reader's Guide to the Short Stories of Mark Twain*. Boston: G. K. Hall, 1987.

Wonham, Henry B. *Mark Twain and the Art of the Tall Tale*. New York: Oxford University Press, 1993.

Bret Harte

Although he has been reduced to a minor reputation in American letters, for an extended period in the nineteenth century Bret Harte was the most popular writer of fiction in America. He was widely admired as one of the originators of the Local Color movement, which featured localized settings, colorful regional characters speaking the vernacular, and dramatic plots with sentimental conclusions. Of all the attributes of fiction, his major contribution was the introduction of character types that became stock figures in popular culture for more than a century: the whore with a heart of gold; the softhearted gambler; the tender tough guy; the grizzly miner; the schoolmistress in a rough and tumble town. Harte set his stories in California at the time of the great Gold Rush, and his pictures of Western life made him, for a time, the most original and best-selling writer of the period between 1868 and 1876, after which his familiar figures and plots attracted only a dwindling audience.

It all began with "The Luck of Roaring Camp," a sentimental tale set in a mining camp on the occasion of the birth of a child to the local prostitute, Cherokee Sal, who promptly dies. The child is saved through the intervention of a group of rugged characters who suddenly reveal a soft interior in their devotion to the baby. Among them, Kentuck and Stumpy play a leading role in saving the boy, nursing him with milk from an ass and providing for him from generous contributions from virtually everyone in the community. "The Luck," as he comes to be called, brings about a transformation in the town, as the men clean up in his presence, watching their language around the boy, protecting him from harm. Roaring Camp enters flush times, with the mines yielding abundant gold and the area growing rapidly with the flurry of economic activity. Just at the height of its prosperity, however, a

The American Short Story Handbook, First Edition. James Nagel.
© 2015 James Nagel. Published 2015 by John Wiley & Sons, Ltd.

flash flood wipes out the town, scattering trees and remnants of houses along the gulch, and it is there the survivors find the body of Kentuck still cradling the remains of Luck in his arms. Told by a first-person narrator, who exhibits a greater sophistication than the inhabitants of the camp, the tale set the standard for the early phase of the enormously successful tradition of Local Color stories. It also contained satiric elements greatly appreciated by an Eastern audience: the birth of The Luck is a twist on the gospels with the local whore as a Madonna figure. The men bring tributes to the infant, but what these Magi lay before him are largely the artifacts of their violent lives: guns, tobacco, gold, a diamond ring won in a poker game, a stolen teaspoon. The child becomes a savior figure for a brief period, but then everything is lost in the flood. There is no final salvation.

Among his most popular tales, "The Outcasts of Poker Flat" follows the familiar pattern. It begins at a transitional moment in the life of a rough mining town, when the citizens have decided to clean up the community, hanging two men and running a gambler, two prostitutes, and a drunkard out of the growing community to make room for "decent" folk. Thus it is that the gambler, Oakhurst, the drunk, Uncle Billy, and two disreputable women, Mother Shipton and the Duchess, find themselves in the wilderness gamely making their way toward Sandy Bar and the safety of another camp. On the way, this ragged crew is joined by two innocent young people, Tom Simson and his blushing bride, Piney Woods. The structure of civilization stripped away in the forest, and the outcasts present themselves as the most virtuous of citizens, a matter that becomes crucial when the party is caught in a blizzard without adequate provisions. As supplies begin to run out, the gambler commits suicide to save his food for the rest of the group. Uncle Billy runs off with the mule, but Mother Shipton deliberately starves to death, giving her food to the young Piney. In time, the young girl and the Duchess cuddle together in an attempt to keep warm, and they are later found frozen to death in precisely that posture. The outcasts, similar to the mining ruffians of Roaring Camp, have been redeemed by their sacrifice, by the goodness that was within them despite their social transgressions. An American public responded to this tale with enormous interest, some readers declaring that it was a masterpiece of fiction, and it has remained a frequently anthologized story ever since its first publication.

A more psychologically complex story is "Tennessee's Partner," set in the same general area of Sandy Bar. Tennessee and his friend share a cabin for a time, and then the Partner goes off to Stockton and brings home a wife. In due course Tennessee and the Partner's wife run off, living together near the town of Marysville. Then, the woman dies and Tennessee returns to his original cabin, greeted by a handshake by his friend. They share the cabin for a time, and then Tennessee murders a stranger and is arrested and brought to trial. At the hearing, there is no one to speak for the defense until the Partner appears and offers the judge "seventeen hundred dollars in coarse gold and a watch," an attempted bribe that is bitterly resented, and Tennessee is hanged in the morning. The Partner claims the body and buries it near their cabin. He lives for a brief period and then begins to decline and dies speaking Tennessee's name.

Much has been made of all of this, including the contention that the two men are lovers and that Harte had written an early homosexual account. From this perspective, the Partner's marriage and Tennessee's cohabitation were only a cover for the true relationship, which is warmly resumed when the wife dies. Most scholars of American literature reject this idea, but some of them endorse a counter-hypothesis, that the Partner never forgives Tennessee for the transgression of running off with his wife. His intrusion into the trial with the offer of a bribe is only a means to ensure that there will be a conviction and a hanging. The Partner hauls the body away in a donkey cart, a rude conveyance normally used for the worst jobs, and he glories in putting the remains into the grave he dug even before the proceedings. A more standard reading is that Harte has offered a sentimental tale of western friendship so deep that it transcended the emotional depths of a marriage of convenience and endured beyond the grave.

Most of Harte's tales, even in the period of his best work, do not require extensive exegesis but are notable for their surface features. One such story is "The Idyl of Red Gulch," which introduces Miss Mary as the archetypal schoolmarm from the more civilized East. She teaches diligently and attracts the attentions of a man of the town, an incipient romance until one of the town prostitutes approaches her, begging her to take her child whom Sandy has fathered. Miss Mary agrees on the condition that Sandy never attempts to see his son, and then she leaves with the boy for the more cultivated East. The West has presented too much corruption for her to bear, and a world of greater refinement will present opportunities for the boy that would be impossible in Red Gulch. A related work is "Miggles," which features another prostitute with a warm heart who has given up her remunerative employment to care for an invalid, Jim, who can no longer speak nor care for his basic needs. Miggles buys a ranch and cares for him personally, a sacrifice that impresses the passengers on a stagecoach that put into the ranch during a storm. They observe what few people have ever seen, the tender treatment the woman gives a man who is not her husband, not her lover, not a relative, but simply a person who needs help. In this, the narrator implies, she resembles Mary Magdalene, even to the point of washing the feet of her patient. She is a tough and independent woman, economically secure, who keeps a bear as a watchdog, but she has an enormous depth of sympathy and human generosity, a hallmark of Harte's stories of the rugged West.

Very few of Harte's other tales attained the popularity of these tales, and most have little to recommend them. "Brown of Calaveras," however, presents another kind-hearted gambler, Jack Hamlin, who is of mixed-blood, a fact that does not prevent him from being a local Lothario. He nevertheless assists an Easterner named Brown in saving his marriage, even though Hamlin is attracted to the wife himself. It is clear that the West is too rough and ready for people from the more cultivated section of the country. "Mr. Thompson's Prodigal" reinforces this theme of the corruption of Western life in a twist on the biblical tale of the prodigal son.

Harte's stories often seem trite and overly romantic, almost a comic parody of Western life, but he was among the first American writers to capture the rugged lives generated by the California Gold Rush and to highlight the conflict between the region and the more cultivated East. His somewhat basic representation of the characters of this area made an impact on popular culture that had prolonged imitation, with tender barroom ladies appearing in movies and television programs throughout the twentieth century, to choose just one example. But the language of his cultivated narrators soon began to seem overly formal to the readers of his day, as did his sentimental endings and saintly characters. What is sustained, however, is his introduction of Local Color stories to the stream of American literature, a movement that contributed hundreds of volumes of fiction by the end of the century, and that is his enduring legacy.

Suggestions for Further Reading

Duckett, Margaret. *Mark Twain and Bret Harte*. Norman: University of Oklahoma Press, 1964.

Morrow, Patrick. *Bret Harte*. Boise: Boise State College Western Writers Series, 1972.

O'Connor, Richard. *Bret Harte: A Biography*. Boston: Little, Brown, 1966.

Scharnhorst, Gary. *Bret Harte*. New York: Twayne, 1992.

Steward, George R. *Bret Harte: Argonaut and Exile*. Boston: Houghton Mifflin, 1931.

Henry James

Although he is best known for his publication of a series of internationally celebrated major novels, Henry James was also the most prolific writer of short fiction of his day. When his biographer, Leon Edel, undertook to edit an edition of the best stories, they came out as a twelve-volume set, a stunning level of productivity, especially for an author so prominently devoted to another genre. These works demonstrate the same level of artistic integrity he displayed in his longer narratives, although they enlist fewer major characters and a more limited range of subjects and themes. As a general rule, what James called his "tales" are longer than standard American stories, often reaching the length of the French "nouvelle," a form he greatly appreciated. In his critical writing, he distinguished between the "picture," a brief narrative that summarized for its effects, and the "anecdote," which explored a single character involved in one situation. In either case, his fiction involves complex psychological conflicts dealing with an American in a Europeans setting, with a woman in a broken romantic entanglement, or with the realization of an important failure in life. His style is often more complex and more highly refined than the substance of his plots, and it demands an active imagination to follow, leading to the observation that of all the American writers, the work of Henry James is an acquired taste.

Some of his best stories, however, contain both exquisite artistry and complex thematic development, as does "The Real Thing." In this first-person narrative, an artist is looking back on an earlier situation in which two aristocrats came into his studio. He anticipated an income from painting their portraits; ironically, they are looking for work, something to produce enough money to maintain the façade of their gentility since their inherited wealth has been diminished. They suggest they sit for

The American Short Story Handbook, First Edition. James Nagel.
© 2015 James Nagel. Published 2015 by John Wiley & Sons, Ltd.

portraits of ladies and gentlemen of their social class. The artist's usual models, Miss Churm and the Italian Oronte, are from the lower classes but prove malleable enough as figures to pose for almost any role. The Monarchs, however, are stiff and inflexible, always themselves, and they prove disastrous to the illustrations made from them. Still, the artist keeps them on, in progressively lower functions until finally they have become the servants, cleaning away the dishes and picking up rags from the floor. The artist cannot stand to see them so degraded in their roles, and he gives them money to go away.

Several crucial themes are inherent in this simple plot, the most obvious being the interplay between reality and art. What becomes painfully obvious is that what is "reality" in life is not always serviceable as the "real" in aesthetic representation, that art deals with the "essence" of life, which requires the transmission through the medium employed. Thus the lower-class models are able to better stand for even aristocratic characters in book illustration, whereas the "true" upper-class figures seem wooden and without life. Another prominent idea is that of social-class inversion, as the Monarchs are reduced to servants in the studio whereas the "poor" Miss Churm and Oronte are posing as wealthy characters. But the most important idea is that of moral and psychological growth on the part of the artist, who develops a genuine sympathy for the Monarchs, understanding the pain of their diminishment, the psychic cost of their desperate search for income, the pathetic circumstances of having to accept having fallen so far in English society. This is the emotion on which the story ends, with the artist having grown as a human being through the experience of hiring the impoverished Monarchs.

Another masterful example of James's short fiction is "The Beast in the Jungle," a tale in which John Marcher is loved by May Bartram, but he is too obsessed with the idea that something gigantic was going to happen to him to make any commitment to her. She agrees to wait with him until this thing, this "beast," actually takes place. So they spend their lives in London in constant companionship but without any clear declaration of love, attending concerts and social events as the decades slip away. She seems wiser than he, realizing that they have lost the opportunity for a loving marriage, whereas he remains blissfully oblivious to what is directly in front of him: her complete devotion. Finally, she becomes ill and dies, leaving him with only the surface of grief, with no genuine feeling. Then, some months after the funeral, he visits the cemetery and observes another man consumed with sorrow, and he realizes what he has lost, that her love, their relationship, was the big thing he had anticipated, that it had been accessible to him all along and he had ignored it, and he falls upon her grave consumed with regret.

Another tale with a fundamentally psychological theme is "The Jolly Corner," which deals not only with the differences between European and American culture but with the intriguing issue of an alter ego, a *Doppelgänger*. It is appropriate that such an intimate subject be related by a first-person narrator who also functions as protagonist, since internal conflict and movement will be a central concern. In this case, Spencer Brydon has returned home to America after living in Europe for more than three decades, and his focus is on two properties he owns in New York: a large house he is having revamped into apartment units, and the home he lived in as a child, which he calls The Jolly Corner. As a quasi-European, he has contempt for the mercantile values of the United States, although he looks forward to a handsome income from his tenement building. His ancestral home remains empty, however, entered only once a week by the Irish cleaning lady, Mrs. Muldoon, who finds the vacant structure strangely forbidding as though inhabited by a ghost. Brydon is a self-absorbed man whose thoughts are primarily about himself, and he seems to enjoy contemplating every facet of his motives and realizations, even the personality he might have been under certain conditions. He quickly hits upon the idea of what he might have been had he not gone to Europe, if he had stayed and served in the Civil War, engaged in commerce, lived in the social life of the city. Then, walking through the building late at night, he develops the feeling that there is someone else present in the empty house, a part of himself, the person he might have become under those circumstances. He quickly becomes obsessed with the concept, eager to meet his double, to see himself as he might have been.

Unlike most of James's major figures, he is engaged in a romance with Miss Staverton, who is patiently waiting for him, a bit like May Bartram, even though she realizes he is self-absorbed. She directly says to him that "you don't care for anything but yourself." Still, night after night he wanders through the house, expecting to see his other self around each corner, and he finally does. He is repelled by what he observes, a man very much himself who apparently had some fingers shot away, presumably in the war, and a man whose face inspires in Brydon a sense of horror. He faints dead away and awakens in the presence of Mrs. Muldoon and Miss Staverton, who bends down to kiss him, saying that now she wishes to keep him. She says she also saw the strange figure, the man he might have been, and she is sympathetic, guessing that he has been unhappy, ravaged over the years. But, she directly states, he was not identical to the Brydon who stands before her, and the two embrace in the conclusion of the story.

The *Doppelgänger* was a popular device at the beginning of the twentieth century, a period absorbed in Freudian psychology at the same time it was fascinated by the occult, by supernatural events and attempts to communicate with the dead. Particularly intriguing was the idea of the psychic double, the person one might have been, and James made good use of the idea. What is clear throughout is Spencer Brydon's self absorption, a Narcissistic obsession with not only who he is as a person but with who he might have been under other circumstances. That he seems to encounter his other self one night in the empty house suggests either a supernatural event or a hysterical projection of his obsession, creating a horrible creature whose face is disfigured and who has lost fingers off his hand. Many readers speculate that this is the person he might have become had he served in the Civil War rather than retreat to Europe for its comfortable life. On another level, he has contempt for the "moneyed" life of American free enterprise, even though he has benefitted from his father's wealth and seeks to make a handsome living with the rentals from his proposed apartment building. His saving grace, rare among James's protagonists, is the love he shares with Miss Staverton, a redeeming virtue that the author chose to use as the conclusion of this unusual tale, one of his best.

James wrote scores of other important stories, many of them among the most frequently studied works in American literature, such as "The Turn of the Screw," which also deals with the ambiguity of psychological projection or supernatural manifestation. Many of his tales feature the International Theme contrasting a brash young American, flush with newly-earned money, coming in contact with an arrogant high society living on a landed income they inherited. In general, the stories are intensely personal and focus on human relations rather than on complex plots. His characters are rarely successful in romance, and love often proves a destructive force, obscuring other avenues of fulfillment. "Daisy Miller" is such a tale, although the protagonist is a young woman, one typically ignorant of the European codes of courtship, which leads to her social ostracism. James's artists are generally failures or they attract personal notice while the public ignores their creative work, as in "The Death of the Lion." His short stories exhibit his brilliant intellect, his deft control of narrative method, structure, imagery, and thematic development. The legacy James left literary history is one rich in mastery of style and design. He was, in short, a literary artist himself, one who continues to reward patient scrutiny and sustained interest.

Suggestions for Further Reading

Albers, Christina E. *A Reader's Guide to the Short Stories of Henry James*. New York: G. K. Hall, 1997.

Hocks, Richard A. *Henry James: A Study of the Short Fiction*. Boston: Twayne, 1990.

Kraft, James. *The Early Tales of Henry James*. Carbondale: Southern Illinois University Press, 1969.

Putt, S. Gorley. *Henry James: A Reader's Guide*. Ithaca: Cornell University Press, 1966.

Vaid, Krishna Baldev. *Technique in the Tales of Henry James*. Cambridge: Harvard University Press, 1964.

Wagenknecht, Edward. *The Tales of Henry James*. New York: Unger, 1984.

Kate Chopin

In the twenty-first century, Kate Chopin is best known as the author of *The Awakening*, a novel celebrated for its portrait of a woman who desires independence, economic freedom, and sexual fulfillment. However, until about 1970 Chopin's reputation rested firmly on her stories, especially those in *Bayou Folk* and its companion volume *A Night in Acadie*. These collections featured tales of New Orleans and the surrounding bayous as well as localized characters who speak the dialect of the region. They also reflect the cultural values of a unique Louisiana society, which was founded by the French, sold to Spain, repurchased by France, and finally relinquished to the United States in the Louisiana Purchase. Inherent in the social fabric is the Roman Catholicism from its European origins and its complex ethnic mix of the indigenous Native Americans, French settlers, Spanish politicians, and African Americans, most of whom were free persons of color but including many slaves who worked the plantations. There were also special rules for the gradations of race, for the numerous quadroons, the product of interracial unions, and the octoroons, who often could pass for white. This complex mix, which increasingly included Americans attracted by the economic opportunities and cultural life of a vibrant city and Spanish immigrants drifting in from the Caribbean. Chopin captured the central elements of all of this in her stunning short fiction, so much so, in fact, that literary historians in the early decades of the century pronounced her to be the great genius of the American short story.

Her most celebrated work of short fiction is "Désirée's Baby," originally published, significantly, as "The Father of Désirée's Baby," which puts the emphasis on the parents rather than the child. It is a startling story of racial prejudice and the destructiveness of deep-seated ethnic bias played out on

The American Short Story Handbook, First Edition. James Nagel.
© 2015 James Nagel. Published 2015 by John Wiley & Sons, Ltd.

a plantation in the bayou country west of New Orleans. In it a beautiful foundling, Désirée, grows up to marry Armand, whose parents wed and eventually died in France, leaving their Louisiana property to their son. The couple is happy in their marriage until a child is born who exhibits a hint of black blood, which he assumes is from her, since her ancestry is unknown. He rejects his wife and child, and she takes the baby and commits suicide by walking into the bayou. Later, Armand is destroying everything that reminds him of his wife and child, burning even the baby clothes, when he discovers some old letters in a drawer. Examining them, he discovers that his mother was of African descent. His parents would have married in France, where interracial unions were legal, and his mother writes that she is pleased that her son will never know that he carries black blood. One of Chopin's few stories to touch on miscegenation, a delicate topic in her day, the story was admired for the bravery of its racial theme and for the integrity of its artistry. In accord with the tight restrictions on the genre suggested by Poe, every aspect of the narrative contributes to its central idea, from the style to the imagery and structure. As Fred Lewis Pattee commented in 1923, the story is "well-nigh perfect."

Another thematically powerful tale of race is "La Belle Zoraïde," a complex narrative in which a slave, Manna-Loulou, tells a bedtime story to her white Creole owner, Madame Delisle. Intellectually and humanistically superior to her mistress, Manna-Loulou uses her account to manipulate the thinking of the other woman, threading themes pertinent to their daily issues into her evening recitations. In this case, seeking romantic freedom, the storyteller relates a poignant tale about Zoraïde, who was raised by a wealthy woman as her own daughter and given every convenience money could provide. As the young girl grows into a beautiful woman, Madame tells her that she must marry an appropriate gentleman, a genteel black man who will bring honor to the family. Indeed, Madame has found such a man, M'sieur Ambroise, owned by Dr. Langlé, a local doctor. But the young girl has recently been to Congo Square and has watched a slave, Mézor, perform an erotic dance, and her passions have been aroused. She will have no other. Forbidden to even see Mézor, she nevertheless has a rendezvous with him and becomes pregnant. Outraged, Madame has the African sold to a distant plantation, and when the baby is born it is also spirited away from the mother. Deranged with grief, Zoraïde takes a bundle of rags as her child and cares for it constantly. Madame is shocked at her condition and brings back the infant, whom Zoraïde rejects in favor of her surrogate rags. The story ends with Zoraïde, now an elderly woman, still loving a tattered bundle. Ironically, as Manna Loulou ends her tale, she discovers that Madame Delisle has misunderstood the central idea and can say only that it would have been better for the child to have died.

Beyond stories of race, Chopin most often wrote about courtship and marriage in a broad range of themes that expressed numerous perspectives on relations between the genders. Her eventual fame derived from her celebrated novel *The Awakening*, in which a woman seeks liberation from what she perceives as the confining roles of wife and mother. She sends her children away, engages in an affair, has a prolonged flirtation with another man, and ultimately commits suicide rather than return to a traditional relationship. Unfortunately, many readers have assumed that the novel expressed Chopin's own attitudes on the subject, which is far from the truth. From all available biographical accounts, she was a happy wife and a devoted mother of six children, all of whom remembered their mother as fulfilled in her domestic life. Nonetheless, she wrote stories about many women whose attitudes were somewhat different. "Athénaïse," for example, deals with a young wife who quickly grows contemptuous of her husband, Cazeau, and she hates life on their plantation on the river. She runs away to New Orleans and rejoices in the vibrant cultural life of the city and the handsome gentlemen who find her attractive. In due course, however, she discovers that she is pregnant and, counter to her original instincts, "her whole being was steeped in a wave of ecstasy," and she returns to her husband, who is eagerly waiting for her boat to arrive. This narrative is nearly the inversion of *The Awakening* in its affirmation of marital love and the joy of having children.

On the other hand, "The Story of an Hour" also features a young wife but one who is told that her husband has been killed in a train accident. At first she is shocked at the news, but soon she experiences a sense of profound freedom, a realization that now she could live for herself, a feeling that is "the strongest impulse of her being." She can hardly contain her exultation, her expectation of a richer life in the future. Then, to everyone's surprise, her husband walks in the door and explains he was not on the train, only to find that his wife has dropped dead of a heart attack. In a sharply ironic conclusion, the doctors interpret her death as the result of "the joy that kills," not as the result of her crushed hopes of freedom.

"Madame Célestin's Divorce" deals with a wife married to a listless husband who runs away for months at a time. She decides to divorce him, encouraged by a lawyer who has his eye on her for his own reasons, but at the last moment the husband returns and makes the same insincere promise he has made countless times before, that he will reform. She believes him and cancels the divorce. "In Sabine" takes things a step further in that the young wife runs away from her husband across the Sabine river and into Texas, where it is unlikely he will ever find her. In "The Storm," a man and a woman who were once lovers find themselves alone during a storm, and they seize the opportunity to resume their sexual relationship before returning home to their respective spouses.

Chopin's work in short fiction contains an array of other themes as well, many of them at the center of the unique values of Louisiana. Only in that region is the pride of aristocratic Creole gentlemen a prime concern, but in "A No-Account Creole" it is what inspires a character to relinquish his engagement to a beautiful young woman so she can marry the man she loves. "The Bênitous Slave" depicts an elderly African American, years after the Civil War, who is determined to return to the white family that once owned him because, he feels, that is where he belongs. "A Gentleman of Bayou Têche" concerns a poor Acadian farmer who is chosen for the subject of a painting, one portraying him in his customary work clothes. Sensitive to the possibility that the portrait has an element of condescension, he insists that the caption carry the implication that he is a "gentleman" from his native bayou. "Beyond the Bayou" deals with a former slave who was frightened during the war and now remains in her simple cabin, refusing to cross the bayou to the mainland and a richer life among the population there. She breaks her pledge to herself in order to help a child, and she simultaneously rewards herself by removing the restrictions she has placed upon her mobility.

As even a quick survey reveals, Kate Chopin wrote on a broad range of subjects with impressive psychological insight into issues of race, sexuality, culture, pride, loyalty, and the need for personal sovereignty. She was not a simple propagandist for the women's movement of her day (she was not a suffragette), but her work reveals a startling honesty about feminine needs inside courtship and marriage, a frankness that rankled the publishing standards of her time. Although in her youth her family had owned slaves, as a mature woman she wrote forcefully about the destructiveness of racial prejudice and the evils of involuntary servitude. Although she wrote virtually all her fiction in St. Louis, the city of her birth, her stories are nearly always set in Louisiana, either in New Orleans or in the bayou country to the west and north of the city. These locations she described in great detail, showing not only the lush settings but the fascinating social and racial dynamic of a complex society, one with a cultural history unmatched in its rich background by any other region of the United States.

Suggestions for Further Reading

Beer, Janet, ed. *The Cambridge Companion to Kate Chopin*. Cambridge: Cambridge University Press, 2008.

Bonner, Thomas, Jr., *The Kate Chopin Companion*. Westport: Greenwood, 1988.

Nagel, James. "Kate Chopin's *Bayou Folk*." *Race and Culture in New Orleans Stories: Kate Chopin, Grace King, Alice Dunbar-Nelson, and George Washington Cable*. Tuscaloosa: University of Alabama Press, 2014, pp. 119–59.

Petry, Alice Hall, ed. *Critical Essays on Kate Chopin*. New York: G. K. Hall, 1996.

Rankin, Daniel. *Kate Chopin and Her Creole Stories*. Philadelphia: University of Pennsylvania Press, 1932.

Seyersted, Per. *Kate Chopin: A Critical Biography*. Baton Rouge: Louisiana State University Press, 1969.

Skaggs, Peggy. *Kate Chopin*. New York: Twayne, 1985.

Toth, Emily. *Kate Chopin*. Austin: University of Texas Press, 1990.

Stephen Crane

Stephen Crane is the *Wunderkind*, the child genius, of American fiction. He was dabbling in journalism at the age of twelve and published his first short fiction, "Uncle Jake and the Bell-Handle," when was he was fourteen. Although he died when he was only twenty-eight, his work filled twelve volumes of a collected edition, and it contains some of the best short stories in English. He tended to devote himself to settings, writing *The Sullivan County Sketches* about his favorite hunting and camping area in the mountains of Pennsylvania; the *Whilomville Tales* about his hometown of Port Jervis, New York; the *Bowery Tales* about the Irish poor in a section of New York City; *The Little Regiment* about the Civil War; and various stories in the American west. Since his career as a writer was limited to the 1890s, he was a man on the move, rarely living longer than a few months in any one location. The son of a Methodist minister, he was a typical rebellious young man somewhat given to the excesses of his day, which consisted of drink, recreational drugs, a fascination with danger, and consorting with ladies of the evening, one of whom he presented to polite English society as his wife even though they were never married. Perhaps it was predictable that this unconventional life should produce similarly unique fiction, imaginative work that stretched the boundaries of the principal modes of the day, using accurate description as in Realism, the deterministic nature of environment as in Naturalism, the narrative focus on the sensory life of the major character as in Impressionism, and short fiction that broke the definitions of story, tale, sketch, and novel.

His major stories are among the best in American literature, and they have been constantly in print since their first publication. Among these is "The Open Boat," a fictional account of a real event in which Crane's ship bound for Cuba sank off the coast of Florida, and he was more than a day in

The American Short Story Handbook, First Edition. James Nagel.
© 2015 James Nagel. Published 2015 by John Wiley & Sons, Ltd.

a ten-foot dinghy fighting against heavy seas and the sharks that circled his small boat. He published his journalistic account of all of this and followed it, a few months later, with his story, which contained important elements that he added to the factual events. One of these takes place in the mind of the protagonist as he thinks about the unfairness of Fate in killing some people and saving others, something that happens when Billy, the oiler who worked on the engines, drowns in the breakers as they approach the shore. Another important theme is the development of a sense of brotherhood of the men sharing the experience, a matter not expressed in the newspaper article. But the most important new idea is his growth of compassion for a character in a poem he read as a student about a soldier in Algiers who is dying and there is no one who cares about him. The complex weaving of these ideas into a coherent narrative is one of Crane's great accomplishments in this tale, and it accounts for its continuing popularity for more than a century.

An equally famous story is "The Blue Hotel," which emerged from a western trip to Nebraska Crane took for a newspaper. On that journey he noticed a hotel painted blue not far from the railroad tracks, and he invented a series of dramatic events to take place there. The protagonist is a Swede on his first trip west, and he seems insecure in these new surroundings and fearful that the disputes about a card game will expand into a killing. The hotel owner, his son, an Easterner, and a cowboy, are all startled when the Swede accuses the son, Johnny, of cheating, and the boy insists on a fight. They go outside into a blizzard that externalizes the turmoil inside the men, and the Swede eventually wins the fight, knocking Johnny down. Filled with adrenaline and fury, the Swede leaves the hotel and goes to a bar a short distance away where he sees other men gambling at a table. He offers to buy them a drink, and when they refuse, he grabs the gambler and attempts to force him to accept, and the man stabs him with a knife and kills him. The cash register pops open with the sign "this registers the amount of your purchase." This plot has been the subject of an enormous amount of commentary on the extent of responsibility borne by each of the men and by Nature, Fate, and chance. The story ends with the Easterner confessing that he also saw Johnny cheating in the card game, and he could have prevented the chain of events from unfolding if only he had courage enough to support the Swede in an unpopular cause.

"The Bride Comes to Yellow Sky" is a parody of the western fiction that was popular in the last decade of the nineteenth century, a mode that normally featured a handsome sheriff, idealized for his bravery and skill with a gun, a comely young woman, and a villain in the form of a desperado who attempts to terrorize a town. But Crane's story captures this scenario at a moment of transition, when the marauding gangs had vanished and the marshal feels secure enough to get married. Sheriff Potter is back from his wedding trip as the plot opens, and he is attempting to get to their little house in town without notice when he encounters Scratchy Wilson, an aged remnant of the Old West, who gets drunk and shoots up the town. The three of them collide on the streets, and Scratchy is ready for a fight when Potter explains to him that he has no gun because he has just gotten married. The desperado cannot grasp the concept of a married sheriff, the passing of a way of life, and he calls off the fight, leaving funnel shaped tracks in the sand as he turns and walks away. The humor derives largely from the inversion of the key expectations. The sheriff is not a reckless combatant but a married man with responsibilities and a wife to support. The wife is not beautiful but a plain woman, a bit slow on the uptake, who used to cook for a living. And the desperado, Scratchy, has lived beyond his day and is now well passed his prime. He is attempting, unsuccessfully, to relive his past glory as a gunfighter. In this era of such famous western novels as Owen Wister's *The Virginian*, an American audience well understood the nature of Crane's carefully wrought satire.

Of his other stories, two groups stand out. The first is his treatment of the urban poor in his Bowery tales, which deal largely with Irish immigrants struggling to survive in an era when the influx of people from abroad outstripped the pace of new jobs, especially in American cities. Most of these works depict not only poverty but drink and violence, cruelty and self-deception, and the influence of this environment on the individuals struggling to survive. "A Dark-Brown Dog," for example, shows the sordid daily life of the Johnson family in a tenement of the west side of New York. A young boy, Johnny, brings home a puppy, something to love and care about, but later in the day his drunken father throws the dog out the window to its death. The boy sees the puppy sailing through the air and crashing onto a roof below. "The Men in the Storm" shows derelicts lined up in the street to enter a soup kitchen, where a weak gruel will provide them with their only meal of the day. Outside, as they wait to enter, the wind and snow whips at them, expressing a cruelty of Nature that parallels the social situation the men encounter. Perhaps the best of these tales, "An Experiment in Misery" deals with a wealthy young man who dresses like an impoverished street person and spends the night in a flop house as part of his investigation. In the morning, when the men are naked, he sees that they are strong and handsome; the clothing they put on, an expression of economic rank, marks them as unworthy, losers in the game of life.

Crane's war stories have attracted a great deal of attention, partly because of the enormous reputation of *The Red Badge of Courage*, his famous novel of the Civil War. "An Episode of War" is typical for its restraint and artistic subtlety. None of the characters are named, for example, meaning that what happens in this "episode" is common and the fate of countless young soldiers. A young lieutenant is carving out equal portions of coffee on a rubber blanket when he is suddenly shot in the arm by an unseen enemy soldier. The sword he had handled so skillfully is now held awkwardly by the blade, signifying his transformation from an officer in war to a wounded man no longer part of the conflict. At the hospital tent behind the lines he is reassured that his arm will not have to be amputated, the standard procedure for treating injured limbs in the Civil War. In the conclusion, when he arrives home with a flat sleeve, his family weeps at the sight of him, and he says only, "I don't suppose it matters so much as all that." "The Veteran" is of special interest because it is about Henry Fleming, the protagonist of *The Red Badge of Courage*, many years after the war, and it clarifies some of the issues that the novel left unresolved. For example, Henry, now elderly and talking to his grandson, tells the boy that he was no hero but a frightened young soldier who ran away at the battle of Chancellorsville. Later that day, the barn catches fire on Henry's farm, and his grandson's colt is locked inside. Henry bolts into the flaming barn just as it collapses, killing everything inside. Fleming, who earlier confessed to cowardice in war, proves himself a selfless hero in domestic life, one who gave his life in an attempt to rescue a horse.

Crane wrote scores of additional stories, many of which have continued to garner attention from scholars and general readers alike. One of the most important is "The Monster," part of the Whilomville cycle of tales, because it deals with complex issues of race in America. In it, Henry Johnson is a stablehand at the home of Dr. Trescott and a playmate of young Jimmie, who enjoys his company. When the house catches fire, it is Henry who rushes into the burning structure and brings out the boy wrapped in a blanket. Unfortunately, Henry's face was badly burned, and his injuries seem to have affected his mind as well. Dr. Trescott vows to care for him, despite the fact that Henry's scarred face is hideous in its deformity, and he endures the rejection of the community. His patients desert him, as do his friends and those in his wife's social circle. The story ends with the household parlor empty on a day his wife should have been receiving a large delegation of patients and friends. Dr. Trescott has paid a high price for his loyalty to Henry Johnson.

Stephen Crane did not shy away from uncomfortable subjects for his stories, and he wrote about many of the crucial issues of the day, including urban poverty, racial prejudice, problems with truth and illusion, human sexual desire, and the absurdity of concepts of heroism and bravery amid the chaos of war. He personalized narratives about military conflict, showing how ordinary soldiers, who do not understand what is going on, suffer and die as a result of the commands of their officers. His Bowery fiction suggested that the environment of urban poverty largely ensures the misery of children growing up in that neighborhood. He showed that self-delusion is a destructive force, especially when it lends a sense of moral superiority, as it often does. Crane depicted life honestly and directly and revealed aspects of the human condition that had never been addressed in fiction before, and for that, and for the integrity of his craft, he has long been among the foremost American writers of short fiction.

Suggestions for Further Reading

Halliburton, David. *The Color of the Sky: A Study of Stephen Crane*. Cambridge: Cambridge University Press, 1989.

Holton, Milne. *Cylinder of Vision: The Fiction and Journalistic Writings of Stephen Crane*. Baton Rouge: Louisiana State University Press, 1972.

Nagel, James. *Stephen Crane and Literary Impressionism*. University Park: Pennsylvania State University Press, 1980.

Schaefer, Michael W. *A Reader's Guide to the Short Stories of Stephen Crane*. New York: G. K. Hall, 1996.

Wertheim, Stanley. *A Stephen Crane Encyclopedia*. Westport: Greenwood, 1997.

Wolford, Chester L. *Stephen Crane: A Study of His Short Fiction*. Boston: Twayne, 1989.

O. Henry

William Sydney Porter, who wrote under the name O. Henry, was the most widely read author of short stories in the early twentieth century, with millions of readers, enormous appeal in the world of popular culture, and an audience of devoted fans who admired his style and emotionally fulfilling plots. The most prestigious literary award in the genre is named for him, the O. Henry Award for the best story of the year, and yet he was never able to garner the respect of professional scholars of literature. Fred Lewis Pattee described O. Henry's work as vapid, without a moral base, and the era of New Criticism found little to admire in the tales that the author spun off at the rate of one a week. In general, critics have regarded the stories as falsely sentimental, contrived, and badly written, with overblown rhetoric and improbable twists of plot. Despite these opinions, O. Henry's stories continue to have sustained appeal to a mass audience not only in print but in film and television as well, with annual showings of "The Gift of the Magi," for example, and the inclusion of "The Ransom of Red Chief" in schoolbooks across the country. His work must have some virtues to explain this continued level of high interest.

It does, although not always for the same reason. Perhaps his most widely read story is "The Ransom of Red Chief," which has been loved by schoolchildren for more than a century. A humorous tale that rides on situational irony, it is told in retrospect by a first-person narrator named Sam, and his voice lends a tone of hopeless resignation to his description of the events. The plot involves two confidence men, Sam and his partner Bill, who are attempting to amass capital for a scam in Illinois by means of a kidnapping scheme in a small town in Alabama, and they choose the son of a wealthy man named Ebenezer Dorset. The boy is a freckled-face lad of

The American Short Story Handbook, First Edition. James Nagel.
© 2015 James Nagel. Published 2015 by John Wiley & Sons, Ltd.

ten throwing stones at a kitten, a perfect expression of his inner character. As they approach the boy, he hits Bill in the eye with a piece of brick, but they take the child to a cave out of town and prepare to send a ransom note to the father. Meanwhile, the boy thinks camping in the cave is great fun, a game, and he becomes Red Chief. Bill is soon covered in bruises and bandages from trying to deal with him, and the boy has no interest in going home at all. His dominant personality is too much for the men, especially for Bill, who continues to sustain cuts and contusions all over his body from thrown rocks. When Sam undertakes to write a ransom letter to Dorset, Bill begs him to lower the request amount from $2000 to $1500. Sam goes to a neighboring village to mail the note, and while he is gone Bill attempts to free the boy and send him home. He refuses to go. Soon, the men receive a reply to their letter, one written by the father requesting that the men pay him $250 to take the boy off their hands. They readily agree, return Red Chief to his father, and flee the town as quickly as possible.

The story is well wrought in several senses. Its narrative tone of helpless frustration with pulling off a kidnapping gives the entire plot a note of ironic humor and an inversion of expectation. The kidnappers become the victims. The portrait of a boy of ten as a holy terror was one that a large audience could understand and appreciate. The language of a minor-league thug such as Sam is wonderful in its high-blown attempts at sophistication. Sam says to his accomplice "it has not yet been discovered that the wolves have borne away the tender lambkin from the fold," which adds linguistic irony to the mix. The major characters are developed just enough to support the comic events. The plot moves quickly and is well structured, and it leads to an outcome foreshadowed by the first appearance of the boy. The return letter from the father suggesting that the crooks pay him to take the boy back is a masterful stroke of irony, one well-understood by readers of the day, and the entire scenario is one that has been enjoyed for more than a century without loss of humor despite enormous technical innovations over the decades.

Another popular story that has maintained its appeal is "The Gift of the Magi," which maintains a very different tone throughout. It is a serious tale, one deeply sentimental in plot and tone, and one that resonates through-out American marriages, many of which went through periods of economic struggle at some point. Jim and Della are happily married and love each other deeply. As Christmas approaches, they both realize there is no money for a proper present for the other, and in due course each sacrifices a precious possession to get the money to buy a gift. The touching irony is that Della sells her long hair to purchase a watch chain for her husband. He, meanwhile, has sold his watch and bought jeweled combs for her. Each sacrificed dearly for the other, and the presents are utterly without use to either of them. What has not been lost, however, is the revelation of love they have expressed, the deep emotion that binds them together.

O. Henry wrote scores of other stories, of course, but nearly all of them follow either the sentimental pattern or that of the surprise ending, the twist of events he made famous. Some of them develop a theme of redemptive virtue, usually one born of a newly found sense of humility and generosity. In "Whistling Dick's Christmas Stocking," the first of the tales he signed under the rubric "O. Henry," rather than his own name, the protagonist is a hobo who warns a family that they are to be set upon by thieves on Christmas Eve, and in gratitude, the family invites him in and gives him a job on their plantation. In the course of the plot, the lowly tramp demonstrates nobility, generosity, and kindness, the kind of humanistic reversal that invests many of the tales. In a related story, "A Retrieved Reformation," a safecracker, and former prisoner resumes his life of crime when he is released. Later, however, he moves into a pleasant small town and marries the daughter of the local banker even though he is wanted for his crimes and is pursued by a wily detective, Ben Price, who comes to town looking for him. Price quickly sees that Jimmy Valentine has formed a new life under an assumed name, and that he is a model citizen. One day a little girl is mistakenly locked in a safe in the bank, a vault on a time lock that cannot be opened by normal means. Jimmy sees that Ben is watching him, but he rushes home to retrieve his safecracking tools and quickly opens the safe with them, thus revealing his true identity to the detective. In a gesture reminiscent of *Les Miserables*, Ben Price declares that he cannot recognize Jimmy, and he leaves town, allowing a virtuous man to continue his domestic life.

"Cherchez la Femme" is a bit more complex in that it is a detective tale within a larger story set in the historic French Quarter of New Orleans. It opens with two local reporters, Robbins and Dumars, seated in a small café owned by Madame Tibault, and the upcoming auction of the property of the Little Sisters of Samaria causes them to recall an incident from two years earlier, when Madame lost $20,000 when she entrusted it to be invested by one Gaspard Morin. He took the money from the bank and withdrew it in the form of gold coin, and soon after he personally created and donated a statue of the Virgin to the chapel and came every day to pray before it. It was the color of gold. Subsequently, he stopped by Madame's café and left on the table a stack of curious papers, which she used to wallpaper a crack in the wall. Not long after that, he died, leaving no trace of the money. The two reporters suspect that Morin made the statue out of the gold coins and that it is worth $20,000, so they bid at the auction and win the bid at $350 and quickly take their prize home. They discover it is lead with a thin gold plate covering it. Returning to the café, they also see that the wallpaper covering the crack in the wall is in fact bond certificates worth $20,000. Morin had not stolen the money after all, and his reputation, and the affection of Madame, are restored.

These kinds of stories were popular in their day, attracting readers to the newspapers each week to read the latest O. Henry installment. At one point in his career, he was receiving $500 a week for his tales, an enormous sum in the early part of the century. Readers knew what to expect: a tale told by a confiding and kindly narrative voice with an edge of irony that introduced an account of a renegade who becomes reformed, or a prostitute with a good heart, or an impoverished couple who prove to be rich in love. Often, but not always, there was a surprise ending, one that twisted the plot around, and nearly always it was sentimental. There was generally an edge of humor and wit, but always his stories were entertaining to a large audience, an appeal that has earned him a permanent place in the history of popular culture.

Suggestions for Further Reading

Current-Garcia, Eugene. *O. Henry: A Study of the Short Fiction.* New York: Twayne, 1993.

Èjxenbaum, B.M. *O. Henry and the Theory of the Short Story..* Translated by I. R. Titunik. Ann Arbor: University of Michigan Press, 1968.

Gallegly, Joseph. *From Alamo Plaza to Jack Harris's Saloon: O. Henry and the Southwest He Knew.* The Hauge: Mouton, 1970.

Long, E. Hudson. *O. Henry: The Man and His Work.* Philadelphia: University of Pennsylvania Press, 1949.

O'Connor, Richard. *O. Henry: The Legendary Life of William S. Porter.* Garden City: Doubleday, 1970.

Sinclair, Upton. *Bill Porter: A Drama of O. Henry in Prison.* Pasadena: privately printed, 1925.

Sarah Orne Jewett

Long established among the forefront of American Local Color writers, Sarah Orne Jewett has begun to be appreciated for not only her deft evocation of a regional setting and charming folkways but for her insightful depiction of the psychology of women living in diminished circumstances. In the nineteenth century, Maine suffered a deficit of men because of their participation in the Civil War, the lost ships on the stormy Atlantic, the appeal of Westward migration, and the prospect of inexpensive farmland on the rich prairies of the Midwest. The development of steamships led to the collapse of the building of schooners, the huge sailboats used in trade with Europe, the flinty soil of New England yielded only a meager living on the scarce farmland in a mountainous state, and many communities in Maine entered into a decline that lasted more than a century, a prospect that further depleted the number of men in the population. As a result, many women suffered loneliness in a prolonged spinsterhood or joined together to form what was called a "Boston Marriage," two women sharing a home in a lifetime commitment. The heir to a modest family fortune, Jewett enjoyed such a relationship with Annie Fields, the widow of James T. Fields, the editor of Houghton Mifflin Publishing Company, and she lived during the winter in the Fields' residence in Boston and in her own home in South Berwick, Maine, during the warm months.

A prolific writer more inclined toward the story than the novel, she published ten volumes of regional tales during her career along with numerous stories for children. Some of these works of short fiction are notable for their depiction of the folkways and dialects of villages Down East, but her best stories also reveal a penetrating insight into human psychology and an

The American Short Story Handbook, First Edition. James Nagel.
© 2015 James Nagel. Published 2015 by John Wiley & Sons, Ltd.

appreciation of the ethical struggles central to the development of the Local Color movement and American Realism. One such story, "A White Heron," perhaps her most famous, was written in 1886 as part of the efforts of the newly formed Audubon Society to save the Snowy Egret from extinction. Stylish women were wearing the feathers from the bird in their hats, and the popularity of that look had severely depleted the population of the herons throughout the United States. The story features Sylvia, a young girl who lives with her grandmother on a small farm in Maine. She is a child of nature, as her name suggests, and she spends her days in the woods and fields around her home with Mistress Moolly, a cow, and the birds and animals of the area for whom she feels a special affection. A handsome young ornithologist comes to the farm one day. He is shooting birds to be mounted for his exhibit, and he wants to kill the white heron he has seen nearby. Sylvia knows where it nests, but she is torn between her desire to save the bird and her longing to win the approval of the young man as well as the money he has offered. This kind of ethical struggle had come to invest American fiction with a central moral conflict by the 1880s, and often it was adolescents who confronted them. In the end, her loyalty to the bird wins out, and he leaves.

Jewett was capable of investing her stories with the conflicts of the elderly, as well. "Miss Tempy's Watchers" illustrates her sensitivity to the lives of country women and their delicate social interactions in a laconic society near the bottom of the economic scale. Thinking of her closest friends even while she was declining with a terminal illness, Temperance Dent arranged that Sarah Ann Binson and Mrs. Crowe would sit at her bedside during the traditional watchful night before the burial. Miss Tempy has done so because these two old friends have become estranged based on the fundamental differences between them. Mrs. Crowe is comparatively wealthy but reluctant to spend any money, especially on charity. Impoverished in comparison, as was Tempy, Miss Binson is generous with her meager resources and with her judgment of others. But the two have long been friends in a small village, and Miss Tempy has apparently had the feeling that an evening together would renew the relationship that they once enjoyed. In the course of the night the two women recall how Tempy had given most of her money to Lizzie Trevor to pay off her education debts and have a trip to Niagara Falls, even though it meant that Tempy would never be able to go herself. The two visitors are moved by the enormity of the gesture, especially Mrs. Crowe, who says she is "humbled to the dust." As the two women develop greater compassion for each other, they have the feeling that Tempy is the watcher, has seen to them while they dosed through the night, and that her transcendent goodness and humane generosity has drawn them together even after her death.

Some of Jewett's stories have a satiric rather than a sentimental edge, as is the case in "The Dulham Ladies," which features the oldest form of humor in English, that of congratulatory self deception. The two titular characters are Miss Dobin and Miss Lucinda Dobin, the daughters of a local minister who once held sway in the society of Dulham. Their mother descended from a Boston family and was once invited to have tea with the governor of the commonwealth, an event firmly planted in family history. But in time the parents grew elderly and passed on, but the Dobin sisters have lived as though nothing substantial had changed, basking in the historic stature of their family and perpetually resistant to even the slightest suspicion that they were not as young and attractive as they used to be.

Despite their slightly addled view of the social life of the town, they come late to the admission that their hair has grown a trifle thin beneath the bonnets they have adopted to hide their baldness, a matter so blatantly obvious to others that one day during a meeting of the sewing society, a child was heard to ask "Do Miss Dobbinses wear them great caps because their bare heads is cold?" At long last the two ladies come to the decision that it is time to travel to nearby Westbury to purchase wigs, as had their father a generation earlier. There they fall into the clutches of a French businessman (the French are always the villains in Maine literature) who sells them both ridiculous bangs long out of fashion and grossly incompatible with the color of their eyebrows. Outfitted with anachronistic frisettes, the Dobin ladies once again delude themselves that they look not a day over thirty as they parade the main street of the city, confident that they once again cut quite a stylish figure. The conductor on the train they take back to Dulham has quite a different view, thinking that they look humorously like poodle dogs. They return home basking in their delusions of timely beauty, confident that they are leaders in social fashions and "prepared for anything."

Even these few examples illustrate the generic pattern for Jewett's short fiction: the central characters are village women, usually living alone in reduced circumstances, who take pride in knowing the customs of local society, the traditions of their families, and the history of their Downeast communities. The conflicts they encounter are rarely physical; most often they focus on ideas, friendships, and new realizations. The central issues of "Marsh Rosemary," however, are of more dramatic moment. Ann Floyd is one of Jewett's rare spinsters who decides to marry, in this case a handsome young man who has a reputation as a listless gadabout. Not long after their wedding, he runs off, leaving her alone once again. In due course she discovers that he is living happily with a young woman and their child. Rather than disrupt what appears to be a happy domestic unit, she quietly withdraws to her former life, resigned to the knowledge that the wedded love she had sought is forever denied to her. Some of Jewett's tales of superannuated courtship are more hopeful, however. "A Winter Courtship" portrays Jefferson Briley as an elderly bachelor who takes an innocent wagon ride one morning and ends up engaged to a widow "on the make." In "The Quest of Mr. Teaby," it is the older gentleman who is eager for matrimony and the coquettish Hannah Pinkham who maneuvers his proposals as she wishes. "The Town Poor" is an unusual story in that two women, Ann and Mandy Bray, live together in their poverty. In a pathetic scene, they attempt to entertain visitors, a situation that emphasizes the extent of their desperation and the distance between their situation and the relative wealth of the community about them.

In these and scores of other stories, Jewett used her consummate skill as raconteur to tell Yankee tales of Downeast women, especially those who reside alone in impoverished circumstances as the last survivors of once proud families. Her deft touch in handling dialogue and narration grant a regional charm to her gentle accounts of the interactions of these characters who strive to retain some dimension of self-respect and social standing despite their financial limitations. When visitors "from away" intrude into this quiet world, it is nearly always with unfortunate consequences based on cultural misunderstandings and social disparities. Jewett's skill in describing the old homes, little villages, vibrant nature, and emotional life of Maine women in what she called her "little postage stamp" of a world is what has given her work a permanent place in literary history and a standing at the forefront of the Local Color movement.

Suggestions for Further Reading

Blanchard, Paula. *Sarah Orne Jewett: Her World and Her Work*. Reading: Addison Wesley, 1994.

Cary, Richard, ed. *Appreciation of Sarah Orne Jewett: Twenty-Nine Interpretive Essays*. Waterville: Colby College Press, 1973.

Cary, Richard. *Sarah Orne Jewett*. New York: Twayne, 1962.

Donovan, Josephine. *Sarah Orne Jewett*. New York: Ungar, 1980.

Nagel, Gwen, ed. *Critical Essays on Sarah Orne Jewett*. Boston: G. K. Hall, 1984.

Silverthorne, Elizabeth. *Sarah Orne Jewett: A Writer's Life*. Woodstock: Overlook Press, 1993.

Sougnac, Jean. *Sarah Orne Jewett*. Paris: Jouve et Cie, 1937.

Toth, Margaret F. *Sarah Orne Jewett*. Minneapolis: University of Minnesota Press, 1966.

Westbrook, Percy D. *Acres of Flint: Writers of Rural New England, 1870-1900*. Washington, D.C.: Scarecrow Press, 1951.

Charles W. Chesnutt

Charles Chesnutt enjoys the reputation of being the first African American writer to produce a sustained body of substantial fiction admired in both the black and white communities. His work in the story is important in a number of ways, including the fact that he located struggle against racial prejudice in characters from both races, wrote in dialects drawn from both communities, and developed complex themes with depth and grace. His two most important volumes of short fiction are *The Conjure Woman* and *The Wife of His Youth and Other Stories of the Color Line*, both of which appeared from Houghton, Mifflin, in 1899. His stories originally came out in the leading periodicals of the day, notably *The Atlantic Monthly*, and were celebrated by an enormous audience of avid readers.

Part of the widespread appeal of his stories was that he was able to write within standard traditions while enriching them thematically with the racial complexity of the post-bellum South. The prevailing mode of the Local Color story provided a framework for the tales in *The Conjure Woman*, which in some respects resembles the dialect narratives of Joel Chandler Harris and the idyllic plantation fiction of Thomas Nelson Page. Chesnutt employed the familiar pattern of a sophisticated frame narrator from the North, speaking in standard English, who sets the stage for a regional internal character to deliver a highly localized tale in the lexicon of his social class and region. In "The Goophered Grapevine," Chesnutt established how this pattern could be used to develop a good deal of interest: the attempt of an impoverished former slave to manipulate a wealthy white man with an improbable tale.

In this case, the initial narrator seems to be a gentleman from northern Ohio who has come to North Carolina looking for an opportunity to buy property, perhaps an old plantation, and grow grapes to make wine.

The American Short Story Handbook, First Edition. James Nagel.
© 2015 James Nagel. Published 2015 by John Wiley & Sons, Ltd.

Charles W. Chesnutt

He arrives in Patesville with his wife, Annie, and they are taken a few miles from town to the old McAdoo estate, where they see old Uncle Julius sitting on a log eating scuppernong grapes. He has had the run of the neglected grounds during a long dispute among the heirs to the estate, and he especially has enjoyed consuming all the grapes he wanted. Now, faced with the prospect of a white man purchasing the property, he attempts to dissuade the narrator from acquiring the land by telling him that the property has been "goophered," bewitched.

The recitation of the goophering of the vineyard is told by Julius in black dialect, and it is a tour de force of language, subterfuge, and manipulation. He relates how Master McAdoo raised scuppernongs but lost much of the crop because the local slaves surreptitiously ate the grapes in the night. To counter the loss, McAdoo first set traps and spring guns to catch anyone approaching the vines in the dark, but, ironically, he was shot in the leg by his own devices. Julius is thus hoping to prevent any such approach by the new owner of the property. The Master then hired Aunt Peggy, the local conjure woman, to put a curse on the vines so that anyone eating them would die. Julius presents evidence that the curse had worked because a runaway horse killed a coachman who had eaten some of the grapes. He then transitions into a marvelous account of a slave named Henry who put juice from the vine on his head in the spring and grew vine-like hair to cover his baldness all summer while at the same time becoming youthful and vigorous while the vines were growing. In fall, at harvest time, he began to lose his vitality and his hair and barely could survive until spring, when his energy returned. Henry had become the human embodiment of the grapes themselves. But the thriving industry on the plantation was ruined when a Yankee came down South with new farming techniques that ruined the vines. Henry died, and the plantation has been in ruins ever since. Julius thus warns the narrator not to buy the plantation, hoping to keep his unearned sinecure in place, but the property is purchased nonetheless. The narrator returns, to complete the frame, in standard dialect, to relate how, despite the goophered grapevine, he bought the plantation and hired Uncle Julius as a coachman.

The opening story establishes a paradigm for the rest of the tales in the volume: a white narrator sets the stage in standard English; Uncle Julius takes over in dialect to deliver a fanciful account with manipulative intent; and the frame narrator returns to comment on the final result. What is patently obvious is that Julius believes not a word of his transparently manipulative yarn but hopes to sustain his easy access to all the grapes he wants. Julius knows the fruit is not poisonous since he eats it all the time. The narrator understands the technique, being aware of confidence men, white and black, but he is entertained by the narrative, as were tens of thousands of Americans. Chesnutt used the pattern repeatedly.

In the case of "Po' Sandy," the initial situation is that the narrator's wife, Annie, desires a new kitchen, one outside of the house, where it would not exacerbate the summer heat. To get the wood for the building, the narrator decides to tear down a school house on the property and use the lumber for the new structure. At this juncture, Uncle Julius intervenes with one of his tales, this one about a slave named "Sandy" who lived on a contiguous plantation. Sandy was an extraordinary worker who was often loaned out for long periods to other slave owners for special projects. When he returned from one of those, his master had sold Sandy's wife and purchased a younger female slave, "Tenie," whom Sandy quickly marries. She, according to Julius, turned out to be a conjure woman. On one occasion, to prevent the master from sending her husband away yet another time, she turns him into a pine tree, one that gets cut down for the lumber to build the school house. In essence, Sandy is now in the wood of the building and, Julius emphasizes, can be heard moaning and groaning in the night, haunting the building. All of this is, of course, a fabrication to prevent the narrator from tearing down the school building because Julius wants to use it as a church on Sundays for his congregation, yet Annie responds as though it were all local history. She says "poor Tenie!" in an expression of sympathy for the desire of a husband and wife to be together, recognizing the humanity in the characters in Julius' tale. This prompts her to reject the notion of using the lumber from the schoolhouse, and a kitchen is build with new wood. Julius has succeeded in preserving his building, and his church begins holding services in the structure, disregarding the haunted nature Julius claims for it.

All of the conjure tales follow this artistic and thematic pattern, the black coachman attempting to outsmart his white employer by means of a tale of metamorphoses involving supernatural "goophering" on the plantation. This stratagem elevates Julius from servile fidelity to a more fully human status as a person who is part of a family, and he has lived on this soil his entire life. His legend of Sandy is fundamentally one of dehumanization, a man turned into a tree because he does not want to be separated from his wife, and Julius is not above subterfuge to achieve his own ends, a church where his people can conduct their own services. He is resourceful and can contrive inventive fictional situations in an attempt to maneuver his listeners into behaving in a desired way. The former slave is in some ways wiser than the white community, especially in pointing out the transgressions of the antebellum slave system.

The tales in *The Wife of His Youth and Other Stories* are more complex with a variety of narrative stances and themes deriving from moral conflicts within both the black and white communities. In "The Sheriff's Children," a former Confederate officer is forced to confront the ethical consequences of his pre-war behavior. He had a son with a slave and then sold both mother and child down the river, never contacting them again. Now, two decades later, the young man comes back to challenge his father with what he had done. The sheriff has another family by that time, and he has arrested his mulatto son for murder even though the young man is innocent. At the end, the young man commits suicide in the jail cell, leaving a stunned father to contemplate the deeply troubling moral lapses in his past.

"The Wife of His Youth" puts moral conflict within the black community, in this case one closely resembling the light-skinned society in Cleveland where Chesnutt grew up. In this case, this group of free blacks, known locally as the Blue Vein Society, has known a good deal of social and economic prosperity, and they exhibit the same prejudices toward their darker brethren as does the white community. The protagonist, Mr. Ryder, hails from the South, but he has grown to be one of the leaders of the organization and a preserver of its most conservative principals. He is hoping to marry a beautiful and well educated younger woman. He plans on announcing their engagement at a society ball when an astonishing event takes place. A small, very dark, old woman shows up at his doorstep looking for her long-lost husband, a younger man she married when she was a slave in the South. Her husband was not enslaved and promised to work and save money to purchase her freedom. But her owner sold her just as the Civil War broke out, and the two were separated. She obviously loved her husband since she has searched for him for twenty-five years, assuming that he would be eager to be reunited. She does not realize that Mr. Ryder, now a well-dressed professional man, is her husband, and he could easily send her away with the comment that he knows nothing about the case. He is torn between his moral obligations to this faithful woman and his desire to wed a charming young woman who belongs to what is now his social class. All of this conflict is played out at the ball, where Mr. Ryder, after a long period of reflection, introduces the old woman as the wife of his youth. Although he thus gives up his future with a wealthy, young woman, he attains a standing of moral consequence by adhering to his ethical standards and by embracing the faithful old woman who has searched for him for more than two decades.

None of the other stories in the volume have the ethical power of these two, but all of them present significant issues in the racial consciousness of American society. In "Her Virginia Mammy," Clara is about to marry a physician from a distinguished white family from the North even though she was an adopted child of uncertain background. She hesitates, fearing that she may have mixed blood. At that juncture a small woman of olive complexion appears, probably a quadroon or octoroon, and they exchange biographical accounts. As a baby, Clara had survived a steamboat explosion on the Mississippi, and she was raised by a white family, educated at a fashionable school, and she became a schoolteacher. But all along she has known that she was darker than her adoptive parents, and she has been concerned about it. She feels it not right to marry the doctor if she is of mixed blood. Her guest, Mrs. Harper, who resembles Clara in several respects, then recites her own story of how she was the mammy of a white child on the very boat that sank into the river, and that the girl's parents were both white from the best of families. Mrs. Harper is lying, of course, since she is obviously Clara's mother and wants her daughter to marry the man she loves. When Dr. Winthrop hears this account, and looks upon the two of them, he immediately sees that it is a protective fabrication, but he is above racial discrimination and pretends to accept the story as fact, and they move directly to the wedding. All of this is precisely the situation and outcome of George Washington Cable's "Madame Delphine" of a decade earlier.

Chesnutt's stories thus exceeded the expectations of some elements of the white community, which assumed an African American writer would deal only with racial issues, by focusing on moral conflicts of universal application. His work also suggests that social and ethnic prejudices are not reserved for Southern whites but can be found across the spectrum of society, especially in those areas where there is significant contact between racial groups. His emphasis, somewhat in the tradition of George Washington Cable, is on protagonists of mixed race, who face the prospect of social ostracism on all sides. Since black society often involved its own stratification based on skin color, these characters faced conflicts in romance, courtship, and marriage. In terms of the literature of race, the issues of passing and unknown parentage gave Chesnutt's stories an ethical dimension unique in the last decade of the century.

Suggestions for Further Reading

Andrews, William L. *The Literary Career of Charles W. Chesnutt*. Baton Rouge: Louisiana State University Press, 1980.

Duncan, Charles. *The Absent Man: The Narrative Craft of Charles W. Chesnutt*. Athens: Ohio University Press, 1998.

Izzo, David Garrett, and Maria Orban, eds. *Charles Chesnutt Reappraised: Essays on the First Major African American Writer*. Jefferson: McFarland & Co., 2009.

McElrath, Joseph R. Jr., ed. *Critical Essays on Charles W. Chesnutt*. New York: G. K. Hall, 1999.

Paulin, Diana Rebekkah. *Imperfect Unions: Staging Miscegenation in U. S. Drama and Fiction*. Minneapolis: University of Minnesota Press, 2012.

Render, Sylvia Lyons, ed. *The Short Fiction of Charles W. Chesnutt*. Washington, D.C.: Howard University Press, 1974.

Wright, Susan Prothro. *Passing in the Works of Charles W. Chesnutt*. Ed. Ernestine Pickens. Jackson: University Press of Mississippi, 2010.

Willa Cather

Willa Cather's sterling reputation as a consummate writer in American literature rests securely on her brilliant novel of 1918, *My Ántonia*, widely regarded as among the finest works of fiction in English. During her lifetime, however, she was regarded as equally adept in the creation of short stories, especially for those collected in *The Troll Garden*, *Youth and the Bright Medusa*, and *Obscure Destinies*. It was here, in her early tales, that she first explored her ability to capture the lives of immigrant farmers struggling to establish a life for their families on the harsh plains recently opened for settlement. Her penetrating understanding of the restrictions such circumstances required, the longings for culture as well as the fulfillment in family interactions that such a setting demanded, had never been captured so sympathetically or presented in more realistic terms.

Some of her early stories involve character and incidents that later reappear as important elements in her novels. For example, "Peter," her first completed tale, deals with an immigrant father from Prague who is devoted to his violin. Disabled by a stroke, he dreams of his lost life in the old country until he finally kills himself with a shotgun, a situation and outcome repeated in *My Ántonia* in the death of Mr. Shimerda. Similarly, "The Bohemian Girl" uses the same basic materials as Cather's great novel, albeit with a different conclusion. The son of a Nebraska farmer, Nils Ericson went East for his education and greater opportunity for a more cultivated life. In the opening, he returns home on the train to visit the people and the life he has left behind. There he falls in love with his brother's wife, Clara Vavricka, who loves music and dancing and the vibrant world he describes in New York and Europe, and he convinces her to run away and start a more fulfilling life with him. She does so, quite unlike the ending

The American Short Story Handbook, First Edition. James Nagel.
© 2015 James Nagel. Published 2015 by John Wiley & Sons, Ltd.

of *My Ántonia*, in which Jim discovers the rich family life that his old friend enjoys and could never leave. Still, the themes of the restrictions of a hardscrabble life on the plains, the possibility of escape to a wider world, and the revisiting of rich memories of early life establish ideas that Cather would use repeatedly throughout her career.

"A Wagner Matinée" deals with Aunt Georgiana, who returns from Nebraska to Boston for the settling of the family estate. Her nephew, Clark, who narrates, grew up on the plains and knows the rough life, the remote setting, and the distance from any kind of cultural refinement that environment entails. As she steps off the train in the East, he can see what the Western experience has done to her, the stoic hardness of her face, which has been ravaged by the wind. Knowing that she had attended the Boston Symphony regularly when she taught music in the city, he arranges for them to fill an afternoon with music. From the opening overture to the end, she is transfixed with overwhelming emotion, and she weeps through the second half of the program and protests that she does not want to go back to Nebraska. But she must. In this one afternoon, she has once again experienced aesthetic transcendence, while her nephew has come to a new appreciation of the depth of feeling within his aunt and the enormity of sacrifice her life in the west requires.

In this early story, Cather brought together her two most important themes: the essential role of the arts in human existence and the differences between life in the cultured East and the rough fight for survival in the West. Her most famous story, "Paul's Case," offers a variation on the concept in that the protagonist grows up not in Nebraska but in Pittsburgh, where he comes to know the dull routine of high school and the mundane world of his working-class neighborhood. What relieves the dreariness of his existence is the arts, which he regards as vital to his being, not an external entertainment. He finds satisfaction in viewing paintings, in the opera, and, especially, in the concert hall where he works as an usher. Here he could find aesthetic escape from a sordid reality, an artistic transcendence that carried him away into another realm. But a degrading world is always waiting for him when the theater closed for the evening, and when a school incident threatens to take this special experience away from him, he steals money and runs away to New York to indulge himself fully in the world he has longed for all his life. He checks into the Waldorf, eats in the finest restaurants, buys new clothes, and immerses himself completely in the pageantry of the opera. For more than a week he floats on the dream of a perfect world, but then the newspapers inform him that his crime in Pittsburgh has been discovered and that his father is on his way to retrieve him. Unwilling to return to life away from the artistic graces of New York, he jumps in front of a roaring train and commits suicide.

"The Sculptor's Funeral" not only develops the theme of the importance of an artistic temperament but adds to it what was becoming known as the "village virus" motif, the idea that a small town can become insulated to new ideas, petty in its attitudes, and cruel to anyone who deviates from the accepted pattern of behavior. In this case, an isolated community in Kansas is depicted in all its cruelty, its predilection for destructive gossip, its lack of human decency in the ways in which the citizens react to one another. The situation for the revelation of these appalling attitudes is the death of Harvey Merrick, a sculptor of considerable reputation in the East who had grown up in this environment. As a youth, he was sensitive, gentle, and somewhat effeminate, not a conventional young man in a society devoted to practical, mercantile values. He cared little for money or possessions, and he was clearly drawn to artistic beauty, a deviation from the norm that led to his social ostracism.

Upon news of his death, and the pending arrival of his coffin on the train, members of the community gather at the station in the opening of the story. They are a non-descript sort with a few exceptions, a red-bearded lawyer named Jim Laird who stands apart from the crowd both physically and intellectually, as does a young man from Boston, Henry Steavens, who has accompanied the body on its long journey. He embodies the culture of the East, its sensitivity to the life of the mind and the value of the arts, and he wishes the ceremonies to be conducted in a suitable manner for a widely respected man. In contrast, the boys of the town are described in the negative imagery of eels, slimy creatures that uncoil themselves from the baggage trucks or slide from the wagons. As the casket is unloaded, the crowd is indifferent to the fact that it carries a palm leaf on the lid, a symbol of peace and the victory of the soul over adversity, an indication of stature and respect.

The coffin is taken to the Merrick family home, which so exudes poor taste in every aspect of its decoration that Steavens concludes they must have come to the wrong home. From the Rogers Group of John Alden and Priscilla to the plush upholstery and the cheap bric-a-brac, every aspect of the room seems discordant with the nature and taste of his friend, as is the behavior of the family. Merrick's mother has a face that seems distorted by violence and the "fiercer passions," and her maudlin expression of grief is offensive to him. One exception to the garish behavior is that of Roxy, a mulatto woman, a servant in the household, whose face is "pitifully sad and gentle" and who sobs silently in the corner. Significantly, Steavens moves over to stand beside her.

The other person Steavens respects is the lawyer, Jim Laird, who is as drunk now as always but whose face reveals a genuine "feeling, the understanding, that must exist in some one, even here." What is shocking is the treatment of Roxy by the Merrick family. She has forgotten to make the dressing for a salad, and the abuse she takes from Mrs. Merrick is shocking in its "excruciating cruelty" and violence, and Laird is moved to close the door to the kitchen, disgusted by what he has heard. Laird explains to Steavens that it is a wonder that a person such as Harvey could have sprung from a "dung heap" such as this. Steavens is shocked by the ugliness and shameful attitudes he has heard expressed at this gathering. He feels a revulsion from the general disappointment that Merrick had little regard for practical things, for acquiring money, remaining in his home town and adopting its social ethic. The story ends with Jim Laird, who was educated with Harvey in the East, delivering a Jeramiad to the group, who have made a moral and intellectual "hog-wallow" out of their community. It is a devastating speech, and Laird and Stevens shake hands at the end of it.

Such a negative portrait of a small town is unusual in Cather's fiction, although the distinction between a society that values the arts and one devoted exclusively to mercantile values is evident in nearly all of her work, including "Paul's Case" and "A Wagner Matinée," among the best of her short fiction. The fundamental conflict between the Hellenistic concern for aesthetic beauty and the more practical pursuit of wealth and security runs throughout her work, and her protagonists are nearly always devoted to the arts. Even the title of "Coming, Aphrodite!" indicates the nature of the central themes through the direct reference to the Greek goddess of love and beauty. It is appropriate, thus, that it be the most sexually explicit of all of Cather's stories and that the plot concerns artists obsessed with both love and their artistic ambitions. Eden Bower is devoted to her music, even though she has an affair with Don Hedger, an artist equally committed to his craft, until it becomes increasingly clear that they cannot immerse themselves in love and still achieve their highest aesthetic goals. Romantic love in Cather's fiction is rarely the source of deep satisfaction. In "Uncle Valentine," the protagonist, a composer, does his best work during a single year of creativity prior to moving to Paris, where he is killed in an accident. "Neighbor Rosicky" returns the focus to a Bohemian immigrant who realizes that life in the city is bereft of the spiritual underpinning that derives from living close to the soil, so he moves west to Nebraska, marries, and raises a family in one of Cather's few portraits of a mutually satisfying marriage. Close to the end of his life, he instructs his children, and his daughter-in-law, in the meaning of family and the importance of the land they have settled, the inner strength that comes from working hard to make a living from nature. Often anthologized, this story recalls the situations in Cather's most popular early novels, and it has helped sustain her reputation as one of the great American writers of short stories.

Her stature as a writer is unusual in some respects. Although she will always be remembered for her vivid evocations of the Nebraska plains, her work is not essentially that of the Local Colorists. She did not write in the vernacular, and the dialogue in her fiction is not notable for its regionalisms. The intense distinction between the cultured Eastern seaboard and the great unwashed of the plains could equally have been true about characters from many different regions of the country, as in Hamlin Garland's depictions of life on the middle boarder of the upper Midwest. Her concentration on the life of the arts is unique in the fiction of her period, and it gives her work a distinctive thematic edge. Unlike other writers identified with a particular setting, she did not write in dialect but embraced a cultivated but unpretentious lexicon that made her work seem graceful, unobtrusive, and sensitive, and her readers came from every level of American society. Most of all she portrayed characters who seemed profoundly common, who faced conflicts understood by the legions of settlers who spread across the country in the decades after the Civil War. Their feelings of cultural duality, of isolation, and of growing community reflected the life they had known and gave it memorable artistic dignity. That dimension of her work will never be duplicated.

Suggestions for Further Reading

Arnold, Marilyn. *Willa Cather's Short Fiction*. Athens: Ohio University Press, 1984.

Gerber, Philip. *Willa Cather*. Boston: Twayne, 1975.

Giannone, Richard. *Music in Willa Cather's Fiction*. Lincoln: University of Nebraska Press, 1968.

Meyering, Sheryl L. *A Reader's Guide to the Short Stories of Willa Cather*. New York: G. K. Hall, 1994.

Murphy, John, ed. *Critical Essays on Willa Cather*. Boston: G. K. Hall, 1983.

O'Brien, Sharon. *Willa Cather: The Emerging Voice*. New York: Oxford University Press, 1987.

Rosowski, Susan. *The Voyage Perilous: Willa Cather's Romanticism*. Lincoln: University of Nebraska Press, 1986.

Wasserman, Loretta. *Willa Cather: A Study of the Short Fiction*. Boston: Twayne, 1991.

F. Scott Fitzgerald

F. Scott Fitzgerald's reputation since his death in 1940 has rested firmly on his superb novels *The Great Gatsby* and *Tender is the Night*, but during his lifetime he was equally well known for his stories. In fact, most of the money he made in his lifetime came from his short fiction, and in the 1920s he commanded the highest fees in the country from the popular magazines. His volumes established the "terms" to describe the period, as did *Flappers and Philosophers* and *Tales of the Jazz Age*, and they depicted the hedonistic frenzy of young society after World War I, drinking heavily in the period of Prohibition, defying Victorian standards of behavior for women, speaking and writing about sexual relationships, and treating middle-class American traditions as outmoded and embarrassingly old fashioned. A new generation was taking over, and they knew better how to think, how to act, and how to live. By the end of the decade it was starting to be clear that this lifestyle was proving to be disastrously self-destructive, and the people who had most heavily engaged in it had worn themselves out and retreated to mental institutions, alcoholic treatment centers, or more conventional patterns of social behavior.

Fitzgerald's stories captured this turmoil brilliantly in over 160 pieces of short fiction, some of which were published only after his death. His standard protagonist was a young man from a modest background who is striving to be accepted into the glittering world of the upper crust, the embodiment of which is a beautiful young woman. This underlying pattern, the subject of many of his early stories, provided the central plot for *The Great Gatsby*, but before it did so it was already used in "Winter Dreams," in which a golf caddy, Dexter Green, sees Judy Jones at the country club and becomes obsessed with winning her acceptance and affection. If he can

The American Short Story Handbook, First Edition. James Nagel.
© 2015 James Nagel. Published 2015 by John Wiley & Sons, Ltd.

in some way possess her he will have made it into the social level he has observed but never experienced. But over the years she reveals herself to be cruel and destructive, unworthy of his idealization, just as Daisy ultimately proves to be unworthy of Gatsby's obsessive devotion. These winter dreams, hollow at their core, based on fantasy and illusion, sustained Dexter's early years and then collapsed, leaving him without a sense of direction and ambition, revealing to him that the vision that had informed his very being had been based on the false surface of things, a dramatically deflating realization.

Another early story, "Absolution," also played a role leading up to *The Great Gatsby* in that it was part of an early draft of the novel and the protagonist was, in a sense, a preliminary formulation of the character who became James Gatz before he reinvented himself as Gatsby. The setting is in the Red River Valley region of Minnesota, an agricultural area filled with Scandinavian and German settlers. In this environment a Roman Catholic priest struggles with the "hot madness" of his sexuality every day when the blond Swedish girls come home from school and walk by the windows of the rectory. At the same time, a boy of eleven, Rudolph Miller, is awakening to the sensual impulses within himself and is likewise torn by a sense of sin and remorse, as he attempts to confess to the priest. He also feels confined, as did Gatsby, by the mundane world about him, with its economic and social restrictions, and he longs for a more adventurous life. Toward that end he enjoys thinking of himself as Blatchford Sarnemington, a suave figure of means and charm that young Rudolph longs to possess. This would seem to be the origin of Gatsby's Platonic conception of himself and an experiment that explains much about the early life of Fitzgerald's most memorable character.

The portrait of Rudolph's father is revelatory of the world his son wishes to escape. A freight agent, Carl Miller is a devout Catholic who, as did Gatsby's father, admires the wealth and accomplishments of James J. Hill, who built the Great Northern Railroad and whose mansion was at the end of Summit Avenue, the very street the Fitzgeralds lived on in St. Paul. Carl insists on strict religious observance for his son, and he beats him severely for minor offenses, such as drinking water before confession. There is a rage smoldering within the father, who does not share a bedroom with his wife, who has shut himself off from the normal experiences of middle-class life, and his frustrations seem to be destroying him from within. But the heart of the story is with Rudolph, with his progressive distancing from the strict theology of the church, with the sense that there is something "ineffably gorgeous" about life that has nothing to do with religion. Father Schwartz is nearly driven mad by the intensity of his sexual desires, by his imperfect attempts to sublimate his impulses, and he is profoundly unhealthy in his role as a priest. Rudolph is moving away from the church's attitudes about sexuality and toward a more fully human participation in the society around him, an exciting world of Northern girls and tall boys and the fertility of nature.

Another pre-Gatsby story is notable for its portrait of a Southern Belle, a Daisy figure named Sally Carrol Happer, who serves as protagonist and center of intelligence in "The Ice Palace." She is nineteen at the time of the action, listless, bored, and focused entirely on courtship and marriage. Her fascination with her region is underscored by her interest in the cemetery for the Confederate dead from the Civil War, a suggestion that the old civilization of the South has exhausted its useful life. She desires adventure and an escape from the South she has always known, and she rejects a proposal from a local young man, Clark Darrow, in favor of Harry Bellamy, a Northern boy, because she sees him as the means to a new life.

She finds it when she journeys to visit him in a city that suggests St. Paul, Minnesota, in part because of the tradition of the ice palace at the Winter Carnival. Harry's family is part of the upper set of the city, as is clear from the elegance of their home and the educational background of their friends, many of whom went to Ivy League institutions. She finds them socially cold, but one of them, Roger Patton, is warmly gracious, and he has come from Harvard to teach French at a local university. She immediately likes Mr. Bellamy, Harry's father, who grew up in Kentucky, but she detests the rest of the family even though she plans to marry in March. At first Sally Carrol tries to enjoy the winter sports that are so much part of outdoor life in the North, but she dislikes the cold, the people, the area. Her feelings reach their apex when she becomes lost in the ice palace, a gigantic building, three stories tall, made of huge blocks of ice cut from the surrounding lakes. She is terrified of freezing to death, and as she loses consciousness, she confuses blocks of ice with the tombstones she frequented in a local cemetery at home, and she is intent on returning to the South. The last scene has her safely home, unmarried, resuming the way of life she had rejected in the opening.

Sally Carol Happer is also a character in "The Last of the Belles," which is set largely in Tarleton, Georgia, and deals with the same issues as "The Ice Palace." A retrospective narrative, it is told by Andy fifteen years after the activities of the story, which take place during 1918, the last year of World War I. The conflicts involve the standard concerns of flirtation, courtship, and marriage, with a special emphasis on the Southern Belle. Andy is a Harvard graduate, and a fellow student during his years there was Bill Knowles, another suitor of the belle, the nineteen-year-old Ailie Calhoun. Much is made of the North-South dichotomy, with the commercial North measured against the plantation world of gallant gentlemen and genteel ladies and a background of wealth, tradition, and proper manners. Ailie parallels Sally Carol in her longing for the adventure she thinks might await her in the North and her feeling that she cannot marry a Southern man. Ailie encourages a spectrum of beaus, one of whom commits suicide because she becomes engaged to someone else, but she breaks off that relationship before the wedding. At the end, Andy realizes that he has been in love with Ailie all along, but she is going to marry someone else and the South will have lost its meaning for him forever.

These early stories utilize much of the materials that went into *The Great Gatsby*: the attractive Southern Belle who longs for a broader range of experience; the young man who creates a new identity for himself out of his romantic idealizations; the conflict between the cultures of the North and South; and the destructive potential of a party that has gone flat, the fun that went on for too long. The portrait of the Belle is one of empty beauty, of superficial attractiveness based entirely on externals. Ailie, like Daisy, is uneducated and reveals little or no depth of thought or feeling. For her, romance is a matter of surfaces, and she has little genuine feeling for any of the sequence of men she encourages. Indeed, there is so little beyond her beauty that she seems as false as the romantic idealization of the South as a setting. Indeed, it would seem unlikely that Andy, with a Harvard education and training as an aviation officer, would be obsessed with a young lady so intellectually unsophisticated. As with Daisy in *The Great Gatsby*, the idealized woman ultimately proves to be unworthy of the intensity of feeling the key young man invests in her.

Fitzgerald's greatest story, and one of the best in American literature, is "Babylon Revisited," written in 1930. It is nearly perfect as a work of short fiction, with impressive thematic congruence, tight narrative progression, deft character development, and a coherent structural design. It is basically a chronological plot that is rather simple on the surface. In years past, Charlie Wales and his wife, Helen, drank too much, partied too hard, and she died after a drunken incident in which he locked her out in the cold. Now, a year and a half later, he has been through alcohol treatment and has a business in Prague. He has come to Paris in hopes of bringing his daughter, Honoria, back with him, but he must convince his wife's sister, Marion Peters, that he is capable of assuming his responsibilities. He loves his daughter desperately, and she loves him, and everything is in place for the plan to succeed. Then, one evening, two drunken celebrants from the old life break in on the group in the Peters apartment, and their riotous humor ruins everything. Marion is reminded of the destructive past and sees Charlie as not entirely free of it, and at the end he is to return to Prague alone, still paying the bill for the hedonistic party of the 1920s.

That simple plot is a brilliant evocation of the end of an era, one that Fitzgerald and Zelda lived through, and the situation is tragically similar to the events of his own life. Indeed, the conclusion is all the more poignant in biographical context: even after he had written so pointedly about Charlie and Honoria, Fitzgerald continued his downward slide into alcoholism and an eventual breakdown, dying young, at age forty-three. What gives the story its power, however, is its artistry, including its close identification with Charlie's mind, his fervent hopes, his longing to make up for the mistakes of the past, his sense of guilt for his wife's death, his desire to establish a quiet domestic life in Prague. In only one scene does the narrative identification shift to the minds of Duncan and Lorraine and their feelings about him, but all of the other assertions reflect Charlie's thinking, and the tone is restrained in accord with the serious purpose of his journey.

Structurally, the action opens and closes with Charlie talking to the bartender in the Ritz, the locus of the human degeneracy of so much of the "good life" of a few years before. It is no longer the "American" bar: "It had gone back into France." The stock market has crashed, taking many fortunes with it, including Charlie's, and what is clear from the beginning is that Paris as "Babylon" is over, and in its wake floats a good deal of human damage. The gang of perpetual celebrants he had known a few years before is gone, leaving emotional debris behind, lives broken by too much money, too many parties. As Charlie says to the bartender at the end of the story, he was not ruined by the stock market crash, he lost everything he cared about in the boom.

The opening and closing scenes thus share a setting that is a reminder of what went wrong. In contrast to the Ritz is the Peters' apartment, the embodiment of middle-class domesticity. The issue is whether his new personal life can escape the residue of a past that clings to him. He has accepted his responsibility for the tragedies, and he embraces the acts of penance that might bring him the redemptive new family life he wishes to establish. Charlie wants his daughter to come live with him, but legal custody was given to Marion and Lincoln Peters, and he needs their approval. He is on his best behavior. The internal sections of the story deal with that issue, beginning with a tender scene of father and daughter declaring their love for each other and their wish to live together. They are playful in their interactions, much on the same wave length, and it is the most positive section of the action. At first Marion can find no justification to deny Charlie his request to take the girl, but then, at just the wrong moment, two of the old drunken celebrants burst into the Peters' flat, ruining everything. Marion is outraged at the intrusion and not at all convinced that Charlie has broken with his past life, and his request for Honoria is denied. It is an emotionally devastating conclusion, the most powerful moment in all of Fitzgerald's work, and it is a demonstration of the brilliant potential that was within him and that was never fully realized because of his susceptibility to the allure of his own Babylon.

What is abundantly clear is that Fitzgerald's stories came out of his own life, out of personal circumstances that allowed him to understand a spectrum of issues central to the Jazz Age and its aftermath. His early stories deal with a protagonist from a family of modest resources who longs to be accepted by the upper crust, especially so because he was educated among them, played sports with them, and was infatuated by the young ladies in that social stratum. Other characters undergo military training and fall in love with a Southern Belle, a character type that persisted as the embodiment of feminine allure. In his most mature stories, Fitzgerald could draw on his own marriage for portraits of riotous good times, the heartache of betrayal, the devastation of the breakdown of his wife and his own destructive lifestyle in the 1930s. Throughout, his stories demonstrate that he was acutely aware of the psychological drama of this personal trajectory, and his insights into the characters he created were presented with searing conviction and artistic integrity, the final testimony to a remarkable career in fiction.

Suggestions for Further Reading

Bryer, Jackson R, ed. *New Essays on F. Scott Fitzgerald's Neglected Stories.* Columbia: University of Missouri Press, 1996.

Bryer, Jackson R, ed. *The Short Stories of F. Scott Fitzgerald: New Approaches in Criticism.* Madison: University of Wisconsin Press, 1982.

Curnutt, Kirk. *The Cambridge Introduction to F. Scott Fitzgerald.* New York: Cambridge University Press, 2007.

Donaldson, Scott. *Fool for Love: F. Scott Fitzgerald.* Minneapolis: University of Minnesota Press, 2012.

Higgins, John A. *F. Scott Fitzgerald: A Study of the Stories.* New York: St. John's University Press, 1971.

Kuehl, John. *F. Scott Fitzgerald: A Study of the Short Fiction.* Boston: Twayne, 1991.

Mangum, Bryant. *A Fortune Yet: Money in the Art of F. Scott Fitzgerald's Short Stories.* New York: Garland, 1991.

Petry, Alice Hall. *Fitzgerald's Craft of Short Fiction: The Collected Stories, 1920-1935.* Tuscaloosa: University of Alabama Press, 1989.

Ernest Hemingway

Ernest Hemingway enjoys an enviable position as one of the foremost novelists in American literature as well as one of its greatest writers of short stories. From the earliest appearance of his fiction in the 1920s until the end of the next decade, he produced a remarkable body of work in the genre that is virtually unmatched for artistic integrity while at the same time addressing many of the central concerns of the period, including the trauma of an impersonal war that resulted in a psychologically damaged "lost generation," changing patterns of social and sexual behavior, the expatriate movement centered on the left bank of Paris, and a general sense that a younger, more modern, civilization had made a dramatic shift from the Victorian assumptions of their parents. The writers of this era lived in a new world, and it was proving to have a level of tumult and painful disruption quite beyond anything Americans had ever known, and no one captured the essence of all of this better than did Hemingway.

Although his stories deal with a wide range of subjects, in his early work a common theme is the psychological effect of violence, and the protagonist is often a young person who undergoes a traumatic initiation into the harsh realities of the adult world. In "Up in Michigan," for example, Liz Coates lives in Hortons Bay, Michigan, and she has an infatuation with Jim Gilmore, the local blacksmith. When Jim comes back from a deer hunting trip, he gets drunk, and when they are alone he kisses her and feels of her breasts. They go outside, and he makes love to her on the dock by the lake, even though she asks him not to do so. It is a crude and disillusioning experience for her. Jim falls asleep immediately, and Liz kisses him on the cheek and covers him with her coat, wresting a thread of decency out of an anti-romantic encounter that proved painful in every sense. The story ends with a metaphor that sums up

The American Short Story Handbook, First Edition. James Nagel.
© 2015 James Nagel. Published 2015 by John Wiley & Sons, Ltd.

the emotional context: "A cold mist was coming up through the woods from the bay."

It is significant that Hemingway's first "mature" story dealt with the point of view of a young woman undergoing a rude awakening to sex and romance. Another early tale, "Indian Camp," is even harsher in the initiation of a very young boy into some of the same issues. It takes place in nearly the same location, in a summer cottage across the lake from an Indian settlement of bark-peelers. It also marks the introduction of Nick Adams, one of Hemingway's continuing characters who in a series of stories grows from his age of seven or eight to his last appearance when he is a father himself taking a car trip in "Fathers and Sons." The situation in "Indian Camp" is that Nick's father is an obstetrician who is on a fishing trip when he is called upon to deliver a baby. Dr. Adams is forced to perform a Caesarian section with only the equipment in his tackle box, a skinning knife and some gut leader to use for stitches. He does not have anesthesia, so the process is horrifyingly painful for the mother. Nick observes the entire process, but he is bothered by her screaming even though his father informs him that it is not important. When the baby is born, Dr. Adams takes pride in a successful delivery under such circumstances, but then he sees that the Indian father has committed suicide by slicing open his throat. Nick sees it as well. On the boat ride back to their own camp, Nick asks his father why the man killed himself. Dr. Adams replies that "he couldn't stand things, I guess," an oft quoted line with biographical as well as literary applications. Nick trails his hand in the water, which feels warm in the chill of the early morning.

This first story about Nick Adams involves a painful initiation to an adult world of pain, death, and psychological wounds that rarely ever heal in Hemingway's fiction. Nick has observed things that are too rough for a boy his age, and he bears the psychic scars of it the rest of his life. In later works he suffers from insomnia, for example, and he needs a light to sleep. When he goes off to World War I, he sees things that are similarly ghastly, and they leave him psychologically damaged, the situation in "A Way You'll Never Be." In the opening Nick, an American recently released from a hospital, is riding his bicycle back to the front lines. He observes that there has been a brutal battle that left many dead behind with their papers spread all about them and their pockets inside out. When he reaches his unit, his friend Captain Paravicini asks him about his new uniform, and Nick explains that the point is to reassure the Italian soldiers that more Americans will be coming. Nick seems to have worked in the canteen service, distributing cigarettes and chocolate, as did Hemingway himself. Paravicini is quick to realize that Nick is not well, has not sufficient emotional stability to resume his previous duties. As the narrative perspective shifts to stream of consciousness, revealing the flow of Nick's thoughts, it is clear that his mind is non-sequential, flitting from scenes in Paris to a yellow house near the river where he was wounded. His mind works abnormally rapidly, running out of control, and Paravicini is sensitive to the situation and orders him back away from the front. At the end, Nick is about to ride his bicycle back the way he had come, having been at the front only a matter of a few hours.

In "Soldier's Home" Krebs, a young man very much like Nick Adams, with much of his family and psychic history, returns home late from the war in Europe. Everything about his homecoming is anti-heroic. He has photographs of him with some German girls, but they are not beautiful and his uniform does not fit properly. Since the American troops did not enter Germany in World War I, the origin of the pictures is somewhat suspect. Worse than that, the other men have been home for months, and they have told the stories of their heroic service in the key battles so many times that Krebs has to lie about his deeds to get anyone to listen to them. His father is in the real estate business (as was Hemingway's paternal grandfather), his mother is a devout protestant, and Krebs has two younger sisters who idolize him, especially Helen, who plays softball. But Krebs has lost interest in middle-class American life and has no sense of purpose or direction. The atrocities he has seen, the trauma of the war, has left him empty, a forerunner of the Lost Generation Hemingway was to write about later in the 1920s.

"A Clean, Well-Lighted Place" is among the best of Hemingway's "mature" stories, works written in the 1930s about adult issues in the modern world. The action of the plot is divided into two settings, with two main characters but a continuing thematic center dealing with the loneliness of age and the existential emptiness two different men face every day. In the first half, an old deaf man stops in a café late at night for a brandy and a moment of quiet dignity in a pleasant atmosphere. Two waiters attend to him: a young married man eager to get home to his wife, who is insulting to the old man, and an older waiter who empathizes with him and shares much of his need for a clean place that is pleasantly lit. The two men discuss how the old man had attempted suicide the week before, and the older waiter confesses that he is like the old man in many ways. When the old man and the younger waiter leave, the older waiter reflects on the need for a clean place and says a mocking prayer to the nothingness in his life: "Our *nada* who art in *nada*." When he leaves to go home he stops in a bar for a drink, but it is not satisfactory because it is not properly clean. He knows he will go to his room and, suffering from chronic insomnia, be unable to sleep. But, he thinks, universalizing his condition, "many must have it."

"The Short Happy Life of Francis Macomber" is an unusual Hemingway story in that the protagonist in the opening scenes is a hapless weakling who has absorbed the humiliation of having run from a charging lion prior to his wife's affair with the professional hunter who serves as their guide. Macomber's wife has dominated him throughout their marriage, as their conversations reveal, and the British guide holds him in contempt. The next day they hunt water buffalo, and in the excitement of chasing a bull Macomber is suddenly reborn, and for the first time he is without fear and performs well on the hunt. Filled with a sense of elation at his new confidence, he makes it clear that he will no longer be subservient to his wife, Margot, and she also is aware of the transformation. In the next buffalo encounter, a bull charges him and as he is about to shoot he is killed by a shot in the head. Margot, the text reports, had "shot at the buffalo" as it seemed ready to gore her husband. Wilson, the guide, interprets the shooting as deliberate on her part, although he is willing to report the death as accidental. Much critical controversy has ensued over whether there was a deliberate killing or an accidental shooting, and the lines of motivation suggest that she meant to murder her husband. However, in literary terms, the omniscient narrator reports that she was aiming at the charging buffalo. If she wanted him dead, she did not need to do anything since the bull was about to gore Macomber. Despite such logic, the controversy rages on, one of several such debatable outcomes in Hemingway's work.

"The Snows of Kilimanjaro" is widely regarded as one of the greatest stories in American literature and, in a sense, a culmination of the thematic and artistic development of Hemingway as a writer in the genre. The situation in the opening is that a writer named Harry is bedridden with a gangrenous wound to his leg and is waiting for a plane to take him to a hospital. He knows the situation is hopeless, that he will die before help arrives, a feeling reinforced by the growing collection of vultures in the trees surrounding the camp. As he waits, he argues with his wife, who has a sharp tongue, and they exchange bitter jibes based on her wealth and his resentment at having been purchased by money. At times he lies, telling her he loves her, sacrificing what little integrity he has left. During the quiet moments he reviews the meaningful highlights of his life that he has always meant to write about, his love of Paris being one of the positive reflections. Many of his other memories feature snow as a destructive force, as in the brutal winter of the Greco-Turkish War, or skiing in Austria above the Madlener haus when Herr Lent lost his entire fortune playing poker.

He resents his wife's enormous wealth and his sense that he does not belong in the circle of her family. Most of all he resents how her money shifted his focus away from his work, from the writing that meant a great deal to him. As his mind rambles on in stream-of-consciousness passages, scenes sometimes have important biographical resonance for Hemingway himself, such as his residual love for the woman he had met during the war. Most of his memories involve money or death, however, progressively more obsessive subjects as he faces the reality of his situation. In the first publication of the story, Harry remembers how F. Scott Fitzgerald had said that the "rich are different from you and me," and someone had answered "yes, they have more money." Subsequently Hemingway revised the passage so that it is now about someone named "Julian," which is less interesting but removed a direct insult to a writer who was in desperate straits at the time of initial publication. Some of his reflections are ghastly, such as a war scene in which an artillery officer has his stomach blown open and begs his comrades to kill him.

The conclusion has occasioned a good deal of critical comment because it seems to contain a post-mortem scene in which Harry's mind continues to work in the morning even though he has died the night before. Most likely Hemingway was influenced by the ending of Ambrose Bierce's "An Occurrence at Owl Creek Bridge," in which the conclusion represents a fantasy that the protagonist has at the moment of death or, perhaps, just after, for he has been hanged for attempting to burn a bridge during the Civil War. Here, in a directly parallel passage, Harry seems to die in the evening when "the weight went from his chest." But the next morning he imagines that the plane has come for him and he says goodbye to his wife and children and flies over Mount Kilimanjaro. Suddenly the time of action has shifted back to the night before, and his wife realizes that Harry has stopped breathing and is dead. There is no final explanation of the conclusion, no clarification of what appears to be post-mortem consciousness, only the human drama of death on an African safari.

In these stories, and in scores of others, Hemingway established himself at the forefront of American writers, although the world he portrayed is rarely pleasant. Romances, for example, never end well, and there are no happy marriages among the major characters in his fiction. The underlying theme of all his stories is that life is an inevitable tragedy and, in the final analysis, there is no way to win. What counts is how his characters conduct themselves in the process of losing. His strongest characters understand a set of codes by which they can live with some semblance of dignity, although they realize that the universe around them is ultimately devoid of larger meaning. Hemingway's fictional world is existential in this sense, and the only enduring values his fictional people can find are the ones they invent themselves. The world about them is violent, deadly, uncaring, and there are few people in it who can be relied upon to act honorably. It is not a pretty portrait of the modern world, but there have been very few attempts to argue that it is not a fairly accurate picture of the first half of the twentieth century.

Suggestions for Further Reading

Benson, Jackson J. ed. *The Short Stories of Ernest Hemingway: Critical Essays.* Durham: Duke University Press, 1975.

DeFalco, Joseph. *The Hero in Hemingway's Short Stories.* Pittsburgh: University of Pittsburgh Press, 1963.

Flora, Joseph M. *Hemingway's Nick Adams.* Baton Rouge: Louisiana State University Press, 1982.

Johnston, Kenneth G. *The Tip of the Iceberg: Hemingway and the Short Story.* Greenville: Penkevill, 1987.

Nagel, James, ed. *Ernest Hemingway: The Oak Park Legacy.* Tuscaloosa: University of Alabama Press, 1996.

Smith, Paul. *A Reader's Guide to the Short Stories of Ernest Hemingway.* Boston: G. K. Hall, 1989.

Smith, Paul, ed. *New Essays on Hemingway's Short Fiction.* New York: Cambridge University Press, 1998.

Waldhorn, Arthur. *A Reader's Guide to Ernest Hemingway.* New York: Farrar, 1972.

John Steinbeck

John Steinbeck is revered as a writer in the Naturalistic tradition who used the techniques of that mode to depict American life during the first half of the twentieth century. His greatest novels, among them *East of Eden, Of Mice and Men,* and *The Grapes of Wrath,* use common characters engaged in a harsh struggle to survive and to preserve some dignity, some self respect in an uncaring world. Since these people little understand the broad picture of civilization and their place in it, their narratives are most often related not by them but from an omniscient point of view. Unlike most Naturalists, however, in the best of his fiction Steinbeck strove to limit expository comment on the causes of human tragedy and to allow the central ideas of his fiction to emerge from the action and dialogue.

Before he had written the best of his novels, however, he produced two volumes of short stories that demonstrate both the aesthetics and the central themes of American Naturalism, *The Pastures of Heaven* and *The Long Valley,* both set in the Salinas Valley of California that the author knew well. *The Pastures of Heaven,* in fact, is a compendium of Naturalistic art and thought in stories told from an omniscient point of view and using patterns of imagery that link characters with the natural world. Unlike his more mature fiction, these tales often develop characters through expository comment rather than through action and dialogue, and their plots are driven by deterministic forces beyond the volition of individuals. It is also a fictional cycle inspired by Sherwood Anderson's *Winesburg, Ohio* with a central family, the Munroes, playing a key role. Steinbeck also followed Anderson in using a common setting for all the stories and in his portrayal of people who are in some sense "grotesque" or limited, including two who suffer from retardation, several who are either neurotic or insane, and one who is

The American Short Story Handbook, First Edition. James Nagel.
© 2015 James Nagel. Published 2015 by John Wiley & Sons, Ltd.

a retarded savant with a gift for artistic representation. Even his "normal" characters are often obsessed with compulsive needs that override their decision making and lead them to either humiliation or disaster.

Although the stories in *Pastures* do not have individual titles, only numbers, they are quite distinct from one another. Each tale deals with a different family, a central conflict, and a resolution, and each was capable of independent publication. The prologue establishes what is unique about the location and some of the continuing themes, religion, for example, and the desire for establishing a dynasty. There is also the suggestion that there is a curse on the valley and that life there will ultimately be tragic, which proves to be true. Even one of the most prominent families, the Munroes, is haunted by disaster, and they appear throughout the volume. The account of Shark Wicks enriches the domestic theme with a basic idea: that his obsession with financial investment obscures from him the real treasure of his life, his wife and daughter. The most entertaining tale is the one about the Lopez sisters, who are devout Roman Catholics who are left to their own devices after the death of their father. They decide their best gifts are for cooking enchiladas, but no one is interested in buying them. That is when they decide to encourage their customers by giving sexual favors to men who buy three or more enchiladas, and their business booms. Throughout they are capable of intense self-deception, seeing in their activities only the most innocent of marketing practices. When the Munroes enter the scene, however, they demand that the sisters admit that they are prostitutes, and the two women are forced to leave the valley. These and other family episodes constitute an intriguing series of tales in the Naturalistic mode, but they never approach the depth and artistic skill of the stories that came next in his career.

Steinbeck's greatest short fiction appeared in *The Long Valley*, a volume not as tightly unified as *The Pastures of Heaven* except for four closely related tales grouped under the title *The Red Pony*. Indeed, these four were later published as an independent volume under that title. Some of the other stories in *The Long Valley*, however, became famous in their own right. "The Chrysanthemums," which introduces the volume, is perhaps his most frequently anthologized work, one read in classrooms throughout the United States and Europe. In accord with Naturalistic themes, it features a protagonist trapped in a stifling situation. Elisa, the wife of Henry Allen, lives on a dreary ranch with a dull husband, and her satisfactions in life derive entirely from her gardening, especially her cultivation of especially fine chrysanthemums. While Henry is engaged in negotiating a business deal, Elisa sees a tinker come into the yard. He is a large man, uncouth in many respects, but he represents escape for her, and she is clearly drawn to him. He repairs damaged pots and pans, and he has learned to manipulate customers, so when she says she has no work for him, he praises her flowers. She responds romantically to his comments, her breasts swelling while she fawns before him, and she realizes she wants to depart with him, share his transient life. When he leaves, she gives him a pot of chrysanthemums, something for him to remember her by, and her lips whisper "goodbye" at his departure. He is gone, but she has been transformed, and she looks younger and stronger to her husband. He suggests that they take the wagon into town for dinner, and as they slowly make their way she spots her flowers thrown down on the road. The tinker has kept the pot for sale. Humiliated, she is once again transformed into a defeated old woman, crying weakly to herself in her resignation to a submerged life on the ranch. The imagery tying her to the animal kingdom, the tone of hopeless resignation, the point of view that reveals her hopes and feelings, all serve to underscore the theme of pessimistic determinism, the idea that she has no chance for a fulfilling life.

"The Harness" is set in the Salinas Valley, an agricultural area Steinbeck knew well, having worked in the fields as a young man. The gritty existence wrested out of the soil seems to have had an effect on the people who work the land, and they tend to be rough and realistic, ready to face the harsh life they can project for themselves, and sensitivity is often a luxury they can ill afford. In this case, the plot deals with a farmer, Peter Randall, who is dominated by his wife to the extent that the imagery describing him suggests an animal that has been "caged" like a "bad dog." He has enormous spirit but it has been submerged by the force of his wife, Emma, a "little skinny bird of a woman." His only revenge is a weekly trip to San Francisco to drink and visit the houses of prostitution. They have no children: dogs do not mate with birds. He works hard on the farm and makes it a success, even earning the respect and envy of the neighbors. When Emma becomes ill, he tends to her needs himself, but she eventually dies, freeing him of her domination. His friend, Ed. Chappell, only then, in watching him undress, discovers that she had forced her husband to wear a harness that pulled his shoulders back to give him better posture, and he wore a girdle to disguise a growing paunch. Now free, Peter feels he can live his own life.

What is intriguing about the situation is that he has internalized his wife as a super-ego, forming her as a conscience that censors all his actions. When he plants his acres in field peas, he has a bumper crop and goes off to San Francisco to celebrate. Ed sees him there, drunk, coming back to the hotel from a night of debauchery, and in his stupor he reveals that his wife "didn't die dead," that she is still active, dictating what he can do. She was worried all growing season about planting peas, he reports, and he is still rebelling against her demand that he wear the harness. Before he drops into a drunken stupor, he tells Ed that he is going to put in electric lights, just as Emma has always wanted. In typical Naturalistic logic, Peter is not a free man who enjoys moral agency, directing the course of his life. He is psychologically trapped in a situation of life he no longer wishes for himself, and he is powerless to break free.

"The Gift," the first of the four linked stories that constitute *The Red Pony*, is set on a ranch in the Salinas Valley, and it deals with Steinbeck's familiar theme of the loss of something valuable but irreplaceable. In this case, what is at issue is a pony, a gift that Carl Tiflin gives his son, Jody, a boy of ten. He loves the young horse and tends it carefully, but one day, on the advice of the ranch hand, Billy Buck, he leaves it outside when he goes off to school. It rains, the pony becomes ill, and despite Billy's best efforts, it dies. Jody is distraught at the enormity of the loss. If this plot is simple, the character development, themes, and artistry of the story make it much more complex. For one thing, Steinbeck's fiction is patently Naturalistic, albeit with a greater sophistication of methodology than is common in this ideological mode. The idea that life is a constant struggle against the forces of Nature is a common one, reaching back to Jack London and Frank Norris, and before that to Hamlin Garland and Stephen Crane, but the deep love that Jody develops for the pony is not characteristic of the tradition. Gabilan is not simply an "animal" for the boy; he is special, representing a gift from his father, a bond between them. Carl Tiflin finds it difficult to express affection in any other way. Beyond that the pony is a nearly sacred "life" placed in his care and guided by the experience and wisdom of Jody's surrogate patriarch, Billy Buck, who is a code hero among the men. Billy is wise in nearly all things related to horses, but he was wrong about the weather. It was he who advised Jody that it would be all right to leave Gabilan out for the day while the boy was in school, but it rained and the pony never recovered from the pneumonia it contracted. The death of the pony signals the end of the admiration Jody has had for Billy, and his bad judgment is a violation of a sacrosanct position, the collapse of an icon. From his point of view, Billy knows that he has failed the boy, who trusted him with his most precious possession, and he loses not only the pony but his stature. The story is thus about loss on multiple layers: the loss of a father's gift, the loved pony; the respect Jody had for Billy; and Billy's pride in being able to mentor the young boy in the proper care of a horse. Jody has also learned a lesson about the enormity of pain that death can bring, a difficult realization for a child but one that will help prepare him for what is to come.

In accord with the conventions of the story cycle, "The Great Mountains" features many of the same characters on the Tiflin ranch and develops related themes, particularly concerning death. It opens with Jody, still a boy, displaying an inherent and gratuitous cruelty toward the other living creatures around him. He torments his dog and kills a bird with his slingshot, cutting off its head with a knife, disemboweling it, and pulling off its wings. His lack of sensitivity is shocking. He is curious, however, about life in the mountains on either side of the valley, the Gabilans to the east and the Great Mountains to the west, the location of one of the former battles with the Mexicans for possession of California. One day an elderly peasant, Gitano, arrives at the ranch saying that he has come home, come back to die where he and his father were born. Jody's father, Carl, does not want him on the property and orders him to leave on the morrow. Billy Buck, the ranch hand not remarkably better off than Gitano, is sympathetic to the old man and to an old horse of thirty, barely able to walk, believing that they have a right to a peaceful old age after a lifetime of work. Carl clearly thinks both the man and the horse should be put out of their misery, and he has no feelings for either. Gitano demonstrates that, like Billy, he has a way with horses, and he comforts old Easter. Later he shows Jody a prize rapier he was given by his father, something he has had all his life. In the morning, Gitano is gone, having taken the old horse and ridden off into the mountains to die, taking his rapier with him, presumably to ensure death comes swiftly for both himself and Easter. Jody now has confronted death emotionally, as he did with the Red Pony, and the story ends with him sprawled out on the grass, looking off into the mountains, filled with a "nameless sorrow" he has never known before.

"The Promise" is more directly related to the opening story in *The Red Pony* cycle in that the death of Gabilan is an important element in Carl Tiflin's decision to allow his mare, Nellie, to be bred so that Jody can raise the colt. Billy Buck will supervise the process, teaching the boy about horses. In return, the boy agrees to work on the ranch all summer and to be dutiful in seeing to his chores. In a series of stories about death, this episode seems a counterpoint to the dominant Naturalistic themes, the birth of the colt restoring life to a locus of pain and death. The titular promise is not simply the breeding, however, but Billy's reassurance that nothing will happen to the colt, and for nearly a year of gestation there are no major problems with that pledge. However, when the time comes for the delivery, the colt is turned the wrong way. Normally, as Billy had earlier explained, he would have to tear the fetus apart to save the mare, but since he recently proved a failure in his attempt to save Gabilan, in this case he kills Nellie with a hammer and extracts the colt in a bloody Caesarean that Jody observes. Billy rips the placenta covering the foal with his teeth and, covered with blood, presents it to Jody. At the moment when he should be filled with joy, he is shaken by the barbarity of it all and by the haunted eyes of Billy, who seems destroyed by the violent emotion inherent in what he has just done. Even the moment of birth is invested with death, and once again a boy is confronted with the harshest of realities.

"The Leader of the People," a domestic drama in the Tiflin family, is the last story in *The Red Pony* sequence. In it Jody's maternal grandfather comes to visit, a garrulous old man obsessed with the time, long ago, when he led a wagon train of settlers into California despite Indian raids and limited supplies. He was a leader of men in his younger days, and the memories are alive in him, still vibrant after decades have past. But the other family members have heard all the stories repeatedly, and one morning, in a thoughtless moment, Carl openly expresses to his wife his feeling of annoyance at sitting through the same monologue scores of times, and her father overhears the remark. It is a deflating experience for him. He had been a man of stature, a mythic leader, and now he is a mere irritant, diminished in his role in the family, looking "small and thin and black." He was once part of something grand, a vital community of people "westering" through danger for the promise of a new life, and now he is an old man nobody cares about. Jody senses his grandfather's despair, his feeling of being worthless and unwanted, and he offers to make him some lemonade. The story closes with this simple act, an expression of sympathy by a boy for a man who has lived past his time and must confront the emptiness of that realization.

As was *The Pastures of Heaven*, *The Red Pony* is nearly perfect as a story cycle, with a continuing setting on a ranch in a fertile but demanding valley the family has lived in for two generations. The core of the characters is the same in all four of the tales, normally with something or someone that arrives to present drama, young horses in two of the stories, an old *paisano* in one, Jody's grandfather in another. Another key element of unity is the emphasis on the emotional impact of the action on Jody's psychological growth, on his development from childish carelessness to the capacity for compassion. In the environment of the ranch, a locus of life drawn from nature at the expense of death, Jody has experienced a great deal of pain, and he has learned some harsh lessons. The methodology throughout is patently Naturalistic, with an omniscient narrator, patterns of imagery drawn from the animal kingdom, and the portrait of human life engaged in a fight for survival against hostile natural forces. In other words, Steinbeck's stories served as precursors to his most important novels in both aesthetic strategies and thematic constructs, and *The Red Pony* must be regarded as among the greatest of his works of fiction.

Suggestions for Further Reading

Fontenrose, Joseph. *Steinbeck's Unhappy Valley: A Study of* The Pastures of Heaven. Berkeley: Joseph Fontenrose, 1981.

Hayashi, Tetsumaro, ed. *A Study Guide to Steinbeck's* The Long Valley. Ann Arbor: Pierian Press, 1976.

Hughes, R. S. *Beyond the Red Pony: A Reader's Companion to Steinbeck's Complete Short Stories*. Metuchen: Scarecrow Press, 1987.

Hughes, R. S. *John Steinbeck: A Study of the Short Fiction*. Boston: Twayne, 1989.

Lisca, Peter. *The Wide World of John Steinbeck*. New Brunswick: Rutgers University Press, 1958.

Hayashi, Tetsumaro, and Thomas J Moore, eds. *Steinbeck's The Red Pony: Essays in Criticism*. Muncie: Ball State University Press, 1988.

Timmerman, John H. *John Steinbeck's Fiction: The Aesthetics of the Road Taken*. Norman: University of Oklahoma Press, 1986.

Timmerman, John H. *The Dramatic Landscape of Steinbeck's Short Stories*. Norman: University of Oklahoma Press, 1990.

William Faulkner

William Faulkner is widely regarded as the most important single author in American literary history, a remarkable stature for a writer who rarely left his home town and whose range of settings for his fiction was limited to one fictional county closely resembling his own in Mississippi. The cast of characters in his Yoknapatawpha County, the social and psychological issues at the center of life in the region, and above all the historical circumstances emanating from the Civil War and the ensuing racial tensions that pervaded the South during Reconstruction and the decades that followed, gave his work an unmatched depth of focus. In this sense, Faulkner's work is the culmination of the objectives of the Local Color movement, to capture in fiction the settings, language, people, and issues of a specific location. If this aspect is sometimes provincial in its limitations, the inventiveness and artistic experimentation of his work set the ideas free from the parameters previously associated with this mode of literature, and the result was a fictional legacy that transformed the twentieth century.

Since virtually everything he wrote contributes to his pervasive Yoknapatawpha saga, his novels and stories coordinate in using not only the same settings but often the same characters and themes. As a total body of work, Faulkner's fiction presents a coherent myth of the South that explains the cultural dynamic that motivates the fallen aristocracy of plantation owners whose wealth was built on slavery and whose pride and courtly manners emulated those of the European gentry. Their legacy is one of building a Southern civilization quite unlike that of any other area in the United States. In financial terms, they constructed their plantations wisely, made enormous sums of money, and created family dynasties that carried on traditions that ran through several generations. They believed in honor and gentlemanly

The American Short Story Handbook, First Edition. James Nagel.
© 2015 James Nagel. Published 2015 by John Wiley & Sons, Ltd.

codes of conduct. The women of this world were virgins until marriage and devoted themselves to their families and their social class. When the Civil War destroyed their economic base, these families went into a prolonged social and psychological degeneration, the manifestations of which are central. The ultimate trajectory of all of their narratives is toward tragedy.

"A Rose for Emily," one of Faulkner's most frequently anthologized works, presents a ghastly manifestation of this concept. Told from the collective perspective of the community of Jefferson, a gossipy social construct given to reviewing the peculiarities of the collapsing upper classes, it covers activities upon the death of Emily Grierson, the last remaining member of her once distinguished family. She had lived alone after the death of her father, and she rarely went out after the disappearance of her lover, Homer Baron, who was presumed to have returned north to his homeland. But upon inspection, his corpse, long decayed, is found in her bridal chamber, where she had apparently slept with his body for some time. The Gothic horror of this realization by the neighbors suggests the psychic pathology attendant to a dramatic social collapse, that there are elements of insanity in the attempts of the aristocracy to somehow preserve the social prerogatives they once enjoyed. Necrophilia, in this sense, is the perfect expression of corruption of the human mind, a deterioration in this case wrought not only by romantic rejection but by economic decline.

Many of Faulkner's stories about the aristocracy show them in a more favorable light, as does "Skirmish at Sartoris," in which Colonel Sartoris ran the carpetbaggers off the property at the end of the Civil War and saved the dignity of the family. "An Odor of Verbena" takes place about a decade later and covers the death of the colonel and the escape of his killer. "That Evening Sun" deals with the Compson family and with Nancy, a black woman who washes clothes for them. Taking place in 1898, the action is important because the Compson children are all young and yet they reveal the internal values that drive each of them: Quentin's need to preserve the propriety of his sister, Caddy; her more libertine attitudes about decorum; and Jason's selfishness and emotional distance from the rest of the family. Although Faulkner's most important fiction about this social group is in the form of the novel, particularly in *Sartoris, The Sound and the Fury*, and *Absalom, Absalom!*, his short fiction fills in chronological gaps and helps explain the motivation of many of the continuing characters.

A second part of the Faulkner myth is the rise of the poor white social class that has come down from the rocky hillsides to do the labor that was previously done by slaves. They are the sharecroppers who work the land, mind the stores, and do the jobs at the bottom of the economic spectrum. They have little knowledge, few skills, and almost nothing to offer the economic structure they are entering, but their most powerful weapon is an almost complete lack of social decorum and moral scruples. They will do anything for money: cheat in a horse trade; sell tickets to people who wish to watch a demented relative make love to a cow; trade sexual privileges with one's wife in exchange for a position at a bank. They steal, murder, betray, conceal, and misrepresent without hesitation. Many of these accounts involve the Snopes family, a ubiquitous family in the area. Part of the brilliance of "Barn Burning," however, derives from these kinds of family values coming in conflict with those of the faded aristocracy. Sarty Snopes has watched his father, Abner, a sharecropper perpetually in conflict with the landowners he serves. His pigs get in the garden of a landowner, but Abner's fierce pride will not allow him to put up a fence, even when the wire is supplied by someone else. Later, when he deliberately ruins the expensive rug of Major de Spain and is expected to pay for it, he decides to burn down the man's barn, something he has done before in other conflicts. But his son, Sarty, has absorbed some of the decency and regard for other people that his father lacks, and he warns de Spain of Abner's intentions, and then he runs off never to be seen again. It is a powerful story of conflicting values that bring about a break between father and son that mirrors the broader contrasting ethics of the old families and the new people who have come down out of the hills. These kinds of conflicts are played out most powerfully in the Snopes trilogy of novels, *The Hamlet, The Town,* and *The Mansion,* with other families involved in *Intruder in the Dust* and *The Reivers,* as well as in a series of stories.

The third part of the mythological structure is the fate of the African Americans whose families lived and worked on the plantations that surround the county seat of Jefferson. Many of them are genetically related to the aristocratic old families, and they take pride in the connections of blood. Some of them have themselves become land owners through inheritance, and they have emulated aspects of the sense of pride and decorum they observed in their former masters. These characters tend to stay on the land they have farmed for generations, some of them becoming servants in a white household. Other black characters depart for the opportunities of the North and never appear in Faulkner's work again. The best of these stories constitute *Go Down, Moses,* a short-story cycle with a central focus on the black families of Yoknapatawpha. These tales are complex because they are often based on the interactions between the races with conflicts that have moral and psychological consequences for all involved.

The volume begins with "Was," with a time-shift to action in 1859 dealing with a runaway slave. In the present there are references to Ike McCaslin and the discovery of a financial ledger of payments made to the slaves who worked the family plantation. These issues remain important throughout the entire collection of stories. Also important is "The Old People," in which Ike is initiated into the sacred rite of hunting by a man of mixed race, Sam Fathers, a ritual of moral maturation with profound implications for the South. "Delta Autumn" also covers Ike on a hunting trip, but this one takes place when he is an old man. The key element in the book is the concluding "The Bear," perhaps the most important work of short fiction in American literature.

"The Bear" is a long story in five parts, all of which deal with Ike McCaslin, his moral and social initiation into manhood, and the consequences of his realization that the family wealth derived from a long tradition of slavery. The first three parts deal directly with the significance of hunting, an activity that, in the primitive forests of the delta, require a reversion to a primitive state in Nature that strips away the social and racial structures that subsequent generations imposed on the South. For this reason, true hunting in its most meaningful sense involves a rejection of the modern world and its implements, codes, and social stratification. In the wilderness, there is a new ranking based not on wealth or race but on knowledge of the woods, on courage, on an understanding of what is sacred in this environment. In this world, a man of color, Sam Fathers, rises to the top of the group as the clear leader even though in civilization he lives, impoverished, in a simple cabin with no stature whatever. In the wilderness, his virtue is recognized as supreme among the men.

With Sam's guidance throughout his initiation, young Ike comes to realize that he must leave behind the artifacts of modern civilization if he is to become worthy of seeing a great bear who roams the woods, and when he discards his compass and watch the bear immediately appears. This event occasions in Ike a profound spiritual rebirth that changes the course of his life. Such a dramatic moment is of mythic significance for the boy, and it involves not only the ultimate death of the bear but of Sam Fathers himself, an expiration inevitable with civilization encroaching into the wilderness, a threat that culminates when the old hunting camp is sold to a logging company. In a sense, Ike is the last young man who will experience the religious significance of hunting in the wild, and its internal effect on him requires that he relinquish his family inheritance and the whole idea that human beings can "own" the land and profit from slavery. Of all of Faulkner's characters, Ike realizes that race and social position do not finally matter and that Sam was the greatest person he will ever know. He was close to the earth, free of the guilt of slavery, apart from the artificial social structure modern life has imposed on the South. That a white boy, born to one of the "old" families, can admire and learn the most important lessons of his life from a poor man of mixed race calls into question the entire social and moral structure of Southern society, one of the central themes of Faulkner's fiction.

Faulkner's stories are important for more reasons than the exploration of these three social components, of course, but his depth of understanding of human psychology is astonishing in a man of such limited education and experience. It is in literary experimentation, however, that his tales make their greatest contribution to literary history, for he changed nearly every dimension of the standard fictional aesthetic. His narrative methods were inventive and nearly always productive in expanding the themes of the narratives related. He employed not only the omniscient narrators common among the Naturalistic writers of the two decades before his career began but the limited first-person tales favored by the Realists. In many of his works, the narrator is a local character whose mind, and lexicon, provide the source of information from which a coherent narrative can be constructed, a method closely related to the tradition of Local Color. Beyond these standard methodologies, Faulkner also used stream-of-consciousness and shifting narrators in parallax whose contrasting frames of vision complement and enrich the unfolding plot. Most of all, his use of multiple narrative techniques in a single story brought a depth of artistry previously unknown in American fiction, and for this, and for his profoundly meaningful insight into the history of his region, Faulkner's stories stand at the forefront of a rich tradition of fiction in the American South.

Suggestions for Further Reading

Carothers, James B. *William Faulkner's Short Stories*. Ann Arbor: UMI Research Press, 1985.

Harrington, Evans, and Ann J Abadie, eds. *Faulkner and the Short Story: Faulkner and Yoknapatawpha*. Jackson: University of Mississippi Press, 1992.

Ferguson, James. *Faulkner's Short Fiction*. Knoxville: University of Tennessee Press, 1991.

Jones, Diane Brown. *A Reader's Guide to the Short Stories of William Faulkner*. New York: G. K. Hall, 1994.

Kinney, Arthur F. *Go Down Moses: The Miscegenation of Time*. New York: Twayne, 1996.

Labatt, Blair. *Faulkner the Storyteller*. Tuscaloosa: University of Alabama Press, 2005.

Skei, Hans H, ed. *William Faulkner's Short Fiction: An International Symposium*. Oslo: Solum Fortag, 1997.

Towner, Theresa M., and James B. Carothers. *Reading Faulkner, Collected Stories: Glossary and Commentary*. Jackson: University of Mississippi Press, 2006.

Volpe, Edmond L. *A Reader's Guide to William Faulkner*. New York: Noonday Press, 1964.

Jamaica Kincaid

Fundamental to understanding of the early life of Elaine Potter Richardson, who later took the name "Jamaica Kincaid" when she began publishing, is the fact that she was born in Antigua, educated in the British tradition, and broke from her mother when she left the island for the United States. Although many writers use their own lives as a point of departure for their early fiction, Kincaid's early work displays what is essentially an obsession with coming to terms with her relationship to her mother, with her awareness of her colonial legacy, and with her sense of cultural duality in America. Out of her personal experience, she has drawn the material for her best short stories, especially those dealing with Annie Victoria John, who closely resembles the author.

The eight separate stories about this young woman constitute a feminine *Bildungsroman* tracing the conflicts inherent in her developmental stages. The stories, however, are told in retrospect so that an older narrator is relating earlier events, presumably those moments salient in the transformative process toward maturity. The earliest story about Annie is "Figures in the Distance," which features her at age ten. It is an "establishing" narrative recording the central facts of Annie's home and family, her friends, and the people in her neighborhood. Basically, it shows that she lives in a childhood world of adoring parents and carefree friends, with nothing to do but to enjoy the sun and the beach of her island. All of the objects in her home speak of the love of her parents, and many of them were made by hand. Her mother would seem to celebrate even the smallest details of her daughter's life, down to the aromatic bark she floats in her child's bathwater. Her father built the furniture within the house and handcrafted even the spoon she uses at breakfast. Beyond the attentions of her overly attentive parents, the most

The American Short Story Handbook, First Edition. James Nagel.
© 2015 James Nagel. Published 2015 by John Wiley & Sons, Ltd.

important fact about her is her lively imagination, for she is bright, playful, and sensitive. In the perverse logic of childhood, all of this leads her to an obsession with death.

Annie is fascinated by the death of Nalda, Sonia's mother, Miss Charlotte, and a young girl with a humpback, whose passing reveals that Annie feels not grief or compassion but interest in discovering whether the hump is hollow. This obsession is especially curious at the time of the telling because by then Annie has left the island and become a nurse who must see death on a regular basis. At the time of the action, however, she visits funeral parlors, and on one occasion lingers so long that she forgets to bring home the fish for dinner. Her mother forgives her, even for lying about it, and it is clear that as a child Annie lived in a warm and caring home with loving parents and an almost total absence of responsibility.

The next story that traces Annie's gradual maturation is "The Circling Hand," which takes place two years after the opening "Figures in the Distance." She is now twelve, a key year that Kincaid covered with four closely related tales focused on the love-hate relationship she has with her mother. In this case, instead of an obsession with death, Annie is now repulsed by sex beginning when she sees her parents making love. It is a new experience for her, and she seems to resent the expression of affection by her mother for anyone but herself. This scene also introduces the familial trunk that the mother took with her when she ran away from home in Dominica. Now, it contains not her mother's possessions but artifacts from every stage of Annie's life, further testimony of her mother's affection for her. Annie is shocked, however, when her mother suggests that she should now begin wearing clothes designed for her and not small imitations of her mother's dresses. It would seem to be a classic confusion in the life of a child: a desire for independence coupled with fear and resentment of anything that suggests separation from her mother.

The paradox of love-hate is given further development in "Gwen," as Annie moves to a new school. The pervading theme is that of the unconditional love she receives from her parents and her dependence upon them, a fact emphasized in a class assignment when she writes a theme about her horror when her mother momentarily slipped from view while swimming one day. But Annie also has a simultaneous desire to reach out to a more expansive world beyond the family, a feeling intensified by the new affection she feels for a classmate, Gwen, who comes to replace her mother as the object of her love. Her initial attempts at an emotional separation from her mother is further intensified in "The Red Girl," yet another story when Annie was twelve. The opening event is her first menstruation, which her mother says makes her just like her, but almost every other activity increases the divide between mother and daughter. When she becomes infatuated with the Red Girl, she rebels against her mother's rules by stealing and lying and, worst of all, playing marbles. The Red Girl is free from discipline and concern for convention, and this autonomy makes her fascinating for Annie, who now desires to form her own sense of identity.

That powerful quest manifests in the most important of the stories in the series, "Columbus in Chains," in which Annie's rebellion is not simply against her mother but also the legacy of English domination of the African peoples who live in Antigua. It is in a lesson on Columbus that she first realizes that it was his voyages to the New World that expanded the colonial reach of the European nations and resulted in the importation of slaves from Africa, so she takes special pleasure in the picture of Columbus returning to Spain in chains, accused of the mistreatment of people of color in the Caribbean. Now she is forced to think about the social history of her part of the world, the legacy of bondage under British colonialism, the implications for her ancestors who were enslaved. She has never thought much about race until this point, although most of the figures of authority in her life are white, but now, in the last story about her at age twelve, she comes to an awareness that will give direction to the rest of her life.

One indication of how she is changing comes in "Somewhere, Belgium," in which Annie is fifteen and has her first fantasy about escape from Antigua. The emotional struggle with her mother, and her bitterness about the history of slavery, have developed into a deep emotional schism that results in depression. Her family life is still warm and protective, but outside of her home the situation is somewhat tenuous. She has been promoted two grades and no longer sees Gwen or her other friends. Her mother finds it difficult to accept her daughter's burgeoning maturation, and she calls Annie a "slut" for flirting with boys. She needs her mother but wishes she were dead, and this duplicitous emotional construct makes it difficult for Annie to establish any integration of self. Her only solace is a daydream of escape from Antigua and a new life in Belgium where she would be free of constraints, a desire encapsulated in the image of the trunk, which signifies her need to break out of the shadow of her mother.

That is the subject of Kincaid's final two stories about Annie, beginning with "The Long Rain," in which Annie sleeps for three months, apparently as a mechanism to escape dealing with her ambivalence about her mother, with her emotional irresolution. What becomes progressively more clear is that as long as she remains in Antigua her sense of herself will be circumscribed by her mother's expectations for her. But it is only by being free that her formation of a new identity can allow her to integrate the cultural, sexual, and psychological conflicts she is experiencing into a coherent new emotional construct.

The final resolution of these themes comes in the final Annie story, "A Walk to the Jetty," in which the two major issues of her life come together: her need for individuation, to break from the domination of her mother; and her conception of herself as part of a society formed by British colonialism and slavery. Her escape from both of these struggles comes in her departure from Antigua. The plot covers a single day, hour by hour, when at seventeen she prepares to leave her island forever. As she walks to the jetty she confronts the central artifacts and places of her life, the Anglican church, the library and schools and stores that have been so important to her. As a character of seventeen, the young woman is attempting to do what the narrator, a much older Annie, has apparently achieved, an integration of all of these experiences into a single conception of self, a synthesis of disparate aspects of her childhood into one mature woman. The implication is that she has done this through her narration, through her detailed memory of the progression of her early years, and the structuring, forming, and recitation of these reflections constitute an act of reconciliation.

What is clear when the eight Annie stories are arranged in chronological order based on her progressive age is that they constitute a classic cycle, a group of interrelated works of short fiction. Each tale is complete in itself; indeed, they were all published independently in *The New Yorker*. On the other hand, they gain in significance, and intelligibility, when brought together. In temporal progression, lines of motivation become clear, including why Annie would want to leave her island. The meaning of the trunk, for example, is not particularly important when it first appears, but with each successive story it takes on greater significance focused on escape from a confining life, of liberation first for Annie's mother and then for the young woman herself. Young Annie's burgeoning sexuality is another linked marker, moving from menstruation to flirtation to a more serious interaction with boys at seventeen.

The stories are unified in other ways as well. All of them have the same setting, the island of Antigua. A small cast of characters interact with Annie and help define her character and development, and her mother plays a central role throughout. Annie's incremental growth of insight into the history of the Caribbean also links key scenes beginning with her realizations in "Columbus in Chains." The narrative perspective is consistent throughout the group: all are told by an older Annie, reflecting on the salient events of her life from England, where she has gone to become a nurse. The motivation for the telling is never stated directly, but it would seem to involve her attempt to understand the meaning of her life through this insightful review of important events, and those reflections provide thematic unity and aesthetic congruence to all eight of the Annie stories.

Nearly all of Kincaid's other stories are drawn from the same basic character types and develop related themes. One of her earliest, "Girl," also concerns a mother–daughter relationship, in this case one in which a mother attempts to instruct her daughter in how to be a proper young lady. Her instructions are formulated to imply criticism, as when she says "try to walk like a lady and not like the slut you are so bent on becoming" or suggests that the girl sings calypso songs in Sunday school. All of these regulations seem drawn from a rigid conception of behavior, perhaps one influenced by the British customs at the center of social life in Antigua. The girl, by implication, wants to be free to establish her own codes of deportment; she resents being told to squeeze the bread to make sure it is fresh or to refrain from throwing stones at blackbirds. This story introduces the foundation of the struggle between mother and daughter, a conflict not resolved in "Girl" but concluded thematically in "A Walk to the Jetty" when Annie strikes out to find a life of her own.

Kincaid's stories about Lucy Josephine Potter parallel those about Annie John in narrative method, characterization, and theme, although Annie left home to go to England and Lucy for New York. There are solicitous mothers in both cases, although the families differ in some respects: Lucy has three younger brothers, for example. But both collections of stories feature a young girl from Antigua who resents the background of slavery and British colonization, and they both chafe against their British educations and the dominance of the Anglican church. Annie's chronicle concludes with her departure from the island at seventeen, whereas Lucy is a bit older, nineteen when she arrives in New York and twenty as the stories progress. The final one, "Lucy," similarly concludes with her process of forming a new self. She has rejected the person she was growing up in Antigua, resents her role as an *au pair* for a woman named Mariah, and she has enrolled in a photography course, a direction of her own choosing. Indeed, as a body of work, Kincaid's short fiction deals with the existential process of self-definition, a journey fraught with a sense of separation, loneliness, and travail, but its final rewards involve the joy of self-discovery and independence. The solemnity of this crucial theme of individuality, and the unique integrity of craft that Kincaid brings to her writing, have established her among the preeminent writers of short fiction in America.

Suggestions for Further Reading

Alexander, Simone A. James. *Mother Imagery in the Novels of Afro-Caribbean Women*. Columbia: University of Missouri Press, 2001.

Bouson, J. Brooks. *Jamaica Kincaid: Writing Memory, Writing Back to the Mother*. Albany: State University of New York Press, 2005.

Burrows, Victoria. *Whiteness and Trauma: The Mother-Daughter Knot in the Fiction of Jean Rhys, Jamaica Kincaid, and Toni Morrison*. New York: Palgrave Macmillan, 2004.

Covi, Giovanna. *Jamaica Kincaid's Prismatic Subjects: Making Sense of Being in the World*. London: Mango, 2003.

Edwards, Justin D. *Understanding Jamaica Kincaid*. Columbia: University of South Carolina Press, 2007.

Ferguson, Moira. *Colonialism and Gender Relations from Mary Wollstonecraft to Jamaica Kincaid: East Caribbean Connections*. New York: Columbia University Press, 1993.

Ferguson, Moira. *Jamaica Kincaid: Where the Land Meets the Body*. Charlottesville: University Press of Virginia, 1994.

Nagel, James. "Jamaica Kincaid's *Annie John*: Genre and Cultural Duality." *The Contemporary American Short-Story Cycle: The Ethnic Resonance of Genre*. Baton Rouge: Louisiana State University Press, 2001, pp. 56–79.

Paravisini-Gebert, Lizabeth. *Jamaica Kincaid: A Critical Companion*. Westport: Greenwood Press, 1999.

Snodgrass, Mary Ellen. *Jamaica Kincaid: A Literary Companion*. Jefferson: McFarland, 2008.

Tim O'Brien

Tim O'Brien's well-deserved reputation as the foremost writer of short fiction about the Vietnam War rests almost entirely on the twenty-two stories brought together in *The Things They Carried* in 1990. Five of these had appeared independently in *Esquire*, three in *Quarterly*, and the rest in a variety of magazines, most notably "On the Rainy River," which came out in *Playboy*.

As a body of work, these tales are connected by setting and situation and the war in Southeast Asia, although there is no single protagonist who ties them all together. However, all of them deal with members of Alpha Company, sometimes as a group, and scenes take place before, during, and after the war. There are a variety of narrative strategies ranging from the omniscient perspective of the opening story, to many told by a fictional character named Tim O'Brien, to some related, unreliably, by Rat Kiley, and two third-person stories derived from an unknown vantage point. Save for "The Things They Carried," the narrative perspective of all the rest is unreliable, suggesting that in the horror and chaos of war it is difficult to distinguish what is real from what is imagined. Although the brutal scenes of battle depicted certainly give the book an anti-war tone, there is no dominating single theme but rather a coalescence of related ideas: the moral horror of war, the terrible responsibility placed on young men, the ethical burden they all must carry. These basic ideas, along with the continual uncertainty about how to tell a "true" war story, constitute the elements that give the volume coherence.

Even in isolation, however, the best of these stories have power and thematic brilliance, presenting concepts rarely included in previous war fiction.

The American Short Story Handbook, First Edition. James Nagel.
© 2015 James Nagel. Published 2015 by John Wiley & Sons, Ltd.

One of those motifs derives from the fact that never before in American history have young men been so reluctant to serve in the armed services of the United States as during the Vietnam War. The country was swept with widespread skepticism about the wisdom of becoming involved in ground combat in Asia, about the justification for American participation, about the fundamental issues at dispute. One side saw the conflict as an attempt to stem the spread of communism throughout Southeast Asia, the other as an effort to expel foreign influence from Vietnam. Whatever the causes or justifications, for the men involved in the fighting it seemed to be horribly destructive physically and psychologically, and the damage could not be measured by a simple body count.

The opening story "The Things They Carried" has multiple functions since it presents its own narrative but also establishes the situation for all the tales that follow. The location is crucial throughout the book, but in this opening the emphasis is on the psychological and emotional weight the men must carry in a context of violence and death. The specific issues focus on the death of Ted Lavender and the responsibility born by Lt. Jimmy Cross, both matters that play a role in many of the stories that follow. The central metaphor deals with what the men must "carry," the literal application of what they must hump through the jungle and the mountains, the physical artifacts of war from rifles to chewing gum.

The subjective weight of what they carry is much more important, however, for they take with them their memories of home, their fear and love and hope, their terror and grief from what they have witnessed in country. The metaphor is individualized by the omniscient narrator who has access to the minds of all the characters. Jimmy Cross carries love letters from his girlfriend, and because he was thinking about them and not about the strategies of battle, Lavender was killed. Subsequently, Cross also carries self-recrimination and determination to expiate his guilt through strict discipline. The death of Lavender on patrol recurs throughout the book, a common horror shared by all the men, but only Cross lives with the responsibility. He is thus the protagonist of the opening story, the person with the internal conflict, the one who is psychologically transformed, the one for whom the central event has the greatest significance.

It thus makes sense that he should also be the focus of "Love," the second story in the volume and one written specifically for the book. It shifts the setting to the United States, the time of the action to some point after 1979, and the narrative point of view to an unnamed writer who would seem to be the fictional O'Brien. Cross has continued to love Martha despite the fact that his affection is unrequited, and he still feels guilt for the death of Lavender, something he says will always be with him. The events of the war years are thus shown to be of deep emotional importance, transformative in their power to resonate years after they have taken place.

Also set on American soil is "On the Rainy River," which again shifts the time scheme to a period just before O'Brien goes off to war. When this story first appeared in *Playboy* in 1990, the readers had no way of understanding that it was not direct autobiography, but as more of the author's short fiction about the Vietnam War appeared, it became clear that the O'Brien character differed from the author in several important respects: the actual O'Brien, for example, has no daughter, but the fictional one does, and he argues with her about writing about the war. The key psychological drama would seem to be parallel with what the author went through in 1968 when he received his draft notice and contemplated going to Canada to escape service, something relatively easy to do in Minnesota where rivers and lakes separate the two countries and a fishing boat is all that is required to cross the border. The narration takes place twenty years after the action, in 1988, when the narrator is still weighing the morality of the central ethical conflict of that period of his life, his decision not to run away but to enter the military. It would have taken courage to go to Canada, he maintains, because it would have meant risking the judgment of his home town and, especially, his father, who served in World War II. Knowing that at some point he would have to face his father, he could not run away: the weight of it would have been too heavy to carry.

If "Rainy River" has persistent ethical consequences, so does service in Vietnam, as is clear in "Sweetheart of the Song Tra Bong," which moves backward in time to a period when Curt Lemon was still alive and went trick or treating in the nude in the local village. Equally as important as the events, however, is the manner of the telling of them, for the story is a study in narrational unreliability. It is told by the fictional O'Brien who heard about it from Rat Kiley, who lived through parts of it and learned of the other parts from guys in the company. Rat learned from Eddie Diamond that Mary Anne, a young American woman who came to Vietnam to be with her boyfriend, had gone out on patrol with the Green Berets. Diamond did not actually witness the events but heard about them from one of the men involved. There is thus no single telling of the tale. The multiplicity of narration introduces a great deal of uncertainty, and most of the guys in Alpha Company are skeptical about the truth of it.

The heart of the story is that Mary Anne Bell was flown over to Vietnam by her boyfriend, Mark Fossie. She arrives innocent and unafraid, walking alone through a Viet Cong village and swimming in the Song Tra Bong river while it was under fire, which inspires one of the men to comment that she has "D-cup guts, training bra brains." She is fascinated by the Green Berets, and one night she goes out on patrol with them and begins to change. Not long later, she moves into their tent, where there is a stack of bones with a sign that reads "assemble your own gook!" Horrified, Mark Fossie then discovers that she has a necklace of human tongues, and soon she has disappeared into the jungle for good. The transformation of Mary Anne is a dramatic metaphor for the corruption of innocence wrought by the violence of war and its moral and psychological degradations. An obvious point is that her gender does not prevent psychic alteration, and the consequences are permanent.

Many of the other stories deepen these basic themes offering variations on the concepts of fear, guilt, morality, and internal corruption. One critical episode occurs in "The Man I Killed," a first-person narrative in which the fictional O'Brien kills an enemy soldier on a jungle trail. It would seem to be a routine event in war, but O'Brien is obsessed with the sight of the dead body and finds it difficult to deal with the moral consequences of an unnecessary shooting. He was hidden when the young Vietnamese soldier came down the trail, and he most likely would have simply passed by, but O'Brien killed him anyway. As he reflects on it, he realizes that the dead man had been a person very much like himself, someone with a girl friend, a family that cared about him, and a future. The emphasis, however, is on O'Brien, his moral awareness, the personalized recognition of the enemy soldier's humanity.

If "Sweetheart of the Song Tra Bong" presented the metaphoric substance of the corrupting power of modern war, "In the Field" is one of the stories that uses setting to describe the degrading environment itself. Three of the tales in *The Things They Carried* involve the company being pinned down by mortar fire while attempting to cross a field the local village uses as a refuse lagoon for its latrines. One of the men in the outfit, Kiowa, was killed there the night before, and now the men are searching for his body in the shit field. There could be no more humiliating context for a story about combat, and the men have no option but to submerge themselves in it. When they find the corpse, Jimmy Cross lays back in the muck, floating. He has been composing in his mind the letter he will write home to Kiowa's parents, a difficult task because he was culpable for his friend's death having given the order to camp in a field where they were vulnerable to enemy fire. It was a blunder that resulted in death, and he wrestles with the extent to which he should acknowledge his responsibility. The character Tim O'Brien also feels guilty for he turned on a flashlight that night to show a buddy a photo of his girlfriend, and that brought in the enemy mortar attack. From Tim's perspective, Kiowa clearly died because of the light. Norman Bowker also struggles with psychic anguish since it was he who pulled the body out of the soil and found that Kiowa's shoulder had been ripped off in the explosion.

Kiowa's death is not only a literal event, it is also a metaphor for the squalor that surrounds Alpha company and a focal point for the men to ponder their ethical and psychological participation in horrible experiences.

Another continuing theme throughout is the morality of narrating fiction about war. The issue is how to tell about it and make it both real and "true," containing the intimate details that convey the physical reality of military combat and also portray the psychological and moral horror of it. The idea is at the center of "Spin," which briefly introduces the complex interaction of experience with memory and how storytelling can put "spin" on the events, giving an element of humor to horrible events. Much of this takes place in the character O'Brien's mind as he thinks about comedic moments in the midst of battle, as when Kiowa taught Rat Kiley and Dave Jensen a rain dance. Humor and horror comingle in a war story, the implication is, and it is difficult to get the mixture right, to convey the mental reality of the situation. O'Brien reflects, "stories are for joining the past to the future.... Stories are for eternity, when memory is erased, when there is nothing to remember except the story."

These ideas are central to "How to Tell a True War Story," O'Brien's reflection on the relationship between the actual events and the fictional portrayal that makes the telling seem "real." One focal point of his thinking involves how to tell about the death of Curt Lemon, who was blown to bits by a mine, reduced to shreds hanging from the trees. Another concerns the strange music that seemed to emanate from a listening post even though there would have been no way to produce it. The third depicts a horrible scene in which Rat Kiley needlessly kills a baby water buffalo. What is revealed in each case is that none of these events actually happened in Vietnam but that all of them are "true," all of them represent the ethical and psychological nature of the experience of the war. In an important sense, the three episodes are fictionally true stories.

The collection concludes with "The Lives of the Dead," a powerful narrative that takes on the responsibility of recapitulation for all that has happened and of closure for a volume of interrelated stories. It features O'Brien reviewing his experiences, going over the key deaths that haunt him at the time of the telling, including not only the military killing of Lavender, Kiowa, Curt Lemon, and the Vietnamese soldier on the trail but the civilian passing of Linda, the girlfriend O'Brien left behind who died of a brain tumor. The title seems to suggest that although they are all dead, they can be kept alive in a story, an expression of his ironic quest for synthesis of life and death. He reviews all of these events, revisiting the horror and the guilt associated with each, and it helps explain to O'Brien why Norman Bowker committed suicide when he got home from Vietnam. Each tale in the volume deals with a specific event that carries psychic and moral implications, but collectively the twenty-two episodes are thematically overpowering, demonstrating in the aggregate that the entirety of the war is impossible to grasp or portray. In a sense, each small event conveys the emotional whole of it, expressed in the form of a story, and that is the way fiction becomes true.

Suggestions for Further Reading

Calloway, Catherine. "Pluralities of Vision: *Going After Cacciato* and Tim O'Brien's Short Fiction." *America Rediscovered: Critical Essays on the Literature and Film of the Vietnam War.* Eds. Owen Gilman, Jr., and Lorrie Smith. New York: Garland, 1990, pp. 113–24.

Farrell, Susan Elizabeth. *Critical Companion to Tim O'Brien: A Literary Reference to His Life and Work.* New York: Facts on File, 2011.

Heberle, Mark A. *A Trauma Artist: Tim O'Brien and the Fiction of Vietnam.* Iowa City: University of Iowa Press, 2001.

Herzog, Tobey C. *Tim O'Brien.* New York: Twayne, 1997.

Kaplan, Steven. "The Undying Uncertainty of the Narrator in Tim O'Brien's *The Things They Carried.*" *Critique* 35.1 (1991): 43–52.

Kaplan, Steven. *Understanding Tim O'Brien.* Columbia: University of South Carolina Press, 1995.

McNerney, Brian C. "Responsibly Inventing History: An Interview with Tim O'Brien." *War, Literature, & the Arts* 6.2 (1994): 1–26.

Smith, Lorrie. "'The Things Men Do': Gendered Subtext in Tim O'Brien's *Esquire* Stories." *Critique* 36. Fall (1994): 16–39.

Vernon, Alex. *Soldiers Once and Still: Ernest Hemingway, James Salter, & Tim O'Brien.* Iowa City: University of Iowa Press, 2004.

Louise Erdrich

Louise Erdrich has a well-established reputation as not only the leading Native American writer of fiction but as one of the great authors of short fiction in the United States. One of the difficulties of assessing her work is that her stories do not adhere to the standards established by Edgar Allan Poe in the early nineteenth century. They are not tightly unified narrative units, told from a single perspective, involving one major character, and the conflicts are not nicely resolved at the end. Quite often her tales involve a family rather than an individual and are told from shifting points of view. They move forward and backward in time, visiting scenes by association rather than by linear event. Very little is finally resolved in her fiction other than by death, and situations are simply integrated into ongoing life rather than concluded. Furthermore, after their initial publication in magazines, her stories have been brought together in volumes of inter-related tales, as with *The Beet Queen* and *Love Medicine*. These books deal with Chippewa life along the Red River of the North, the area where Erdrich was raised by a German father and a mixed-race mother, both of whom had positions in the Indian School in Wahpeton, North Dakota. Some of these settings are located in the Turtle Mountain reservation on the Canadian border north and west of Grand Forks, the largest town for nearly a hundred miles.

Part of what makes Erdrich's fiction so compelling is that she draws not only on traditional methods of Chippewa narration, in which the point of view is a communal voice that seems to share in the aggregate knowledge of the events, but on a central mythological matrix involving a limited number of figures in a few closely related families. Thus, the same characters appear repeatedly in various stories, the setting is limited, and the themes are drawn from the continuing social and economic situation, similar to

The American Short Story Handbook, First Edition. James Nagel.
© 2015 James Nagel. Published 2015 by John Wiley & Sons, Ltd.

what William Faulkner did with his stories of Yoknapatawpha County in Mississippi. Erdrich also has a firm grasp on the history of the area, especially with regard to key developments for Native Americans, and dates and places often contain a significance not immediately apparent but that is ultimately important in understanding the flow of events.

For example, many of her stories take place in 1934, a crucial year for the Chippewa of the Midwest. In the nineteenth century, that tribe had been relegated to living on reservation land on the theory that there was no way they could ever become assimilated into the general population of European immigrants. In 1887, however, Senator Henry Dawes rejected that idea and introduced the Indian Emancipation Act which sought to make Native Americans citizens of the United States, getting them off the reservations. His plan, which was quickly passed, allotted 160 acres of land to each Indian family, treating them exactly as the Europeans settlers had been by the Homestead Act of 1862. The assumption was that because the Europeans had established successful farms, formed communities, and prospered, the Chippewa could do the same. This Allotment Act proved a failure, however, because the Indian men, who had been hunters for thousands of years, refused to plant the seeds they were given and generally rejected the concept of work as ignominious. It was a disastrous situation until 1934, when the commissioner of Indian Affairs established the Indian Reorganization Act which bought back the allotments in return for monthly checks, and the attempt at assimilation was over. The Chippewa returned to the reservation and the towns surrounding it, fighting poverty and lack of opportunity.

That is the background for "Saint Marie," published in the *Atlantic Monthly* in 1984, and which won the O. Henry Award for the best short story that year. It involves a young girl, Marie Lazarre, and her teacher, Sister Leopolda, in a Roman Catholic elementary school. Marie narrates in first person, focusing on the nun who instructs her. The teacher's name is significant in that Christianity was initially brought to the Chippewa by the Leopoldine Society of Austria in 1829, and the theology and social codes of that organization have held sway ever since. Sister Leopolda administers a severe regimen for the children and demands absolute discipline. In one instance, she scalds Marie with boiling water as a punishment, seeking to purge her of evil impulses, and in another she throws the girl to the floor, stepping on her neck.

Marie, however, has a counter religious construct from Chippewa mythology, one that promises to give her magical powers drawn from Native American gods and legends. Inherent in the situation is an irreconcilable ideological conflict of spiritual assumptions and ways of life, one that frequently erupts into violence. At the end of this story, which takes place in a schoolhouse,

Marie attempts to kill Sister Leopolda by pushing her into a stove, and in the scuffle the girl is stabbed in the hand by a fork. The crux of the plot is that this incident is grossly misinterpreted by everyone not involved, for the nun reports that Marie's wound is a stigmata that appeared spontaneously, a miracle. Thus Marie becomes famous and is revered, and the tale ends on this ironic note, a falsehood that is not refuted, a holy event that is worshipped but is entirely without spiritual foundation.

An early story, "Celestine James," set in 1933, demonstrates how deeply engrained Roman Catholic mythology is in the Native American community. Celestine provides the account of an incident involving her best friend, Mary Adare, an elementary student who went down a slide at Saint Catherine's school face forward in winter time. Snow and ice covered the playground, and there is the usual confusion of playing children. Then Mary smacked her face into the snow and came up covered in blood. Sister Hugo looked not at Mary but at the impression in the snow, indentations that seemed to resemble not Mary but Christ himself. She shouts that there has been a miracle, and Sister Leopolda comes running with her camera to record what becomes known as The Manifestation at Argus. Late that night, Sister Leopolda worships at the sight of the image, scourging herself until her arms bleed into the snow. Later, she is canonized using the manifestation as part of the evidence justifying her elevation. Mary Adare also becomes a sacred person, and her life is changed because of this ironic incident in the playground. Despite the fact that Christianity was a religion superimposed on a people who already had their own spiritual traditions, Roman Catholicism is a powerful force in the lives of the Native Americans in Erdrich's fiction, a pattern of values and icons that are present in their everyday lives.

"Scales" appeared in the *North American Review* in 1982 and is narrated by Albertine Johnson. Her tale is about Dot Adare and Gerry Nanapush, whose last name is resonant of "Nanabozho," a mythological Chippewa trickster obsessed with his appetites for food and sex. Another of his attributes is pertinent to Gerry, his total distrust and disregard of law. The title, as is nearly always the case with Erdrich's fiction, is meaningful in several ways. A scale is a mechanism for the weighing of things, a concept with both literal and metaphoric significance in this story. The literal one is that the gravel trucks have to be weighed in order to calculate the value of the sand they carry. The metaphoric meaning measures the proportional weight of responsibility. Gerry was in a fight in a bar one night over an insult to Indians as a race, and he kicked a white man in the scrotum. Later, out of prison, he kills a state trooper who was attempting to arrest him. Gerry was trying to get home to see Dot and their baby girl, Shawn, but now he has a death sentence. Gerry did not trust American law, a set of regulations superimposed on his people, who already had their own system of justice. The implication is that the scales were tipped against Gerry and his people from the very beginning, an insight further emphasized when Dot has the baby weighed on the truck scales. She does not register at all. She has no weight and no value, one of a people who do not count in the grand scheme of things.

"Crown of Thorns" appeared in *Chicago* in 1984 and deals with the consequences of the death of June Kashpaw, an event that takes place in "The World's Greatest Fisherman," which was published in 1982 in the same magazine. This inter-textual reference is one of the things that makes Erdrich's stories complex in that the motivational strands sometimes reach out to events not in the immediate work. June died in a snowstorm on Easter Sunday of 1981, and the present time of "Crown of Thorns" is one month later. The focus is on June's husband, Gordon, an alcoholic who believes that he sees June's face everywhere he goes, and he has difficulty in dealing with her death. When he hits a deer with his car, the animal is stunned and motionless. Gordie thinks it is dead, and he puts it in the back seat of his car. When he later looks in the rear view mirror, the deer is sitting up in the seat, and he again thinks it is June. Later, he collapses and is taken into custody by the police.

If the plot is simple, the telling is not. An omniscient narrator establishes the background situation, that Gordie had married June, and their passionate relationship produced a son, King. A shift in perspective to Eli Kaspaw's memories then covers another part of June's life, when she left the home of Nector and Marie and came to live with him, learning some Chippewa lore from an elder. Another shift to Gordie's mind reveals their troubled marriage, his ambivalence about her, and his final assessment that he cannot live without her. It becomes clear that she meant a great deal to him. Finally, yet another point of view is introduced, shifting to the perspective of Sister Mary Martin, a lonely and troubled woman, who knew both Gordie and June, and who provides a compassionate conclusion to the story of June's death.

Her most frequently anthologized story, "The Red Convertible" appeared in the *Mississippi Valley Review* in 1982. Its central character is Henry Lamartine Jr., and the plot revolves around his difficulties in adjusting to civilian life after Vietnam. In the earlier "A Bridge," Henry Jr. stops in Fargo, North Dakota, on his way home from the war in 1973. He meets young Albertine Johnson, who at fifteen has run away from the reservation, and they spend the night together in a hotel. The emphasis is not on sex but on emotional instability, for Henry Jr. clearly suffers from post-traumatic stress disorder, turning violent without provocation and weeping at the conclusion of the action. Now, in "The Red Convertible," he makes it home and joins his younger brother, Lyman, who narrates in retrospect, sharing his memories of the incidents. Lyman is ironic and playful in his telling, often hiding key elements of the plot. For example, he begins by saying that he walks everywhere he goes, which is strange given that the story is about the car he owned together with his brother. What becomes clear later is that Henry Jr. committed suicide by jumping into the Red River of the North. Facing uncontrollable grief, Lyman ran the car into the river, giving it back to Henry Jr., in effect.

That the two brothers owned a car is an indication of the extent to which they have assimilated into American society, for an automobile is an artifact of the white world, an industrial product, an expression of modernity. When Henry Jr. arrives home, he has been damaged by another aspect of that world, mechanized warfare, and he cannot deal with it emotionally. He bites through his own lip, bleeding profusely, harming himself rather than an external enemy. That is when Lyman damages the car, knowing that his brother, an excellent mechanic, will repair it, giving him purpose and direction. The plot works, and Henry Jr. devotes himself to the job, achieving a sense of stability, but when he finishes he gives the convertible to Lyman, who understands what that means: that his brother intends to kill himself. Lyman refuses the gift, the two men fight, and Henry Jr. jumps into the river, committing suicide, as had his father. At the time of the telling, Lyman is still coming to terms with the loss of his brother, a painful attempt to integrate a devastating experience into his life and accept the permanency of it, something he is eventually able to accomplish.

As a body of work, Erdrich's short fiction is a complex set of inter-locking narratives dealing with multiple generations of Native American families. In a sense, they constitute a collective character, the story of a people, not a disparate set of individuals with unique desires and needs. They are suspended between two cultures with vastly diverse histories, social values, and relationships, and their intricate romantic entanglements produce brothers and sisters with different fathers and mothers who dominate the household. Unrelated children are often taken into a family and absorbed into the domestic sphere, not certain where they fit into society biologically. Many of the Chippewa characters marry white people, and a few assimilate fully into the European social structure, as did the Erdrich family. Most of them, however, are deeply aware of their unique racial history, the abandoned treaties, the life on the reservation, the broken lives of generations of families who struggled to fit into a foreign way of life. It is a subject fully worthy of the most profound consideration, and Erdrich's stories have provided an important portrait of two centuries of Chippewa life on the western plains.

Suggestions for Further Study

Sarris, Greg, Connie A. Jacobs, and James R. Giles, eds. *Approaches to Teaching the Works of Louise Erdrich*. New York: Modern Language Association, 2004.

Beidler, Peter G., and Gay Barton. *A Reader's Guide to the Novels of Louise Erdrich*. Columbia: University of Missouri Press, 1999.

Chavkin, Allan, ed. *The Chippewa Landscape of Louise Erdrich*. Tuscaloosa: University of Alabama Press, 1999.

Cooperman, Jeannette Batz. *The Broom Closet: Secret Meanings of Domesticity in Postfeminist Novels by Louise Erdrich, Mary Gordon, Toni Morrison, Marge Piercy, Jane Smiley, and Amy Tan*. New York: Peter Lang, 1999.

Hafen, P. Jane. *Reading Louise Erdrich's* Love Medicine. Boise: Boise State University Press, 2003.

Jacobs, Connie A. *The Novels of Louise Erdrich: Stories of Her People*. New York: Peter Lang, 2001.

Kloppenburg, Michelle R. *Contemporary Trickster Tales: The Pillagers in Louise Erdrich's North Dakota Quartet and Their Stories of Survival*. Essen: Verlag Die Blaue Eule, 1999.

Maszewska, Jadwiga. *Between Center and Margin: Contemporary Native American Women Novelists: Leslie Marmon Silko and Louise Erdrich*. Lódz (Poland): Wydawnictwo Uniwersytetu Lodzkiego, 2000.

Stookey, Lorena L. *Louise Erdrich: A Critical Companion*. Westport: Greenwood Press, 1999.

Wong, Hertha D. Sweet, ed. *Louise Erdrich's* Love Medicine: *A Casebook*. New York: Oxford University Press, 2000.

Part 4 **Great American Short Stories**

Benjamin Franklin, "The Speech of Polly Baker"

"The Speech of Polly Baker" was first published in London in *The General Advertiser* in April of 1747 and then in the *Maryland Gazette* in August of that year, when Benjamin Franklin was a largely unknown writer still in his forties. It immediately created a literary sensation, and it was quickly reprinted in newspapers and magazines throughout Britain and in America, which was still a colony at the time. It appeared during the Age of Reason, when the rigorous exercise of rational discourse was highly valued, and one of the primary literary modes of the age was satire, especially that revealing social hypocrisy among the privileged classes. Drawing from classical sources, including Boccaccio and Montaigne, Franklin drafted a Horatian satire, one with gentle humor, aimed at laws and customs regarding sexual behavior. Polly Baker is being prosecuted for having her fifth child out of wedlock, but none of the men in her life have ever been punished for fathering these children, nor does the law even consider their participation in the pregnancy to be a crime. Indeed, one of the men who impregnated the good Polly is now a justice in Boston, highly regarded in a position of esteem, whereas she has been repeatedly fined and jailed for bearing her children. Franklin was not insensitive to this form of gender discrimination even in this period before the Revolutionary War, and his account of her testimony in court is part of the early history of the development of the story as a popular genre in America.

The story begins with an expository paragraph setting the scene for the monologue that follows. Polly is speaking in a court in Boston, the heart of Puritan culture, for having given birth to yet another child out of wedlock.

The American Short Story Handbook, First Edition. James Nagel.
© 2015 James Nagel. Published 2015 by John Wiley & Sons, Ltd.

Since she has no money to pay an attorney to defend her, she pleads her own case directly to the justices mounting such arguments as occur to her and formulating them in her own language, the vernacular of the day. This artistic utilization of common language is significant in literary history since the elevated lexicon of the privileged classes was generally thought to be the only suitable dialect for publication, but this woman of the lower classes could not realistically speak in that way. The wandering, desultory course of her argument is also suitable to her nature, for she has no formal training in disputation, legal presentation, or the forms of debate. Nonetheless, her comments before the judge are sufficient for her to prevail in court, and the logic of that decision is what constitutes the heart of the matter.

In her simplicity and unhesitating honesty, Polly proves to be a persuasive advocate by revealing her personal traits as well as by constructing a convincing logical argument. In the Age of Reason, nothing was quite as appealing as a rational discussion that moved from specific points to logical generalizations derived from them. That such discourse could emanate from an uneducated, lower-class woman suggested that many of the assumptions of American society needed revision, beginning with laws that punished women but not men for the crime of fornication, regulations that allowed only men to vote, and traditions that closed the doors of universities to female applicants.

But Polly begins not with such weighty matters but rather with the presentation of herself as humble and respectful, and she asks not that she be found innocent but only that her fine be remitted so that she might better care for her infant child. She says she is a "poor unhappy woman" who cannot afford to pay a lawyer to argue for her, but she then constructs a defense based on common sense applied to a series of points of law. The first such matter is that the regulation that pertains to her case seems unreasonable and unduly severe. It is unreasonable in that it applies only to women and not to men, not even to the man, now a judge in Boston, who originally seduced her with a promise of marriage. She thus establishes that her moral standing is not inferior to that of a magistrate. She adds that her actions have contributed to the number of the King's subjects and that they are consistent with both Nature's instincts and the biblical injunction to increase and multiply. She reasons that God must approve of her fecundity in that he has seen to the formation of the healthy bodies of her children and granted each of them immortal souls. She thus disarms the counterargument that if the law itself seems unjust she might yet be guilty of a moral crime against religion. But it is in the revelation of her personal values that she is most appealing and convincing, for she portrays herself as lusty but devoted to the man she loves, frugal yet determined to develop the character of a good wife, a loving mother who has provided for her family through her industry and ambition, and eager to wed the first sincere man who would take her as a wife. It is perhaps this last point that convinces one of her judges to marry her the next day, and the force of her reasonable argument convinces the judicial panel to dismiss her charges without punishment.

Polly wins not only her own case but a series of points of logic that society might well wish to ponder: gender inequities; the idea of punishing in a public forum actions that are private and personal; the hypocrisy of persons in high stations who enjoy the respect and esteem of society; and the appeal of a simple woman of domestic virtues who desires to become a good wife. Such a person, the conclusion seems to suggest, may well be worthy not only of marriage but of a statue erected in her honor. Franklin knew well the strategy of Horatian satire as a form that sought not to offend but to reform, thus it had to construct humor that was so gentle that the object of it could laugh and improve. This brief and simple story is, in many ways, the foremost example of this traditional mode in American literature.

Suggestions for Further Reading

Aldridge, Owen A. *Benjamin Franklin and Nature's God*. Durham: Duke University Press, 1967.

Franklin, Benjamin. "The Speech of Polly Baker'." *The General Advertiser* (April 15, 1747): 1.

Hall, Max. "An Amateur Detective on the Trail of B. Franklin, Hoaxer." *Proceedings of the Massachusetts Historical Society* 84 (1972): 26–43.

Hall, Max. *Benjamin Franklin and Polly Baker: The History of a Literary Deception*. Williamsburg: The Institute of Early American History and Culture, 1960.

Lemay, J. A. Leo. "The Text, Rhetorical Strategies, and Themes of 'The Speech of Miss Polly Baker." *The Oldest Revolutionary: Essays on Benjamin Franklin*. Philadelphia: University of Pennsylvania Press, 1976, pp. 91–120.

Newcomb, Robert. "Benjamin Franklin and Montaigne." *Modern Language Notes* 72 (1957): 489–91.

Smeall, J. F. S. "The Readerships of the Polly-Baker Texts." *North Dakota Quarterly* 28 (1960): 20–29.

Ruri Colla, "The Story of the Captain's Wife and an Aged Woman"

In 1789, the *Gentleman and Ladies Town and Country Magazine* published a remarkable narrative entitled "The Story of the Captain's Wife and an Aged Woman." Short fiction was still in its rudimentary form as a genre, but this one was, in many ways, artistically sophisticated even though it shared the standard conventions of the time. For example, it is a didactic tale teaching a moral lesson, a tradition that evolved from the Biblical parable, and such a purpose was often presumed to justify publication. For another, it purports to be a true story related not originated by the narrator but simply reported from what a "clergyman of this Commonwealth" claimed to be the facts of the case. The name "Ruri Colla" was a pseudonym for an unknown writer, also a standard practice. Fiction was ethically suspect at the time, and few respectable persons wanted to be known for having written it, so the taking of a false name became standard practice for writers, a tradition that lasted several decades. Many of the early tales of the eighteenth century contained supernatural elements, as does "The Captain's Wife," although in this case with an unusual twist.

The central fictional elements of the story are thus not startlingly original; what sets it apart from the other fiction of the period is its handling of language, the power of its plot, and the introduction of what several decades later became known as Romantic Ambiguity, alternative explanations for what is related. The expository frame at the beginning and again at the end purports to present not fiction but historical fact testifying to the accuracy

The American Short Story Handbook, First Edition. James Nagel.
© 2015 James Nagel. Published 2015 by John Wiley & Sons, Ltd.

of the internal narrative. It begins with reflections on the theme of hypocrisy, "condemning others for those very things which we practice ourselves," a commonplace human fault that rests on self-congratulation and an unearned sense of moral superiority. The narrator expounds on the idea with some subtlety, proposing that were hypocrisy eliminated, people would have to improve their behavior in order to have the ethical platform from which to criticize others. Society would thus be improved, scandal would be eliminated from daily conversation, and life in the community would be more congenial. These are worthy objectives, logically presented (in the Age of Reason), and illustrated by a tale the narrator heard from a clergyman, who swore it to be true. The narrator acknowledges that it has "incredible" aspects, but that is why the clergyman has kept it a secret for many years and has never written it down. The kindly narrator has now done so, and the tale constitutes the majority of the rest of the story.

The internal narrative is dramatic, containing both action and dialogue woven together seamlessly in a fast moving plot, a skill that was still developing for most writers of the period. It concerns a young woman of twenty-one who married an older ship captain who is away from home for long periods on his voyages, a common problem for seafaring men and their families. Each day the lonely wife walks on the wharf looking for the sails of her husband's ship to appear on the horizon, and her forlorn appearance draws the attention of an elderly woman who tells her to come back to the same location that evening and she will be taken to see her husband and returned home before morning. At first the wife ignores the strange offer, but as the day progresses she sees little harm in finding out more, so she visits the wharf at dusk and is instructed to cast her basket on the water. It is instantly transformed into a sailboat, and the two women put out to sea, quickly losing sight of land. After two hours, a town appears on the shore, and they set into port, where the old woman shows the wife the door to a house and informs her that her husband is within. The wife enters to find him eating his dinner with a singular knife and fork. When he finished his meal, he approaches her saying that she reminds him of his wife back home, and he proposes to spend the night with her. She agrees on the condition that she receive the utensils, a requirement he reluctantly accepts. In the early morning, she leaves the house, finds the elderly woman, and they sail back home together, and the central section of the story is concluded.

Seven months later, however, her husband returns home to find his wife pregnant, at which point he flies into a rage, swearing never to lay eyes on her again, inconstancy being, according to his standards of conduct, an unforgivable crime against the covenant of marriage. He takes separate lodgings and manages to avoid his wife entirely until she enlists the assistance of an uncle, who invites the captain to a party. As he sits down to dine, he notices that his place setting has no utensils, and he calls for them. His wife appears, carrying the knife and fork he had given her for the night they spent together in a foreign city, and he is embarrassed and chagrined, knowing not how to act, having been so blatantly caught violating his own rules. He confesses that he has, indeed, been guilty of hypocrisy, forgives his wife, and they return home together, united by her trick and his contrition.

At this juncture the frame narrator returns to comment on the story he has presented observing that he is not sure this account is true but the character of the person who related it to him was not to be questioned. He also repeats the admonition that people should be careful about finding fault in others when they are themselves guilty of the same weaknesses. No one, he suggests, would want to be caught in the embarrassing position of the hapless captain who was so publicly humiliated by his hypocrisy. It is far better to live a righteous life and forgo passing judgment on the behavior of others.

What is remarkable about this brief tale is not only its integration of exposition, action, and dialogue, but the introduction of what later became known as Romantic Ambiguity, a story with multiple levels of interpretation. For example, "The Captain's Wife" can be taken as simple realism, the presentation of rather remarkable events as they truly happened. Although unusual, these simple actions illustrate the moral lesson perfectly, stressing the dangers of hypocrisy and the frailty of human constancy. From another perspective, the issue is the magical powers of the aged woman, who transformed a basket into a boat, sailed thousands of miles in a single night, and brought about the uniting of husband and wife as she had promised. On this level, there are Gothic implications in the supernatural elements, confirmed by the strange knife and fork, although the ultimate theme remains the same. On yet another level, however, the meaning of the story is quite different. The tale could simply be the fabrication of a young wife who knows the ways of sea captains away from home port and guesses that her husband has been unfaithful. Her story then is a ruse to trick him into a confession of his infidelity that will match her own, she apparently, from this point of view, having been impregnated by someone else. Her elaborate stratagem elicits his confession, paving the way for their reconciliation. The theme of hypocrisy is still present but weakened in this interpretation by the elaborate lie the wife tells to explain her pregnancy and justify it by his admission of inconstancy in a foreign port. Yet another possibility is that the young wife knows she is guilty and suspects that her husband has been unfaithful on his voyages and yet wishes to reconcile if he can find a way to do so without disgrace. She provides a fabricated explanation for her pregnancy that the husband knows to be false, to be sure, but he accepts it because it allows him to be the father of the child in the eyes of the community. He can thus continue in the marriage without public humiliation. These various levels give the narrative an interpretive richness unusual in the eighteenth century, and they make "The Captain's Wife" a key document in the development of the American story.

Suggestions for Further Reading

Current-Garcia, Eugene, and Bert Hitchcock. *American Short Stories*. 6th ed. Boston: Addison Wesley, 1996, p. 5.

Doran, Robert. "The Fantastic Tale: Poe and Scott." *Tale, Novella, Short Story: Currents in Short Fiction*. Eds. Wolfgang Görtschacher, and Holger Klein. Tübingen: Stauffenburg Verlag, 2004, p. 51.

Nagel, James. *Anthology of the American Short Story*. Boston: Houghton, Mifflin, 2008, pp. 48–53.

Hochbruck, Wolfgang, Aynur Erdogan, and Philipp Fidler, eds. *Origins of the American Short Story*. Los Gatos: Slack Water Press, 2008.

Porter, Roy. "Witchcraft and Magic in Enlightenment, Romantic, and Liberal Thought." *Witchcraft and Magic in Europe: The Eighteenth and Nineteenth Centuries*. Eds. Bengt Ankarloo, and Stuart Clark. Philadelphia: University of Pennsylvania Press, 1999, pp. 209–10.

Scanlon, Larry. *Narrative, Authority, and Power: The Medieval Exemplum and the Chaucerian Tradition*. Cambridge: Cambridge University Press, 1994, p. 60.

Werlock, Abby H. P. *The Facts on File Companion to the American Short Story*. New York: Facts on File, 2009, p. x.

Washington Irving, "Rip Van Winkle"

Often described, inaccurately, as the first short story to appear in America, Washington Irving's "Rip Van Winkle" has earned an important place in the literary history of the genre. Although not actually the first piece of short fiction in the country, it was the first to generate international approval and to garner sustained attention for nearly two centuries on the basis of its gentle irony, sustained humor, elegant style, and the force of its mythic tale. There is, quite obviously, something intriguing about the tale, something that has resonated with the American public through many generations and among various age groups, making it one of the most popular works in the canon. Irving was living in Europe when he wrote it, and he drew from a broad variety of earlier folktales that feature legendary sleepers, from the ancient Greek account of Epimenides, to the Norse legends of Odin, to the German tale of Peter Klaus. Working closely with the structure and details of these earlier narratives, Irving infused "Rip Van Winkle" with a setting and meaning that was uniquely American.

Much of what is new is contained in the opening and closing sections, for those are set in a small village in the Catskills of upstate New York and draw on the Dutch history of the area, the transition to an English colonial society, and the dramatic changes wrought by the Revolutionary War, the establishment of a democracy, and the beginning of a new society. The area was formally settled in 1647 and presided over by Governor Peter Stuyvesant, the last Dutch governor before New Netherlands came under English rule, and the citizens built their village in a Dutch design with materials shipped from Holland. When the British gained control of the region,

The American Short Story Handbook, First Edition. James Nagel.
© 2015 James Nagel. Published 2015 by John Wiley & Sons, Ltd.

they did little to change the ambience of the local area, it being remote from the centers of commerce and politics. To these American issues, Irving overlaid the standard elements of the tale he had read and translated in Germany: that his protagonist is a gregarious loafer dominated by a shrewish wife who berates him constantly. His one true friend is his dog, Wolf, and his only relief comes in his trips into the mountains squirrel hunting. This last endeavor sets the stage for the second section, the experience with the strange creatures who seem to be from Henry Hudson's crew from a century or more ago. Later, when Rip returns to his village, this sailor is referred to as "Hendrik Hudson," which is a historical error. He sailed on a Dutch ship, to be sure, but he was a British adventurer with an English name.

The opening is filled with charm, humor, and historical interest. The only developed character is Rip, but his desultory manner and casual approach to life carry their own appeal. But in terms of the art of fiction, this section is not dramatically more sophisticated than what had come out of the eighteenth century, although the elegant style represents a significant artistic advance. As is the case with much eighteenth-century fiction, it is all exposition. There is no present action and no dialogue. It is an excellent set up, in structural terms, but the heart of the story is yet to follow.

That comes in section two, the adventure in the Catskill mountains. This intriguing account is highly derivative of its sources, particularly the myth of Peter Klaus, which this section follows in great detail, even down to the glen in the mountains, the thunder derived from lawn bowls, the cawing of the crows, the silence of the mysterious little men, the keg and the draught Rip takes from it, the sleep for twenty years, the death of the dog, the rusted gun, and the long beard that has grown during Rip's extended slumbers. His hike into the Catskills clearly derives from Peter's hunting trip into the Kyfhauser mountains in Thuringia, although Irving has added some American aspects, the fact that the strange little men are dressed in Dutch fashion, for example. This detail links Rip's adventure to the legend that Henry Hudson, who vanished after his men mutinied in what is now Hudson's Bay, reappears in the Catskills for a day every twenty years, playing bowls with his crew. The balls crashing into the pins generate the sound of thunder that echoes throughout the mountains. Like Rip, Hudson would seem to be another prodigious sleeper who awakens and returns to active life, and the river that winds through the valleys below is named for him.

This section has both action and dialogue, and the narrative is compelling. Rip wanders into a mountain glen with his dog, Wolf, a name derived from Norse legend in which two wolves sat at Odin's feet prior to his long sleep. He hears his name called from a distance, but it seems to emanate from a crow flying overhead. Then a strange man appears below, small but stout, carrying a keg of liquor, and he gestures for Rip to assist with his heavy burden. Rip complies, being one to enjoy the occasional drink, and he is led into a hollow where he sees a company of silent men, dressed in the Dutch fashion of the century before, playing at bowls. The commander, who would seem to be Hudson, fills large flagons from the keg, and everyone drinks, including Rip, who revisits the keg until he becomes quite drunk and falls asleep. It is a fascinating series of events, one that has had an allure in many countries for more than a thousand years, and Irving renders realistic details with both wit and a serious tone.

The most dramatic section of the story, however, is his waking and returning home, a matter handled with compelling action, riveting dialogue, and gentle humor, basically in the asides by the narrator. Rip awakens after his long sleep to find his dog nowhere to be found, his rifle rusted, the crow circling overhead replaced, appropriately, it turns out, by an eagle, the emblem of the new country that has been formed while he slumbered. Rip assumes he has tarried only one long night on his trip to the mountains, and he worries about confronting his termagant wife, something he need never endure. Apart from a stiffness in his joints and a lingering hunger, he seems not to have suffered from twenty years of unconsciousness, but on his trip to the village he begins to encounter progressively greater changes to the world he has known. At first he realizes that his beard has grown a foot long. On the periphery of the village he encounters strange children, a meaningful detail in that the former Rip was, in his perpetual childhood play, a favorite of the youthful set. The community has grown and become more prosperous, with new houses and bustling activity, the result of the recently established free enterprise economy that functions without the taxation the King imposed on his earlier colony. A dog approaches him, one resembling Wolf, but it shies away, unfamiliar with this strange figure. Most importantly, the old village inn has been transformed into the Union Hotel, a name with especial political resonance for the newly formed United States. In short, Rip has slept through the Revolutionary War, the establishment of a functioning democracy with a representative government, the unification of the separate states into a single federal body, and the election of George Washington as president.

This period in history is the most important in the life of the nation, and Rip is entirely innocent of any of it. That detail, nowhere to be found in the antecedent permutations of the myth, is what Americanizes the story. Moreover, he has returned on election day, a new event for a foundling society, and the time of his return would seem to be either 1789, when the first elections were held, or 1792, which resulted in the inauguration of President Washington. These transformations have altered the tone of society, and the sleepy village is now bustling with activity and interest in the voting, and he is immediately asked which side he favors, whether Federal or Democrat, a question he answers in the worst possible way, that he is a loyal subject of the king. About to be cast out as a Tory, an elder of the town begins to question him, only to discover that the people Rip associated with have long passed from the earth, including his wife, and he is declared harmless. Encountering his listless son, a replication of his former self, Rip begins to doubt his identity, but then his daughter appears with her child named after him, and it becomes evident that he has been away twenty years. Even the manner of his wife's death is presented with quiet irony, for she "broke a blood-vessel in a fit of passion at a New England peddler," an eager entrepreneur representing the Yankee head for business. Her death frees him from the tyranny of "petticoat government," and he assumes a new, comfortable life as a chronicler of the history of the village, a sage known to hold forth before the Union Hotel, entertaining all who would listen with the tale of his adventures.

The story ends with an ironic passage, putatively presented directly by Dietrich Knickerbocker, making reference to the German tale about the Kypphauser mountains but giving assurance that he knew Rip personally and could testify to his "perfectly rational and consistent" nature and that his story "is beyond the possibility of doubt." Of course it can be doubted in the same sense that the supernatural tale in "The Captain's Wife" of the century before can be. In that instance, the pregnant wife's relation of a fantastic journey across the ocean on a broom can be read as her desperate attempt to hide her infidelity. In the same way, Rip's tale could conceal the simple fact that he ran off to escape his nagging wife and has now returned, in his dotage, to the community of his youth.

But in either reading, the charm of this kindly naïveté is unmatched in American fiction until Mark Twain's stories and novels, and it signals a significant advance in the art of storytelling. So, too, does the unobtrusive elegance of Irving's style, the skillful drive of the plot, the realistic nature of the dialogue, and the details that tie Rip's tale to the New World despite the European origins of the central legend. "Rip Van Winkle" thus deserves a special place in the historical development of the short story, infusing impressive artistry with compelling action, dialogue, and humor, and it may well be the best tale ever to have been told by 1819, but it is not the first short fiction to appear in America.

Suggestions for Further Reading

Anderson, Donald R. "Freedom's Lullaby: Rip Van Winkle and the Framings of Self-Deception." *ESQ* 46 (2000): 255–77.

Blakemore, Steven. "Family Resemblances: The Texts and Contexts of 'Rip Van Winkle'." *Early American Literature* 35.2 (2000): 187–212.

Horwitz, Howard. "'Rip Van Winkle' and Legendary National Memory." *Western Humanities Review* 58.2 (2004): 34–47.

Kuczynski, Peter. "Intertextuality in *Rip Van Winkle*: Irving's Use of Büsching's Folk-Tale *Peter Klaus* in an Age of Transition." *British Romantics as Readers: Intertextuality, Maps of Misreading, Reinterpretations*. Eds. Michael Gassenmeier, Peter Bridzun, Jens Martin Gurr, and Frank Erik Pointner. Heidelberg: University of Heidelberg Press, 1998, pp. 295–315.

Martin, Terrence. "Rip, Ichabod, and the American Imagination." *American Literature* 31 (1959): 137–49.

McLamore, Richard V. "The Dutchman in the Attic: Claiming an Inheritance in *The Sketch Book of Geoffrey Crayon*." *American Literature* 72 (2000): 31–57.

Pochmann, Henry A. "Irving's German Sources in *The Sketch Book*." *Studies in Philology* 27 (1930): 477–98.

Ringe, Donald A. "New York and New England: Irving's Criticism of American Society." *American Literature* 38 (1967): 455–67.

Shear, Walter. "Time in 'Rip Van Winkle' and 'The Legend of Sleepy Hollow'." *Midwest Quarterly* 17 (1976): 158–72.

Young, Philip. "Fallen from Time: The Mythic Rip Van Winkle." *Kenyon Review* 22 (1960): 547–73.

Nathaniel Hawthorne, "Young Goodman Brown"

Nathaniel Hawthorne's "Young Goodman Brown" was published in the *New England Magazine* in 1835 before being incorporated into *Mosses from an Old Manse* in 1846. Often taken as a quintessential example of American Romanticism, it is a moral allegory that presents the protagonist's resistance to the knowledge of evil; he clings to his dream of perpetual innocence, and it destroys his life. This outcome is related to a general theme in Hawthorne's work of the "fortunate fall," the idea that an awareness of personal weakness and failings can humanize people through humility, allowing them to recognize and forgive the transgressions in those around them. In this sense, sin can bring self-knowledge, insight, and compassion. Hawthorne's Goodman Brown resists such wisdom and thus never gains insight into the duality of human nature.

As an allegory, the story opens with personified characters who function both as literal human beings and as abstract qualities. Brown, the protagonist, is called "Goodman" not because it is his first name but because it was the common means of address for ordinary young men of respectable standing in the community. He is a figure of innocence, uncorrupted by the complexity of life and unschooled in the vagaries of human nature. He is an Everyman character since people begin life with childhood purity and become more worldly as their lives progress. His wife, Faith, similarly plays two roles, as a flesh and blood young woman married for three months and as the abstract religious quality of "faith," of steadfast belief in a creed based on moral commitment rather than on an evidentiary procedure guided by reason. In the opening scene, Goodman is leaving his Faith to attend a

The American Short Story Handbook, First Edition. James Nagel.
© 2015 James Nagel. Published 2015 by John Wiley & Sons, Ltd.

forbidden ceremony. The "Witches' Sabbath" was believed to be an evil religious ceremony presided over by the Devil. Held in Nature at midnight, it presented the temptations of the physical world and threatened the spiritual realm, particularly conviction, as explained by Cotton Mather in his *The Wonders of the Invisible World* in 1693. Why Goodman feels he must attend is not clear, but allegorically the implication would be that everyone, at some point, becomes aware of the potential weaknesses in all human beings, including themselves. Encountering temptation could thus be seen as inevitable, and Goodman must face it.

The opening ends with his departure from home, and the heart of the action concerns his walk through the dark woods surrounding a village near Boston, a midnight journey into the forest and toward a dark knowledge of human nature. The reference to King William's court indicates that the action is taking place between 1689 and 1702, which is confirmed by the historical comment regarding the recent King Philip's War. King Philip was an Indian leader known as Metacomet who resisted the encroachment of Europeans into New England, and he was killed by the British in 1676, essentially ending hostilities. On his journey, Brown encounters an elderly man who, shockingly, resembles himself. It is soon revealed that the figure is the Devil, with a staff in the shape of a snake, who has assumed the visage of Brown's grandfather, a man he knew well. Since the travelers are on their way to a congress of evil, the theme of hypocrisy invests the rest of the experience, as respectable people of the community who by day profess the most holy of thoughts and deeds are here, in the dark, revealed to have knowledge of sin. All the more shocking to Brown is the revelation that his fellow travelers include the most reputable women of his community, a situation also based on historical evidence. Both Goody Closyse and Goody Cory, whom he soon encounters, were condemned as witches in Salem, despite the fact that "Goody" meant "good wife." Further shaking Brown's equilibrium, he soon sees both his minister and Deacon Gookin joining the group. The very people who have instructed Young Goodman Brown into righteous Christianity are now on the path with him headed for an evil ceremony presided over by witches and the Devil. He overhears that a young woman is to be initiated into the group, and soon after he sees, or seems to see, Faith flying through the dark clouds above him, a perception confirmed when one of her pink ribbons comes floating down. It is a transitional moment as Brown explains "my Faith is gone" and concludes that "there is no good on earth and sin is but a name. Come, devil! For to thee is this world given," and he proceeds down the path. There he perceives a nightmare ceremony in front of an altar lit with candles, with the sounds of the forest laughing like "demons" at Brown's exclamations of blasphemies.

Most horrid of all is the realization that Brown's own family had been initiated into evil, that all the revered elders who had led him to holiness were themselves part of this midnight ritual. The Devil explains that here are wives who have murdered their husbands, elders who have attempted to seduce young ladies, unmarried fair maidens who have buried infants in their gardens, all of this being part of the "mystery of sin." The Devil presents a central principle of Puritanism, that "Evil is the nature of Mankind." But just as he and Faith are about to be initiated into the brethren of the unholy, Brown cries out to her that she should "look up to Heaven, and resist the Wicked One," and he finds himself suddenly alone in the forest, his nightmare vision over. The journey concluded, Brown returns home a ruined man, distrustful of everyone around him, unable to accept members of his own family out of the suspicion that they have a dual nature, with dark sin hidden in their hearts. Thus he lives out his days psychologically isolated, emotionally distant from his wife and family, and "his dying hour was gloom."

This story has been the matter of a good deal of critical disputation, with some scholars seeing in it a Freudian journey out of the super-ego and into the dark recesses of the unconscious and others reading it as a condemnation of a rigid Puritan culture that perceived life as a religious struggle between the forces of good and evil. Some readings offer, more simply, the observation that once Brown has recognized the hypocrisy around him, and lost his own faith, he is unable to accept the duplicity in everyone, and he dies estranged from humanity. He cannot accept an awareness that despite their human failings, people can also endorse an essential goodness within themselves. He pays a terrible price for his assumption that he should expect eternal purity outside of Eden.

Suggestions for Further Reading

Bell, Millicent, ed. *New Essays on Hawthorne's Major Tales*. New York: Cambridge University Press, 1993.

Cherry, Fannye N. "The Sources of Hawthorne's 'Young Goodman Brown'." *American Literature* 5 (1934): 342–48.

Cohen, B. Bernard. "*Paradise Lost* and 'Young Goodman Brown'." *Essex Institute Historical Collections* 94 (1958): 282–96.

Cook, Reginald. "The Forest of Goodman Brown's Night: A Reading of Hawthorne's 'Young Goodman to Brown'." *New England Quarterly* 43 (1970): 473–81.

Doubleday, Neil Frank. *Hawthorne's Early Tales*. Durham: Duke University Press, 1977.

Levy, Leo B. "The Problem of Faith in 'Young Goodman Brown'." *Journal of English and Germanic Philology* 74 (1975): 375–87.

Von Frank, Albert J. *Critical Essays on Hawthorne's Short Stories*. Boston: G. K. Hall, 1991.

Edgar Allan Poe,
"The Cask of Amontillado"

Edgar Allan Poe's "The Cask of Amontillado" can be read against the standards the author endorsed in "The Philosophy of Composition," a seminal essay defining the aesthetics of fiction and poetry. Poe maintained that a work of literature must demonstrate both coherence and congruence, that all of the elements should contribute to the ultimate effect, to the underlying artistic idea. Although he was discussing his poem "The Raven," the basic thesis relates to his short stories as well. To be well executed, in other words, the central formal devices must be unified, so that narrative method, tone, structure, characterization, imagery, style, and theme are coordinate in creating a story of integrity and design, as in "The Cask," since all aspects of it function together.

The story is a first-person, retrospective narrative told by an elderly Montressor some fifty years after the night he killed Fortunato and sealed him up in a wall deep in the catacombs of his familial mansion. "The Cask" is thus not one of Poe's crime stories of ratiocination in which the identity of the perpetrator is slowly teased out of the empirical evidence. Rather, it is a revelation of the inner character of the speaker, the motivation for his actions, and the irony with which the plan was executed. The plot, in a sense, begins in the middle, after the offending insult has been given and the revenge planned, and all that is left is the calculated implementation of a series of events staged with psychological precision. The particular offense is not named but seems to involve the stature of the Montressor family, since the victim, Fortunato, is able to recall neither his host's family coat of arms nor motto, implying a social inferiority for what was once a proud

The American Short Story Handbook, First Edition. James Nagel.
© 2015 James Nagel. Published 2015 by John Wiley & Sons, Ltd.

and prominent dynasty. It would seem that the current Montressor is no longer as rich and powerful as were his ancestors.

First-person narration is normally an exercise in self-revelation, since speakers often reveal as much about themselves as they do about the subject they are discussing. In this case, however, Montressor shows little of himself at the time of the telling, probably sometime during the first half of the nineteenth century and certainly by 1846, when the story was published. Since the action is fifty years before that, it would seem to be toward the end of the eighteenth century and at the latest 1796. That time period is confirmed by the costume Montressor dons for the carnival, a "roquelaire," a cloak popular during this era named for the Duke of Roquelaure. Furthermore, wealthy Austrian and British travelers attend the carnival, part of the new moneyed class that emerged near the end of the eighteenth century. But whenever the events occur, the speaker presents a factual and logical account. He relates his tale in an attitude of kindness and calm objectivity, not expressing emotion, the justification for his act of revenge, nor any sense of guilt or regret. He rather calmly describes the events and the dialogue, trusting his audience to see the ironic significance of each.

The setting seems to be Italy, but possibly France, during the carnival season, an ancient, pagan event forty days before Easter. The social significance of the festival is that fortunes are temporarily reversed, a celebrative parody of reality, the wealthy and powerful often dressing in costumes of the poor or powerless, the poor donning the attire of the nobility. It is an evening out of time, a reversal of fortune, a perfect moment for Montressor to attempt to right the wrong that has been done his family. During the celebration, nearly everyone wears a mask, a key element of Montressor's plan since no one would be able to identify either the victim nor his assassin. That evening, Fortunato, befumed by drink and dressed as a fool, is dominated and controlled by a lesser man, Montressor. "Fortunato," the fortunate one, has a position of wealth and social importance, enough so that he is not only respected but feared. He belongs to the Masons, a secret organization of the powerful, and it is clear that he regards himself as being beyond the reach of persons beneath him, namely Montressor, "my treasure," who comes from a family once rich and significant but that has seen a decline in recent years. Given the vast number of ancestors entombed in the catacombs beneath the family home, however, it would seem that the Montressors had been a prominent part of society for centuries. The speaker would seem to derive from a traditional French Catholic family: the last words he speaks to Fortunato before placing the final stone in the wall are "In pace requiescat," "rest in peace," the last line of the requiem mass. What is behind this past insult is not clear, but "Montressor" is a French name, "Fortunato" clearly Italian, and family origins could have played a role in the insult. Still, the bitterness over the slight is without explanation, although, during various wars, the borders between the two countries moved on the basis of treaty, and during Napoleon's reign northern Italy was defeated and the French leader assumed political control of the region. Italians naturally felt resentment at the incursion of another culture into their territory, the change of place names, and alteration of language. In any event, nationality, and pride, play a role even with regard to drink, for "Amontillado" is a Spanish dry sherry and the other liquor consumed during the evening is a French Médoc, this despite the fact that a key motivational aspect of the plot is connoisseurship of Italian wine.

From the very beginning, Montressor treats Fortunato with ironic respect, since he plans to kill him this very evening. During the festivities, he merely mentions his purchase of a cask of Amontillado, a Spanish sherry from Montilla, knowing it will stir Fortunato's interest, and then plays on his vanity by suggesting that he will ask Luchresi to verify the quality of it. This the Italian cannot abide, since he rates his knowledge above that of Luchresi's, and he insists on making the judgment himself, despite Montressor's repeated suggestions that they turn back and rejoin the revelers. Thus they begin the journey down through the catacombs beneath the Montressor mansion. However, virtually every line of their conversation is ironic. When Fortunato coughs from the damp air, he asserts "I shall not die of a cough," and Montressor answers "true—true," knowing the actual means of death awaits them at the end of their descent. Stopping for a taste of Médoc, Montressor offers an ironic toast "to your long life." Virtually all of the conversation is replete with such ambiguity, even when Fortunato boasts of his membership in the Masons and Fortunato produces a physical trowel, the one he will use to seal his opponent in the wall. It is taken as a pun, a jest only, until it is too late. Throughout this rich conversation, Fortunato takes the literal meaning of what is said, and Montressor understands something quite different since he knows the conclusion of the journey to see the cask of Amontillado. Even during the entombing of his adversary, the ironic comments continue, as Fortunato regards the walling process as a joke and suggests that they will have many laughs about it over a drink, and Montressor replies that they will, over the Amontillado. Then, he places the last stone in the wall, covers it with the rampart of bones to match the surroundings, and leaves with his blessing, "In pace requiescat!"

The story is a brilliant exercise in artistic control and fictional economy. Every word contributes to the progression of the plot and the development toward the ultimate revenge. All of it is conducted in the tones of genteel civility, since the aristocratic stature of the two men is very much at issue.

The emotional restraint of the exchanges, the ironic duplicity of much of the dialogue, and the driving progression toward the conclusion combine to create the tension underlying each paragraph. But even beyond its achievement as an individual work of fiction, "The Cask of Amontillado" is an impressive demonstration of the rigorous principles for the short story that Poe outlined in his commentaries on the art of literature.

Suggestions for Further Reading

Baraban, Elena V. "The Motive for Murder in 'The Cask of Amontillado' by Edgar Allan Poe." *Rocky Mountain Review of Language and Literature* 58.2 (2004): 47–62.

Gargano, James W. "'The Cask of Amontillado': A Masquerade of Motive and Identity." *Studies in Short Fiction* 4 (1967): 119–26.

Hammond, J. R. *An Edgar Allan Poe Companion: A Guide to the Short Stories, Romances, and Essays.* London: Macmillan, 1981.

Kennedy, Gerald J. *Poe, Death, and the Life of Writing.* New Haven: Yale University Press, 1987.

May, Charles. *Edgar Allan Poe: A Study of the Short Fiction.* Boston: Twayne, 1991.

Reynolds, David S. "Poe's Art of Transformation: 'The Cask of Amontillado' in Its Cultural Context." *New Essays on Poe's Major Tales.* Ed. Kenneth Silverman. Cambridge: Cambridge University Press, 1993, pp. 93–112.

Thompson, G.R. *Poe's Fiction: Romantic Irony in the Gothic Tales.* Madison: University of Wisconsin Press, 1973.

Herman Melville, "Bartleby, the Scrivener"

First published in *Putnam's Monthly Magazine* in 1853, "Bartleby, the Scrivener" was incorporated into Herman Melville's *The Piazza Tales* three years later. Controversial almost from the beginning, this story has been widely studied, frequently taught, and energetically interpreted from a broad spectrum of points of view. At its center, however, it is a tale about two men, a lawyer who employed Bartleby in his office and who now narrates and Bartleby, who sought work copying legal papers but who quickly lost interest in everything and spent his days quietly looking out a window at a brick wall. Some interpretations focus on an explanation for Bartleby's strange withdrawal from ordinary life, finding him either mentally ill or philosophically profound, having encountered the infinite emptiness of the universe. The counter view regards the narrator, a lawyer who is either an insensitive villain or a somewhat ineffectual, quiet man who was deeply changed by his encounter with his employee.

Fundamental to any intelligent reading of the story is the consideration of its basic artistic attributes. It is essentially a first-person retrospective narrative. Therefore, all of the events have taken place before the narrator speaks the first word of it. The motivation for the telling would seem to be that despite his characteristic reticence, the lawyer's encounter with Bartleby proved to be especially meaningful to him, one that deepened his capacity for compassion and made him think about life in a different way. Although he does not spell out precisely what the scrivener meant to him, it is clear from the numerous passages of soul searching that the experience was transformative. The process of telling the account would seem to be an attempt to come

The American Short Story Handbook, First Edition. James Nagel.
© 2015 James Nagel. Published 2015 by John Wiley & Sons, Ltd.

to terms with the meaning of it, of understanding clearly what happened, why, and what it means to his life and to the fundamental status of humanity.

It is clear from the beginning that the subject of Bartleby is a sensitive one for the narrator, since he begins with descriptions of himself and his office staff, delaying any mention of Bartleby until later. The narrator, a lawyer, describes himself as elderly and quiet, preferring an easy life of peace working on bonds and real estate rather than on the more robust dramas of trial law. He seems to be a man of few accomplishments since the most he can say is that he was once praised by John Jacob Astor, a millionaire who established the first trust and later made a name for himself in real estate in New York City. For his part, the lawyer has had a disappointment in that after being named Master in Chancery, an office of public archives relating to legal transactions, his position was closed, his salary terminated, leaving him in modest circumstances with a room on Wall Street in the back of the building, the cheap space with windows facing the air shaft.

Within the office there is an entertaining cast of characters described in some detail by a lawyer with apparently no family and no close emotional ties, so his staff would seem to represent the sum total of his personal inter-action with civilization. Thus he watches them closely and describes them in great detail, outlining their daily rhythms and habits, their idiosyncrasies, their predilections, with a special emphasis on how they perform in the course of a work day. The Englishman Turkey, for example, is languid in the mornings but hyper-energetic in the afternoons, when he is apt to make mistakes, drop ink on the documents, and become insolent when questioned about it. The narrator stresses several times that Turkey is his own age, roughly sixty, and they share the experience of aging, which creates a tie between them. Nippers is his counterbalance. A young, ambitious man, he is agitated in the morning and compliant in the afternoon. Rounding out the cast is Ginger Nut, a lad of twelve who runs errands for the office and brings in lunches for the men.

Into this smoothly functioning office comes Bartleby, a quiet man who works dutifully in the early term of his employment, writing methodically and initially producing an enormous body of work. The lawyer's comments on the other characters were kindly if somewhat bemused, implying under-standing without sympathy, but from almost the first moment he takes a special interest in his new copier: "His face was leanly composed; his gray eye dimly calm." Within a short period, Bartleby begins to refuse to do various tasks, saying merely "I would prefer not to." The narrator not only records this strange behavior, he begins to feel something for the man, as though the scrivener had awakened a dimension within him that had long lain dormant: "But there was something about Bartleby that not only strangely disarmed me, but in a wonderful manner touched and disconcerted me." If at first his attitude simply seems odd, perhaps a temporary reluctance for certain kinds of work, it quickly becomes evident his living habits are equally idiosyncratic. He does not go out to eat, the lawyer first discovers, and then he realizes that Bartleby does not leave the office at all, living there all day and all night, weekends included. Just when the lawyer might be expected to reject such a man and have him removed from the premises, the narrator instead asserts that he has become "reconciled" to Bartleby, impressed by his quiet and unassuming demeanor, his absolute resolve.

The important interpretive issue in this response is not so much the mysterious behavior of Bartleby but the internalization of his plight by the narrator, who is discovering something about himself that is provoked by this strange man, who seems all alone in the world. The lawyer reflects that "his poverty is great; but his solitude, how horrible!" The narrator would have sympathy for Bartleby on this score for he, himself, seems all alone in the world, without family, without mention of any friends beyond his employees. He feels a kinship with Bartleby and experiences emotions and realizations that his peaceful life had never occasioned before: "For the first time in my life a feeling of overpowering stinging melancholy seized me. Before I had never experienced aught but a not-unpleasing sadness. The bond of common humanity now drew me irresistibly to gloom. A fraternal melancholy! For both I and Bartleby were sons of Adam." Apparently the narrator had never felt part of the human community before, never reflected on his lonely life, the lack of depth in his relationships, his resistance to any sort of empathy with those around him.

Those deepening realizations gradually take on less pleasant dimensions as he internalizes Bartleby's situation, finding fear and repulsion beneath his initial bemusement. At first he feels that the man is ill with some incurable disorder, a medical malady that explains his withdrawal from the world, but then he gives the matter a deeper assessment: "It was his soul that suffered, and his soul I could not reach." Unstated is the possibility that, for perhaps the first time, the narrator has become concerned about his own soul, his inner being, his feelings about himself, about his place in the world. Bartleby has moved him, touched him in an important way, and the lawyer's realizations about the scrivener apply to himself as well: "He seemed alone, absolutely alone in the universe. A bit of wreck in the mid Atlantic." Not all of these new feelings are welcome to the narrator, so he attempts to persuade Bartleby to leave the office, even offering him money to do so. As a last resort, the lawyer moves his office, leaving Bartleby behind as quiet and stationary as ever to haunt the new occupant, who has him removed to jail, to the famous Tombs in New York. It is there that the scrivener dies, discovered lying on the cold stones by the lawyer, who still cannot rid his thoughts of him. The narrative concludes not with Bartleby's death but with further reflection by the lawyer, who has heard a report that the copier once worked in the Dead Letter Office in the city, a repository for undeliverable mail sent to someone who had died, is hospitalized, or has suffered from some other catastrophe. The account is unverified, but the narrator reflects on its implications, that Bartleby was brought to terms with tragedy and death, just as the lawyer is now. He contemplates the inevitable, that the flow of life is to death, a universal prospect that causes the narrator to reflect "Ah Bartleby! Ah humanity!"

Bartleby is ultimately the impetus for the narrative, not the main player in it, for he undergoes little of internal struggle and changes only in the sense that he quietly withdraws into himself. It is the lawyer, the narrator, who does all the reflecting, who is impelled to new realizations and feelings by the experience with the scrivener. As is often the case with first-person, retrospective tales, he becomes the main subject of the story he is telling, the true protagonist. Even at the age of sixty, this encounter has caused him to look into his soul for the first time and to contemplate the limitless universe, the infinite time, the cold emptiness that surrounds each human life on earth. It is a frightening view of existence, and the lawyer assumes, without full justification, that Bartleby has participated in such somber philosophical ruminations. In any event, on a more immediate level, Bartleby has been in despair, and the lawyer, for all his education and professional experience, was impotent in the face of the challenge to help him. Such reflections have changed the narrator, deepened him into a more compassionate, more empathetic person, and that process is the core of one of the great stories in American literature.

Suggestions for Further Reading

Dillingham, William B. *Melville's Short Fiction 1853-1856*. Athens: University of Georgia Press, 1977.

Emery, Allan. "The Alternatives of Melville's 'Bartleby'." *Nineteenth-Century Fiction* 31 (1976): 170–87.

Hardwick, Elizabeth. *"Bartleby in Manhattan" and Other Essays*. New York: Random House, 1983.

McCall, Dan. *The Silence of Bartleby*. Ithaca: Cornell University Press, 1989.

Parker, Hershel. "The Sequel in 'Bartleby'." *Bartleby the Inscrutable: A Collection of Commentary on Herman Melville's "Bartleby the Scrivener*. Ed. M. Thomas Inge. Hamden: Archon Books, 1979, pp. 159–65.

Pribeck, Thomas. "An Assumption of Naiveté: The Tone of Melville's Lawyer." *Arizona Quarterly* 41 (1955): 131–42.

Silver, Allan. "The Law and the Scrivener." *Partisan Review* 48 (1981): 409–22.

Vincent, Howard P, ed. *Melville Annual 1965: A Symposium: "Bartleby the Scrivener'."* Kent: Kent State University Press, 1966.

Frances Ellen Watkins Harper, "The Two Offers"

Frances Harper's first story, "The Two Offers," is celebrated as the earliest piece of short fiction by an African American. Published in *The Anglo-African Magazine* in 1859, it was hailed as a masterpiece by the temperance movement, which she strongly supported, and the related issues of gender equality and the need for an even partnership in marriage gave her fiction a reformist edge that fit well into the issues of her life. These causes, along with the abolition of slavery, constituted the center of her existence, and for two years she toured the United States lecturing for the Maine Antislavery Society. Especially interested in the rights of women, she was the speaker before the World Congress of Representative Women at the Columbia Exposition in Chicago in 1893, an occasion in which she advocated universal suffrage for all Americans. Her early story "The Two Offers" helped to establish her reputation as an artistic reformer, and it has been admired for its style and themes of courtship, marriage, and family life. Equally remarkable is the fact that it is without racial markers, and the ethnic identity of the two main characters is unknown, giving the conflicts a universal application.

Despite the fact that ethnic and gender equality were thought to be progressive issues at the time, the aesthetics of her story reach back into the eighteenth century and the early formation of short fiction, when authors had difficulty in integrating dialogue, action, and exposition. The first section is entirely dialogue, a conversation between Janette Alston, an older, unmarried woman, and Laura Lagrange, a young woman being courted by two eager suitors. Laura remarks that she cannot decide which of the two offers to accept, and Janette replies that she should refuse both. Her logic is

The American Short Story Handbook, First Edition. James Nagel.
© 2015 James Nagel. Published 2015 by John Wiley & Sons, Ltd.

that a marriage should be "an affinity of souls or a union of hearts" and not a matter of bargain or "selfish interest." Laura is frightened by the prospect of becoming an "old maid" who is lonely, but Janette counters that nothing is as bad as a "loveless home," one with a "deficiency of love" and passion. The first section ends where it began, with Laura's indecision.

The rest of the story makes an abrupt artistic shift in that it is entirely exposition with no further dialogue and no action in the present. The narrator intrudes in first person to say "before I proceed with my story, let me give you a slight history of the speakers." It turns out that the two women are cousins but on different economic levels. Laura has wealthy and indulgent parents while Janette's father died leaving his financial affairs in an "embarrassed state," and her mother was left homeless, in poverty, and died soon after. Janette worked hard and established herself in the literary community. Hidden from her cousin is the fact that, earlier in her life, she had a passionate romance with a gentleman who proved untrue to her. They separated, and then he died, leaving her longing for love and trying to forget her "mournful past." At this juncture, the narrator jumps over a ten-year span, and despite her disappointment, Janette has developed a "spiritual beauty" reflecting the fact that "her inner life had grown beautiful" allowing her to bring peace to younger women on their deathbeds.

The narrator then shifts to account for what has happened to Laura over the intervening decade. She accepted one of her two offers and married a man who became an "absent and recreant husband" who regarded her not as his soul mate but as his property. Despite a brief period of happiness, "their souls never met," and Laura suffered through an unhappy marriage. He began gambling, drinking, and enjoying the "pleasures of sin," with little regard for home life. They had a child who died, despite her all-encompassing love, and in due course, suffering from a broken heart and the neglect of her husband, Laura died as well.

Janette lived through all of this with empathy and compassion, and her writing deepened and became more meaningful. She devoted herself to the major social causes, including abolition, temperance, and equal rights for women. In her exemplary kindness and concern for others, she earned a respected place in society, where children spoke her name with affection, the poor saw her as an angel of mercy, and the hungry were fed at her hands. She did not have the pleasures of a loving family, to be sure, and she was indeed an old maid, but she had learned the most precious of life's lessons, the regulation of desire and the cultivation of the full development of her inner nature. Thus Janette, the old maid Laura had feared to become, emerges at the end as the person who has lived most fully and contributed the most to the happiness of those around her.

It is a didactic conclusion, stated directly by the narrator in the fashion of the early stories of the 1780s, but it was also timely in a period in which there were few options for women apart from the traditional role of wife and mother. Despite its rudimentary artistic method, the story deals with many of the salient issues of 1859: the abolition of slavery, which was soon to become the central issue in a massive Civil War; the temperance movement, which resulted in the era of prohibition in the 1920s; political enfranchisement for women, which came with the right to vote in 1919; and the evolution of the concept of marriage from one of chattel ownership and domination to one of a more equal partnership. Frances Harper's "The Two Offers" is thus important in literary history not only because it is the first known story by an African American but because it demonstrates how short fiction can play an important role in presenting salient moral and political issues and lead the way to the transformation of society. Furthermore, because the magazine that published the story, *The Anglo-African Magazine,* was distributed almost exclusively within the black community, it meant that people of color were deeply engaged in the foremost social issues of the day, not a separate segment of the population remote from cultural change and progressive growth. What is even more remarkable, however, is that despite the readership of the magazine and the ethnic identity of the author, nowhere in any part of the narrative is there any mention of race.

Suggestions for Further Reading

Bruce, Dickson D, Jr. *Black American Writing from the Nadir: The Evolution of a Literary Tradition, 1877-1915.* Baton Rouge: Louisiana State University Press, 1989.

Gates, Henry Lewis, Jr. *The Signifying Monkey: A Theory of Afro-American Literary Criticism.* New York: Oxford University Press, 1988.

Harper, Frances Ellen Watkins. "The Two Offers." *The Anglo-African Magazine,* 1 (September, 1859): 288–91; 1 (October, 1859): 311–13.

Rosenthal, Debra J. "Deracialized Discourse: Temperance and Racial Ambiguity in Harper's 'The Two Offers' and 'Sowing and Reaping'." *The Serpent in the Cup: Temperance in American Literature.* Amherst: University of Massachusetts Press, 1997, pp. 153–64.

Scheick, William J. "Strategic Ellipses in Harper's 'The Two Offers'." *Southern Literary Journal* 23.2 (1991): 14–18.

Stancliff, Michael. *Frances Ellen Watkins Harper: African American Reform Rhetoric and the Rise of a Modern Nation State.* New York: Routledge, 2011.

Hamlin Garland, "Under the Lion's Paw"

When "Under the Lion's Paw" first appeared in *Harper's Weekly* in 1889, it was hailed by the burgeoning Populist Movement as a dramatic demonstration of the economic injustice faced by Midwestern farmers in their quest to establish a life for themselves and their families. Inspired in part by Henry George's popular *Progress and Poverty* in 1879, there was growing support for the idea of a "single tax" on land to end speculation and unfair rental agreements that placed tenant farmers at the mercy of predatory landlords and money lenders. The story next appeared in *Main-Travelled Roads* in 1891, and a year later Garland read it at the national convention of the People's Party to a rousing reception, making him a spokesman for the reforms advocated by the Populist movement. It also became a signal work in the growing Naturalistic movement in American literature, which presented either a protest against the intractable and unassailable tragedies wrought by natural disasters or a call for reform of unfair laws and social programs capable of revision. This story featured both elements in a complex artistic structure often ignored by readers obsessed with only the most obvious themes of injustice.

"Under the Lion's Paw" is structured in four sections, each with a distinct set of issues, all of which come together in the shocking conclusion. The first part opens not with the protagonist, Tim Haskins, but with Stephen Council at work on his Iowa farm in the fall, struggling with horses and a single-blade plow to turn the stubble field before the winter snows cover the land. Although he has had to work hard to establish his farm, he has succeeded, raised a healthy family, and established a modest prosperity.

The American Short Story Handbook, First Edition. James Nagel.
© 2015 James Nagel. Published 2015 by John Wiley & Sons, Ltd.

He works from early morning to dark, and his mantra is clearly that "it's purty tuff, but got a be did." When Haskins arrives with his family, desperate for a place to sleep for the night, and seeking some kind of opportunity to support his family, Council and his wife invite them in, guided by the social ethic of the rural Midwest.

Generous with their humble home, the Councils take them in and care for them. Haskins reveals that they were driven off their farm in Kansas by grasshoppers and that they came across much unworked land on their way north, indicating that property was owned by land speculators who had purchased it not for farming but to realize a profit when land values increased, the precise object of populist protest in the 1890s. The issue of grasshoppers is good Naturalistic fare, although there is nothing to be done about them except to lament the destruction. Political action, however, could limit the profit from speculation, although the populist program was never fully implemented. Not common in Naturalism, however, is the kindness and generosity of the Councils, who offer to allow the Haskins' family to live with them and to help them get a new start in life. The first section ends with Haskins' comment that "there are people in this world who are good enough to be angels." Although there is a background of misfortune in Kansas, the present action is presented as imbued with the profound generosity and goodness of spirit common on the farms and in the small towns across the upper Midwest. People with little are willing to share much, the tradition was, and Garland grew up in the midst of this social ethic.

The second part introduces Jim Butler, the antagonist, an embodiment of the greed and heartless exploitation that seems so out of place in the same social context as the opening of the story. Once a hard-working farmer himself, Butler made an enormous profit on the sale of some property and became an entrepreneur owning twenty farms that he rented out or sold at usurious rates of interest. One of the farms was worked by a man named Higley, who was never able to pay off the mortgage, and the property reverted back to Butler. In a negotiation presided over by Council, Haskins is able to rent the farm with an option to buy, although the sales price is never firmly established. Council provides him with seed and cattle, and the Haskins live with his family for the winter. When he complains that this generosity is too much, and that Council will be compensated for all of it in the future, Council says "don't want any pay. My religion ain't run on such business principles," revealing the secular philosophy of the age, when religion was treated with suspicion. Thus the second section emphasizes humane generosity, selfless good will, and a profound sense of human community, values virtually unknown in most Naturalistic fiction. However, the stage is set for a dramatic shift of attitudes.

Section three is also a positive narrative, although Haskins works desperately hard to establish his new farm, and all the members of the family, even the children, contribute to the success of their efforts. They work the land, improve the house, fix the fences and out-buildings, and greatly increase the value of the property. As the omniscient narrator emphasizes, "no slave in the Roman galleys could have toiled so frightfully and lived, for this man thought himself a free man, and that he was working for his wife and babes." As is standard in Naturalism, the ideas are dramatized but also presented in exposition. Realism functioned with implication; Naturalism tended to work with direct statement of the central themes.

The kindness shown the Haskins family in the first three parts leaves them vulnerable in the fourth, for they have come to expect fair dealings and honesty in business ventures from the people in the area. However, when Butler returns from a year in the East, where his wife's brother is a member of Congress, Haskins approaches him with an offer to buy the farm. Butler agrees but at twice the original price, elevating the value on the basis of the improvements Haskins has himself instituted. Butler explains his position by saying that "it's the law. The reg'lar thing. Everybody does it." Outraged, Haskins feels "under the lion's paw," being cheated out of the value of the hard work his family has done, and he grabs a hayfork with the intention of killing Butler on the spot. Just then, Haskin's daughter appears, and he realizes his responsibilities do not allow him this means of retribution. He must allow himself to be exploited, he knows, and the story ends with him "seated dumbly on the sunny pile of sheaves, his head sunk into his hands."

This conclusion had an enormous impact on readers in the 1890s, when poverty was widespread and mortgage rates and interest payments could be easily manipulated, and the story has been regularly anthologized and studied ever since its publication. As an example of the Naturalistic mode in fiction, it has been examined primarily for its social impact rather than for its artistry, for the movement used literature for economic reform rather than for aesthetic pleasure. In this sense, it played a role in bringing about new governmental regulations on the rental and sale of farm land, and these political reactions to a short story demonstrated the impact fiction can have on a society, a principal objective of the movement.

Suggestions for Further Reading

Garland, Hamlin. *Main-Travelled Roads*. Boston: Arena, 1991.

Hazard, Lucy L. *The Frontier in American Literature*. New York: Crowell, 1927, pp. 261–68.

Holloway, Jean. *Hamlin Garland: A Biography*. Austin: University of Texas Press, 1960.

McCullough, Joseph. *Hamlin Garland*. Boston: Twayne, 1978.
Nagel, James, ed. *Critical Essays on Hamlin Garland*. Boston: G. K. Hall, 1982.
Newlin, Keith. *Hamlin Garland: A Life*. Lincoln: University of Nebraska Press, 2008.
Pizer, Donald. *Hamlin Garland's Early Work and Career*. Berkeley: University of California Press, 1960.

Charlotte Perkins Gilman, "The Yellow Wallpaper"

Ever since January of 1892, when *The New England Magazine* first published Charlotte Perkins Gilman's "The Yellow Wallpaper," it has been one of the most controversial stories in American literature. Reprinted more than twenty times even before its "discovery" and publication by the Feminist Press in 1973, it has been widely hailed as an example of the new Psychological Realism that developed toward the end of the nineteenth century. According to the author's account, it grew out of her personal experience of being treated for chronic depression with a form of rest cure, a strategy developed by Dr. S. Weir Mitchell, one of the most famous physicians of the time. Restricted from work or intellectual stimulation, Gilman's condition grew steadily worse, verging on suicide, the manner in which her life eventually ended. Five years later, as she recalls in her autobiography, *The Living of Charlotte Perkins Gilman,* she wrote the story as a objection against this treatment, which led to her nervous breakdown. Throughout the twentieth century, however, the story has been seen not only as a commentary on Mitchell's treatment for emotional pathology but as a broader protest against a patriarchal society that limited the role of women in education, in the political life of the nation, and in social and economic opportunities. In this context, it has become one of the most famous short stories ever published.

In formal terms, it is a masterpiece of fictional artistry based on a dramatically important subject, especially so if the narrator's treatment for emotional pathology is interpreted as a metaphor for the lack of opportunity for

The American Short Story Handbook, First Edition. James Nagel.
© 2015 James Nagel. Published 2015 by John Wiley & Sons, Ltd.

women and their desire for full equality. This theme dominates the narrative throughout, and it has had an enormous impact on the discussion of gender roles in American life. The story also deserves to be appreciated for its aesthetic integrity, however, for it is a model of the discipline and economy in the fictional mode that Edgar Allan Poe advocated half a century earlier. For example, the narrative method, first person, permits the protagonist to reveal a great deal about herself indirectly as she presents her innermost thoughts and feelings. The setting in an old familial mansion provides a Gothic atmosphere that is mysterious and foreboding, underscoring the narrator's progressive paranoia and her projection of herself into the wallpaper that lines the bedroom she shares with her husband. The imagery emphasizes her projection of pathological states into the wallpaper, where she sees threatening and aberrant scenes, all generated within her own mind. Even the structure is congruent with these ideas as it moves toward a progressive fragmentation of scenes, mirroring her rapidly fluctuating and segmented units of consciousness. The overarching theme lends further coherence to the story by demonstrating the pernicious effects of the medical approach of restricting stimulation and intellectual expression, and the narrator's mental health steadily deteriorates, resulting in the startling and deeply disturbing conclusion. All of these artistic dimensions work smoothly together to create the dramatic effect of the rapidly worsening mind of an intelligent woman suffering from post-partum depression exacerbated by the inappropriate treatment she is receiving.

This palliative strategy was devised by Mitchell for the treatment of not women but the thousands of men who suffered post-traumatic stress syndrome in the Civil War, and its efficacy was celebrated throughout the medical world. In the United States, Mitchell used it for women suffering from depression following childbirth, an emotional pathology caused by rapid hormonal changes, and his approach of creating a healthy body through diet and exercise as a precursor to solving the emotional problems through rest won him the gratitude of hundreds of his patients who had quickly recovered, probably because of restored chemical balance. His book *Diseases of the Nervous System, Especially of Women* had appeared in 1881 and quickly became influential. But his method did not work in all cases, and it quite probably worsened the condition of some of his patients. The narrator's husband, also a physician, is apparently an admirer of Mitchell's treatment, as is her brother, also a medical doctor, and they have been roundly castigated in criticism as patriarchal figures who control her and exacerbate her emotional state, and there is justice in this judgment. But it also seems true that they both love her and wish for her recovery, and this approach is the best one within their frame of reference, although the empirical evidence directly in front of them, her deterioration, would seem to suggest some major alterations are in order.

From the opening of the story onward, however, it is evident that the narrator is deeply disturbed. Although thousands of people rent houses along the Maine coast every summer, and John has chosen a large colonial mansion for the two of them, their child, a nurse, and a servant. The size makes it convenient to entertain frequent visits from relatives and guests. Nevertheless, the narrator finds the house "queer," although it is she, herself, who is unusual. The house has been taken for three months for two reasons: the first is so that she might rest and recover from her depression; the second is that their home in the city is being renovated, perhaps to make it more suitable for a child, and it will take all summer to complete the renovations. Self centered, she thinks of the accommodations only in terms of her emotional needs. Her secret passion is her writing, and she records her thoughts surreptitiously since she is forbidden any other means of expression. Her record is valuable for it establishes the context for all that follows. For example, she reveals that her husband is a physician, a rational and calculating man who is suspicious of faith and superstition, and her brother seems to share the same personal qualities. The narrator's assessment of herself is instructive: she knows she is ill but she believes that "congenial work" would be helpful. She is not totally deprived of stimulation, however, because she mentions the "journeys, and air, and exercise" that are part of her treatment. She also longs for more "society and stimulus," something hard to find in a quiet New England village.

There are two things about her room that are often misinterpreted and need correction. The first is that she is not alone in it at night. John shares the room with her, taking one of the "two beds," and she says that he is "very careful and loving." Nor is she locked in the room, despite the bars on the windows. She, in fact, has the only key to the room, and she throws the key out the window in the conclusion. The room, previously a nursery, is on the top floor, and the bars would have been to prevent children from falling out the window during their play; the implements of their games are still evident. Thematically, however, that she is housed in a nursery is important: the narrator has been infantilized by her treatment just as, metaphorically, women have been treated like children in a society that does not allow them full participation. It should be remembered that this story was published more than two decades before women were granted the right to vote.

Her final obsession is with the wallpaper, a matter at the center of the second section. This part clarifies that the narrator knows she is suffering from depression and that part of the treatment is a three-month relaxation at the Maine coast. A nurse cares for the baby, and the narrator seems to have little to do with the child. Her husband seems both loving and demonstrative if somewhat condescending: "He took me in his arms and called me a blessed little goose . . . ." The problem is that in his repression of her writing and intellectual interests, he worsens the very condition he is attempting to cure. She complains that she could get better if only she could write a little, even though she is writing, continually, producing the story itself. The wallpaper about her seems to function as a Rorschach test in that it is indeterminate and varied enough to allow the projection of the viewer's own preoccupations upon it. What she sees indicates the status of her mental health. As a metaphor, the wallpaper has come to take on a spectrum of possible meanings for various scholars, from an expression of her being trapped in an unwanted marriage, to being used as a sexual object, to being socially restricted, to being forced to assume the role of mother. But in all of these approaches, it is clear that early in the story she sees imposing eyes in the wall, eyes that crawl up and down: "There is a recurrent spot where the pattern lolls like a broken neck and two bulbous eyes stare at you upside down." The aberrant issues are clearly an internal mental disorder and not a problem with the house, the room, or even the wallpaper. At this juncture John's sister arrives to assist in taking care of her and the house, and soon other relatives arrive to celebrate the Fourth of July, which must have provided some stimulation for the narrator.

Their departure leaves an opportunity for quiet reflection by the narrator, and what she reveals about her emotional state is not positive: "I cry at nothing, and cry most of the time." This is the section in which John has suggested sending her to Dr. Mitchell for treatment, which never actually happens, a point often missed: she is never treated by S. Weir Mitchell, the physician who cared for Gilman. Her deepening obsession with the wallpaper, which John does not understand, underscores her decline, as does the fact that she now sees grotesque figures in its design. In the fourth section, she first sees a woman in the wallpaper, an obvious projection of herself in an entrapped state. Soon she sees a "woman stooping down and creeping about behind that pattern," and she wishes John would take her away. In line with Mitchell's prescribed treatment of the body as well as the mind, John is encouraged that her color is better and she is gaining weight. She later observes that "I really do eat better" and that in some physical ways she feels better. When he falls asleep that night, however, she lays awake for hours staring at the wallpaper.

A new sensory element is introduced when she begins to smell the yellow color of the wallpaper, a synesthetic suggestion that has been interpreted in many ways. Yellow was a color often associated with pathology at the time, and the yellow fever and various causes of jaundice underscored the association of the color with disease. Some readers have suggested that the smell relates in various ways to urine or menstruation and her role as a woman, a correlation perhaps too specific for the evidence at hand. Whatever the associations, they add a negative dimension to an already disastrous mental condition.

The tenth section of the story presents a further permutation of the identification of the narrator with the woman she sees creeping in the wallpaper. Now, she is aware that it is she who crawls about the room, something she must do during the daytime because John is still sharing the room with her at night: the narrator reflects "I wish he would take another room!" The next section confirms that he, too, has been sleeping under this wallpaper for nearly three months, but he is growing increasingly concerned about her condition. The narrator overhears John asking the nurse about her mental state. The last section reveals that he had just cause for apprehension, but he is away on business for the night. Without his presence, she is free to pursue the figure in the wall, which occupies her entire night, and she says the figure in the wall has been chewing on the bedstead. What is evident is that it is she who has been knawing the headboard; she is unaware of her own actions and projects them onto the imagined woman in the wallpaper so that she will not have to acknowledge them. The sentences she offers have grown shorter and more abrupt, paralleling her mental processes as she becomes more desperate. Significantly, she records that she has locked the door (it has been open all summer) and thrown the key out the window onto the front lawn. She continues to rip away at the wallpaper and bite the headboard, and her projections onto the wallpaper are now even more pathological: "All those strangled heads and bulbous eyes and waddling fungus growths just shriek with derision!" She creeps continuously, obsessively, and when John returns he is startled by her appearance, and he faints. This event is one of the least convincing in the story. Physicians, who are trained to treat severely injured, even dismembered, patients in times of emergency, do not faint at the sight of a creeping woman, even one they love. But she records that he is rendered unconscious, and that she had to creep over him at each circle around the room. It is the fruition of nearly total deterioration of mental health, and it is a clearly insane woman who completes the narration of the story, another bit of poetic license. It would seem unlikely that her condition would allow any form of coherent narration, least of all a beautifully written, carefully structured, and fully coherent short story.

When William Dean Howells reprinted the story in 1920 in *The Great Modern Short Stories: An Anthology*, he commented that "The Yellow Wallpaper" was "too terribly good to be printed," a comment that has been oft quoted. The narrative does offer a harrowing portrait of an insane woman, whatever the cause, and it suggests throughout that the narrator's pathology is to some extent iatrogenic, caused by the medical treatment she is receiving. That point is precisely what Gilman said she was intending to do, and it is a theme of sufficient substance to carry a major work of fiction in an age inclined toward psychological Realism. That the plot affords broader, socially pertinent interpretations testifies to the richness of the artistry of the narration, for the only data available is what she records in her clandestine episodes of writing. Collectively, however, the many conflicting readings of the story indicate the seriousness with which "The Yellow Wallpaper" has been regarded for more than a century, and its consummate artistry is beginning to be equally as well respected. Very few American stories have received so much earnest attention or rewarded it so richly.

Suggestions for Further Reading

Blackie, Michael. "Reading the Rest Cure." *Arizona Quarterly* 60.2 (2004): 57–85.

Gilbert, Sandra, and Susan Gubar. *The Madwoman in the Attic: The Woman Writer and the Nineteenth-Century Literary Imagination*. New Haven: Yale University Press, 1979.

Gilman, Charlotte Perkins. *The Living of Charlotte Perkins Gilman: An Autobiography*. New York: D. Appleton-Century Co., 1935.

Gilman, Charlotte Perkins. "The Yellow Wallpaper." *The New England Magazine*, 11 (January, 1892): 647–56.

Golden, Catherine. "The Writing of 'The Yellow Wallpaper': A Double Palimpsest." *Studies in American Fiction* 17 (1989): 193–201.

Hedges, Elaine R. "'Out at Last'? 'The Yellow Wallpaper' after Two Decades of Feminist Criticism." *Critical Essays on Charlotte Perkins Gilman*. Ed. Joanne B Karpinski. Boston: G. K. Hall, 1992, pp. 222–33.

Hume, Beverly A. "Managing Madness in Gilman's 'The Yellow Wall-Paper'." *Studies in American Fiction* 30 (2002): 3–20.

St. John, Shawn. "An Updated Publication History of 'The Yellow Wall-Paper." *Studies in Short Fiction* 34.2 (1997): 237–41.

Shumaker, Conrad. "'Too Terribly Good to be Printed': Charlotte Gilman's 'The Yellow Wallpaper'." *American Literature* 57 (1985): 588–99.

Henry James, "The Real Thing"

Henry James's famous "The Real Thing" was first published in a variety of newspapers in England and the United States in 1892 before appearing in *The Real Thing and Other Stories* the following year. It was heralded almost from the beginning as a signal work of Realism exploring the nexus between what is "actual" in the material world and what is a convincing portrait of human experience in art. Although scholars eventually enlarged the range of issues in the narrative, this theme alone was enough to draw attention to the story, and it became widely celebrated in Britain and in the United States. Although the ideas are complex, the plot is simple: two English aristocrats walk into the studio of a London artist looking for work as models. They have lost their fortune and, totally unskilled for any sort of useful labor, they are hoping they could pose for characters in illustrations for books and magazines. The artist, who narrates in retrospect, misunderstands their purpose, assuming that such well-positioned people would want to engage him to do a portrait. He is shocked, and touched, as they explain their reduced circumstances, their humiliation, and, although he does not truly need them as models, he engages them for a time. They prove to be stiff and unsuitable for assuming a variety of characters, unlike two of the artist's models who come from the lower class: Miss Churm and Oronte, an Italian immigrant who speaks little English. As these two, originally hired as servants, assume more of the modeling duties, Major Monarch and his wife take on the humble tasks of serving tea and cleaning the studio, a situation that moves the artist a great deal. When he uses them for models, the caricatures are stiff and unsuitable for publication, and he is forced to dismiss them. At the end he looks back on the experience as having had great value for him, even though it damaged him professionally.

The American Short Story Handbook, First Edition. James Nagel.
© 2015 James Nagel. Published 2015 by John Wiley & Sons, Ltd.

A simple summary of the plot does not do justice to the full complexity and richness of the story, however, for it develops not only the central theme of the concept of "reality" in the corporeal sense as opposed to what is convincing in art but also what is real socially and morally. The memory of the experience is presented by the artist in four units of experience, beginning with the arrival of the Monarchs at the studio. The narrator observes them closely, assuming them to be aristocratic clients rather than people looking for employment. Major Monarch is a true gentleman from every appearance, "very high and straight," and his wife is similarly tall and erect, and both are well dressed, exuding a sense of "prosperous thrift." They explain that the major has left the army, that they have lost their money, and they have failed to find any form of employment. They have no skills beyond their "preponderantly social" advantages that are so immediately evident, and they have aged, giving the major an air of stiff nobility and his wife the appearance of faded beauty. At the end of the first part, what is established is that "the real thing" is a social concept, and the Monarchs are genuine representatives of the upper crust of London society lost in a changing world that now regards inherited positions of respect an anachronistic concept. But the artist finds them interesting and, in the next section, engages them on a trial basis to pose for some illustrations.

The narrator, a working artist, is no aristocrat, but he is sufficiently mobile in the city to know and understand the upper class and the Monarchs' feelings, the negotiations with a personal tailor, for example, the declining value of landed income, and the sensitivity of being discovered having to "do" something for money. Although not one of their peers, the narrator likes them, sympathizes with them, and although he already has enough models, he attempts to use them for the illustrations of the aristocrats in *Rutland Ramsey*. In contrast, the artist employs a cockney servant, Miss Churm, who is also able to model, to assume almost any personality in a pose. Major Monarch observes her dressed as a Russian Princess, and he disdains the image, asking the artist if he thinks she looks the part. He replies "when I make her, yes," meaning that for art, she can be transformed into a suitable image. Monarch sees things in a social realm, the artist in aesthetic terms.

In the third section, what matters is aesthetic "reality," and the Monarchs are no good whatever when transformed into art. They are genuine gentility, a social class above that enjoyed by the artist, and he is sensitive to the indications that Mrs. Monarch wishes to maintain the distinctions of their rank: "She was alive to the propriety of keeping our relations markedly professional—not letting them slide into sociability." In their relations with the narrator, their demeanor suggests that although they have been "employed" by the artist, they have not been "cultivated," made into friends and accepted as equals. But their rank also works to their disadvantage in that, as models, they are "the real thing, but always the same thing," with no capacity for adaptability. Miss Churm, being, in a social sense, nothing, can be anything in art, and a young Italian man, Oronte, a lower-class immigrant, exudes the same capacity: "The fellow's a bankrupt orange-monger, but he's a treasure." So it is, within the special world of an artist's studio, that the lower-class characters are valuable and the aristocratic ones practically worthless. In the third section, "the real thing" is artistic, not social, and it leads to a concluding part that adds yet another dimension to the theme.

The final section adds a new character, Jack Hawley, a somewhat unskilled painter himself who is nonetheless a source of good counsel and candid assessments. He says directly that as models the Monarchs are "stupid" and inappropriate, "all convention and patent-leather," and he is also critical of what he regards as an antiquated social system of inherited nobility and rigid levels of caste. His most important observation, however, is that the Monarchs have proven detrimental to the quality of the artist's work, compromising his reputation. The artist is sensitive to the truth of this assessment, but he is intrigued by the complexity of the drama being played out in his own house. As Miss Churm and Oronte assume more of the modeling duties, the Monarchs begin taking on rather menial tasks, serving tea, tidying the room, and washing dishes. The full psychological weight of this social transformation is not lost on the narrator: "When it came over me, the latent eloquence of what they were doing, I confess that my drawing was blurred for a moment—the picture swam. They had accepted their failure, but they couldn't accept their fate." This empathy, which brings tears to the artist's eyes, evokes emotions that are impossible to endure: "It was dreadful to see them emptying my slops." He gives them money to go away, and he never sees them again, but even after a good deal of time has passed, he still treasures the memory.

All of this is typical fare for James's fiction. There is no dramatic action, no direct confrontation, no conflicts between characters that need to be resolved on the dueling ground. The struggle is entirely internal, within the emotions and sensitivity of the narrator, one of the major themes within the growing movement of American Realism. Internal growth and moral transformation had been at the center of Mark Twain's *Adventures of Huckleberry Finn* and William Dean Howells's *The Rise of Silas Lapham*, for example, both published in the decade before "The Real Thing," but James lent the idea an elegant style and a refined emotional sensitivity unmatched in the work of any other writer of the period. In this story he is able to develop multiple thematic dimensions within a rather simple plot, as the artist reviews the social, aesthetic, and moral implications of the experience and the ways in which they transformed him as a human being. Psychological growth is a hallmark of the protagonist in literature, and this process makes the artist into the most important character, not the static and intractable Monarchs, who occasion transformation but do not experience it. It has taken nearly a century for readers to perceive the richness of the story, the subtlety of its motifs, and the artistic skill of one of the finest writers of fiction in the nineteenth century.

Suggestions for Further Reading

Hocks, Richard A. *Henry James: A Study of the Short Fiction*. Boston: Twayne, 1990.

James, Henry. "The Real Thing." *The Real Thing and Other Stories*. New York: Macmillan, 1893.

Johanningsmeier, Charles. "How Real American Readers Originally Experienced James's 'The Real Thing'." *Henry James Review* 27.1 (2006): 75–99.

Labor, Earle. "James's 'The Real Thing': Three Levels of Meaning." *College English* 23 (1962): 376–78.

Monteiro, George. "Realization in Henry James's 'The Real Thing'." *American Literary Realism* 36 (2003): 40–50.

Nordloh, David J. "First Appearances of Henry James's 'The Real Thing': The McClure Papers as a Bibliographical Source." *Papers of the Bibliographical Society of America* 78.1 (1984): 69–71.

Rawlings, Peter. "A Kodak Refraction of Henry James's 'The Real Thing'." *Journal of American Studies* 32 (1998): 447–62.

Ron, Moshe. "A Reading of 'The Real Thing'." *Yale French Studies* 58 (1979): 190–212.

Kate Chopin, "Désirée's Baby"

Kate Chopin's famous "Désirée's Baby" first appeared in *Vogue* in 1893 under the title "The Father of Désirée's Baby," which placed the emphasis on Armand Aubigny, the husband. When the story was incorporated into *Bayou Folk* a year later, it carried the current title, which conveys implications that the central conflict is within Désirée herself. Almost immediately after its first appearance, it was recognized as a brilliant artistic accomplishment with a powerful anti-racist central theme, moving it to the forefront of the important social contributions made by the Local Color movement. Indeed, in his history of the American story in 1923, Fred Lewis Pattee pronounced that Chopin was the greatest writer of short fiction ever published in the country and that she was a supreme master of the form.

The importance of the subject, the humanity of its theme, and the grace of its artistry make the story fully worthy of such commendation in both formal and ideological dimensions. However, its subtlety has sometimes inspired readers to think of it as having a surprise ending when actually the gentle progression of the plot gives ample indication of the final outcome. For example, in the opening scene Désirée's mother, Madame Valmondé, journeys from her plantation to visit her daughter and grandson. On the way, she remembers her profound joy when her husband found a young child at the gates of their property, a foundling they took in and raised as their daughter even though she was of uncertain racial background. Years later, innocent of her origin, Armand Aubigny fell in love with the beautiful young woman and married her, producing a child. Armand's parents were married in France, where his mother died before the family returned to the United States.

In the present, Madame Valmondé, looking at the baby after not having seen him for some time, proclaims, in French, the language of the household,

The American Short Story Handbook, First Edition. James Nagel.
© 2015 James Nagel. Published 2015 by John Wiley & Sons, Ltd.

"this is not the baby." She has noticed suggestions of African features in the child, but Désirée, consumed by maternal adoration, misunderstands the remark, interpreting it to refer to the weight the baby has gained. A moment later, she offers the seemingly innocent observation that the infant cries so loudly that Armand could hear the sound in La Blanche's cabin, all without exploring her husband's motivation, sexual or otherwise, for visiting the servant. La Blanche is a mulatto who has produced quadroon children, signifying that they have a white father. Meanwhile, without saying a word, "Madame Valmondé had never removed her eyes from the child." She then shifts her gaze, significantly, to the quadroon nurse, Zandrine, who has turned to gaze across the fields. It is clear that Désirée's mother is searching for confirmation of her grandson's racial identity; Zandrine clearly sees the baby every day and knows everything but is reluctant to be the one to confirm the suspicions. Madame Valmondé's next comments further clarify the parameters of her concerns: "Yes, the child has grown, has changed," she says, and then asks "what does Armand say?" Désirée innocently observes that since the birth of the baby, he has been kind to the slaves. The scene ends with an offhand remark about Armand's "dark, handsome face," one of several early indications that he is darker than Désirée, suggesting that it could be he who is of mixed blood.

The second major scene occurs some time later, when the baby is three months old and Désirée has grown uneasy at the change of mood in her household. Something is wrong in her marriage, and she has no idea what it is. Then, when one of La Blanche's boys is fanning the baby, she searches the faces of both of them and sees the resemblance. When she questions Armand about the matter, he tells her that it means she is not white and that the child is also of mixed blood. She sends a letter to her mother hoping for a refutation, but the mother knows her daughter is a foundling and instead asks her to come home to the family that loves her and to bring her child. When Armand tells Désirée he wants her to leave the house, she takes the baby from Zandrine and walks with it into the bayou, clearly committing suicide and killing the child.

The final scene drives home the central thematic point of the destructive cruelty and stupidity of racial prejudice as dramatically as any moment in American fiction. Some weeks later, with Désirée and the baby now dead, Armand is burning every household item that reminds him of them. In the process, in clearing out an old desk, he comes upon some old letters from his own parents that indicate that it was his mother who carried African heritage: "I thank the good God for having so arranged our lives that our dear Armand will never know that his mother, who adores him, belongs to the race that is cursed with the brand of slavery." He who so adamantly despised the slightest suggestion of black blood, driving his wife to her death, is shockingly revealed to be the spouse of mixed racial identity.

"Désirée's Baby" is one of only two major stories Chopin set in antebellum Louisiana, both of them portraying women characters whose lives are ruined by a cruel and deeply-seated racism, but intelligent readers of the day would have been aware of the complex cultural history in the background of the plot. Race relations in Louisiana were governed by the *Code Noir* originating in Paris in 1685 to standardize the treatment of slaves in the French colonies in the Americas. Its provisions covered nearly every aspect of the lives of slaves, free people of color, slave owners, overseers, and judges. When those regulations were imported into Louisiana in 1724, they represented a unique set of rules that required that all slave owners be Roman Catholic, that all slaves be educated in the same religion, and that all sexual contact between the races was strictly forbidden. Marriage between two people of differing racial backgrounds was therefore illegal, which explains why Armand's parents wed in France, where the *Code Noir* was not in force, and why their son is so upset when he mistakenly assumes he had been duped into an alliance with a wife of mixed race.

Another point that a contemporaneous audience would not have missed is that it is the older generation that espouses the most enlightened attitudes about race, not the younger offspring. Armand's parents obviously loved one another and married in France when it was forbidden in Louisiana. They placed personal affection beyond local laws and customs, and they seem to have assumed that their son could live out his life happily without knowing that he carried mixed blood. Désirée's parents, the Valmondés, also loved their adopted daughter whatever her racial identity, as is clear in their having taken her in not knowing of her origins. Furthermore, when the evidence suggested that Désirée is of African ancestry, her mother still invited her to come home with her baby to the people who love her. It is the younger generation, both Armand and Désirée, who place utmost importance on pure racial bloodlines, a matter carried with such vehement ferocity that Armand is content to see his wife and child die rather than have them as part of his family. On her part, she directly states that she would rather die than live as a person of color. She apparently applies the same logic to the life of her child. The story thus presents a generational shift in attitudes that somewhat reflects the historical shift that took place after the Civil War. In the post-Reconstruction era surrounding the publication of the story, race relations had become especially unpleasant, with the irony that although all of the slaves had been freed, still some previously free people of color were suffering reduced economic and social status that the old social structure had permitted. Armand and Désirée are representative of that new binary view of racial preferences, and their lives are destroyed by it.

Suggestions for Further Reading

Foster, Derek W, and Kris LeJeune. "'Stand by your man … :' Désirée Valmondé and Feminist Standpoint Theory in Kate Chopin's 'Désirée's Baby'." *Southern Studies* 8.1–2 (1997): 91–97.

Gibert, Teresa. "The Role of Implicatures in Kate Chopin's Louisiana Short Stories." *Journal of the Short Story in English* 40 (2003): 69–84.

Koloski, Bernard. *Kate Chopin: A Study of the Short Fiction*. New York: Twayne Publishers, 1996.

Lundie, Catherine. "Doubly Dispossessed: Kate Chopin's Women of Color." *Louisiana Literature* 11.1 (1994): 126–44.

Peel, Ellen. "Semiotic Subversion in 'Désirée's Baby'." *American Literature* 62.2 (1990): 223–37.

Toth, Emily. "Kate Chopin and Literary Convention: 'Désirée's Baby'." *Southern Studies* 20.2 (1981): 201–08.

Wolff, Cynthia Griffin. "Kate Chopin and the Fiction of Limits: 'Désirée's Baby'." *Southern Literary Journal* 10.2 (1978): 123–33.

Ambrose Bierce, "An Occurrence at Owl Creek Bridge"

One of the most famous stories in English, "An Occurrence at Owl Creek Bridge" has been anthologized continuously for almost a century, and it was made into an award winning motion picture. First published in the *San Francisco Examiner* in 1890, it was later included in Ambrose Bierce's *Tales of Soldiers and Civilians* and then *In the Midst of Life*. Born in Ohio, the author fought for the North in the Civil War and was severely wounded on the banks of Owl Creek at the Battle of Shiloh. After months of recovery, he was assigned as a cartographer to General William B. Hazen's army in northern Alabama, the location of the action in his story. Twenty five years later, during a time of reconciliation between the two regions, he wrote a poignant account of the execution of a Southern planter, one that has impressed readers throughout the world.

The "reality" of the plot is simple: a man is standing on a bridge with a rope around his neck, about to be hanged. After some brief military formalities, he is dropped through the trestles where he spins slightly at the end of the rope before he dies. It is not this simple action that makes the story gripping but rather its artistry, which is used to deepen the meaning of the hanging, the value of life, and, in a sense, the importance of art. Much of the skill of the rendition of the plot is in the manipulation of structure and narrative technique, matters handled by the author with consummate skill.

The story is divided into three sections, each told from a different point of view and each with a separate perspective on the events. The first part is related from an outside vantage point, as though by someone who had happened upon the scene and recorded what could be observed. It is without

The American Short Story Handbook, First Edition. James Nagel.
© 2015 James Nagel. Published 2015 by John Wiley & Sons, Ltd.

emotion, simply describing the scene of "a man" (the narrator does not know who he is) looking down into the river from a bridge. His hands are tied, and there is a rope around his neck. The Union soldiers are performing a formal ritual with a captain issuing orders and a sergeant directing two privates in their duties. On the bank, a company of infantry observes the events, and two sentinels guard each end of the bridge.

The narrator clearly has limited knowledge of the situation: he says the man about to be executed "was apparently about thirty-five years of age." He is dressed as a civilian, and the narrator guesses that he might be a planter, given his clothes. He stands on the end of a plank supported by the weight of a sergeant at the other end. The perspective then moves in to record how things are from the point of view of the nameless man about to be hanged. He looks down at the swirling water below and the slow movement, to his racing mind, of a piece of driftwood. He then hears a regular pounding in his ears, a sharp sound that, in his state of heightened sensitivity, turns out to be the ticking of his watch. He thinks about his wife and children as the sergeant steps aside, allowing him to fall through the bridge.

The second section presents a different point of view, an omniscient perspective that fills in background information to explain the activity on the bridge. The condemned man is Peyton Farquhar, a wealthy Alabama farmer who has not been involved in the war until this rather late date when the Union Army has already occupied parts of his state. He was tricked into attempting to burn the bridge by a Federal scout dressed in a Confederate uniform, a man who was seeking to expose potential saboteurs. He explains to Farquhar that there is dry driftwood at the base of the bridge, and a fire could destroy the Union Army's capacity to transport men and supplies throughout the state. This section, in its all-knowing revelations, seems utterly reliable and trustworthy, the "truth" of the situation, an assumption that sets up a rather different stratagem for the conclusion.

The concluding third part begins where the first left off, with Farquhar falling through the bridge to the end of the rope, where he loses consciousness. This section is a marvel of narrative method, mingling genuine physical sensations with fantasy so skillfully that millions of readers have been surprised at the ending. After the rope comes taut at the end of his fall, Farquhar feels a pain in his throat and the feeling of suffocation followed by "a frightful roaring" in his ears, all of which seem plausible physical experiences, especially when all turns "cold and dark." His mind continues to function for a time, however, and his desires drive his fantasy to reinterpret the data his brain receives. He interprets the dark coldness as evidence that he has fallen into the stream below, and he thinks he sees a dim light above him, probably the last imperfect image of his eyes. Then his imagination takes over with a reinterpretation of sensory data, and he fantasizes that he is swimming in the river. In his dream of life, the men who officiated at his hanging fire at him, and a shell lodges between his collar and his neck, giving him the sense of burning, which, of course, he does feel from the noose. Then he seems caught in a vortex, whirling in the water, the way he must be twisting at the end of the rope. His next fantasy allows him to see his wife and children again, as he imagines running the thirty miles home to them. Then reality sets in, replacing the free workings of his mind, and as he is about to embrace her, he feels a sharp blow on the back of his neck and a "blinding white light blazes all about him, with a sound like the shock of a cannon," and then there is nothing but "darkness and silence!" The narrator, at this point, intrudes to comment, since there are no further thoughts or sensations to report from Farquhar, and he explains that the man is dead with a broken neck, his body swaying on the rope beneath the bridge.

The fantasy during the hanging has humanized the death experience of one man in a horrific war that saw the end of hundreds of thousands of lives, but Peyton Farquhar's longing to be with his family makes his individual execution supremely important in its common simplicity. That a Union veteran, badly wounded in the conflict, wrote so poignantly about a Southern partisan represents a small part of what was a widespread effort at reconciliation and genuine regional unification. Northern magazines ran long articles on the progress of the New South, just as the federal government poured millions of dollars into assisting the rebuilding of the region. Bierce thus joined a host of other writers from the North in sympathetic portrayals of Southern life, although there is little depth to the social representations of this story. But it is ultimately the shocking realization, born of the shifting narrative method, that the protagonist's thoughts are fantasies and not genuine sensations that emphasize the tragedy of the loss of even one human life. That is the central theme that is advanced in this short narrative and, indeed, throughout *Tales of Soldiers and Civilians*.

Suggestions for Further Reading

Berkove, Lawrence I. *A Prescription for Adversity: The Moral Art of Ambrose Bierce*. Columbus: Ohio State University Press, 2002.

Davidson, Cathy N. *Critical Essays on Ambrose Bierce*. Boston: G. K. Hall, 1982.

Davidson, Cathy N. *The Experimental Fictions of Ambrose Bierce: Structuring the Ineffable*. Lincoln: University of Nebraska, 1984.

Fatout, Paul. "Ambrose Bierce, Civil War Topographer." *American Literature* 26 (1954): 391–400.

Grenander, M. E. *Ambrose Bierce*. New York: Twayne, 1971.

Logan, F. J. "The Wry Seriousness of 'Owl Creek Bridge'." *American Literary Realism* 10.Spring (1977): 101–13.

Marcus, Fred H. "Film and Fiction: 'An Occurrence at Owl Creek Bridge'." *California English Journal* 7 (1971): 14–23.

O'Brien, Matthew C. "Ambrose Bierce and the Civil War: 1865." *American Literature* 48 (1976): 377–81.

Owens, David M. *The Devil's Topographer: Ambrose Bierce and the American War Story*. Knoxville: University of Tennessee Press, 2006.

Woodruff, Stuart C. *The Short Stories of Bierce: A Study in Polarity*. Pittsburgh: University of Pittsburgh Press, 1964.

Stephen Crane, "The Blue Hotel"

One of the most discussed stories in American Literature, Stephen Crane's "The Blue Hotel" was first published in *Collier's Weekly* in 1896 before being included in *The Monster and Other Stories* in 1899. It grew out of a western trip the author took as a journalist covering the drought on the plains, and his stop in Lincoln, Nebraska, provided the impetus for this tale of a Swedish immigrant who arrives on the train only to find gambling, fighting, and death at the end of his journey. The plot of the story is complex only in that it is set in two locations, first in a hotel and then in a saloon. Three men arrive in Fort Romper on the train, a Swede, a cowboy, and an Easterner, a laconic observer of most of the events. The proprietor of the hotel, Scully, an Irish immigrant, meets the men at the station and conducts them to his establishment. As they enter the building, his son, Johnnie, is playing cards with a farmer, a game that ends in quarreling, and the Swede is frightened by the conflict. Two more card games end the same way. Then the Swede and the cowboy join the game, and it ends with the Swede saying that he would guess a good many men have been killed in this room. The Swede looks to the Easterner for understanding, but he is reluctant to say anything about the game. Scully takes the Swede upstairs and attempts to reassure him that Fort Romper is not part of the wild west any longer but a progressive, modern town that will soon have electric street cars, a factory, a school, and several churches. Scully and the Swede drink whiskey together and then return downstairs where a new card game is beginning.

The Swede, now boisterous from the liquor, joins the game, which ends suddenly when he declares that Johnnie has been cheating. Johnnie insists on a fight to save his honor, and they go outside in a snowstorm, where

The American Short Story Handbook, First Edition. James Nagel.
© 2015 James Nagel. Published 2015 by John Wiley & Sons, Ltd.

the cowboy yells for Johnnie to kill him. After a scuffle, the Swede knocks Johnnie down and the fight ends. The Swede leaves the hotel and walks to a saloon where another card game is in progress, one involving a professional gambler. The Swede attempts to bully the man into drinking with him, and in a brief struggle, the gambler stabs him and he drops dead in front of the bar. The final section takes place months later, after the gambler has been sentenced to three years in prison for the killing. The cowboy and the Easterner discuss the events, and he confesses that Johnnie was cheating, that he had seen him but was reluctant to speak out on the side of the Swede. He then reflects that many men contributed to the Swede's death and that sin is often the result of a collaboration. The cowboy protests that he did not do anything, and the story ends with this ironic comment.

These events have provided the basis for a spectrum of competing inter-pretations, ranging from the religious approach contending that humanity has been abandoned by God, to the Naturalistic view that everything was predetermined by the hostility of Nature and the paranoia of the Swede, to the Realistic emphasis on the individual responsibility borne by each of the men involved. All of these assessments, as well as the Impressionistic con-cern for the epistemological process of understanding complex events, have made contributions to the full understanding of the story, and all deserve consideration.

After the intense emphasis on religion during the era of American Roman-ticism, which stressed spirituality in nearly every dimension of life, the Real-istic movement brought a period of skepticism about supernatural matters, placing its emphasis on human behavior, morality, and the law. Religion became a subject of humorous satire, with confidence men bilking the trust-ing innocents out of their money with fake salvation, as is famously done in *Adventures of Huckleberry Finn*. In this case, it is more a sense of the deity having abandoned his creation. From this point of view, if God is defunct and no longer functions in the universe, humanity is alone in it, life has no meaning, and existence is absurd. The events of the story thus illustrate the violence and cruelty of an empty world with no controlling intelligence to give it meaning.

A Naturalistic reading would treat the action as the expression of over-whelming forces outside the control of any of the characters. Many readers who confront the story in this way see the storm as the central event in that it expresses the hostility of Nature and the fragility of human existence. Others put the emphasis on the involuntary paranoia of the Swede, who comes to the hotel shaking with fear and provokes a chain of events with his uncon-trollable trepidation. Other Naturalists regard the events more broadly, with a stress on inbred greed or anger or self-protection, but in each case, from this point of view, the responsibility is external to the will and action of individual characters.

From a Realistic perspective, human beings are capable of creating their own codes of conduct and living according to rules of decency and kindness. They understand the world; they have moral agency and can make decisions about their own course of action; they thus bear full responsibility for what they do, a theme that links the movement to the later Modernist and existential thinking of the 1920s. From this point of view, the center of the story is on individual human behavior, and each character does and says things that contribute to the chain of events that lead to the death of the Swede. The story concludes with the Easterner's long speech about how the men bear responsibility. He points out that Johnnie cheated, and he saw him do so. If Johnnie had played the game correctly, there would have been no impetus for the conflict, the fight, and the death of the Swede. Scully provided the liquor that exacerbated the situation, and he later allowed the physical violence, joining the group in opposition to the foreigner. The cowboy yelled for Johnnie to kill the Swede and helped intensify the already strident emotions. The Swede chose to speak out when he saw Johnnie cheat, was eager to fight Johnnie, and bullied the gambler when he arrived at the saloon, finally grabbing him around the neck. The gambler refused to drink with the Swede, which caused the physical action, and then actually stabbed him in the conflict. The bartender had responsibility for maintaining order in the bar, and protecting his customers, and he bears some slight guilt, although everything happened so quickly he had little time to react. But the Easterner, who knew the truth and concealed it, who was hesitant to speak on the side of the Swede when everyone else was against him, would seem to be the key character from a Realistic perspective. It is he who struggles with internal conflict and grows in his insight into his moral responsibility, and he knows at the end that he failed to do what was right. That puts him in direct contrast to the obtuse cowboy, who ends the story by saying "Well, I didn't do anythin', did I?"

These competing interpretations helped keep the story at the center of literary conversation throughout the twentieth century and into the next. It has been examined from nearly every conceivable perspective, from the biographical route of Crane's travels to Nebraska, to the location of various hotels painted blue throughout the United States, to the self-referential role that Crane plays in the action in the character of the Easterner. What all of these angles of approach confirm, however, is that the story presents a morally complex series of actions and conversations that lend themselves to rewarding reflection and ethical consideration. To some extent, the Realistic interpretation seems to have prevailed on the basis that the conclusion emphasizes precisely the point of considering the ways in which each of the men, individually, contributed to the death of the Swede.

Suggestions for Further Reading

Bergon, Frank. *Stephen Crane's Artistry*. New York: Columbia University Press, 1975.

Cady, Edwin. *Stephen Crane*. Boston: Twayne, 1980.

Crane, Stephen. "The Blue Hotel." *The Monster and Other Stories*. New York: Harper & Brothers Publishers, 1899, pp. 109–61.

Gibson, Donald. *The Fiction of Stephen Crane*. Carbondale: Southern Illinois University Press, 1968.

Kent, Thomas L. "The Problem of Knowledge in 'The Open Boat' and 'The Blue Hotel'." *American Literary Realism* 14.2 (1981): 262–68.

LaFrance, Marston. *A Reading of Stephen Crane*. Oxford: Clarendon, 1971.

Monteiro, George. "Crane's Coxcomb." *Modern Fiction Studies* 31 (1985): 295–305.

Frank Norris, "A Deal in Wheat"

A quintessential example of American Naturalism, Frank Norris's "A Deal in Wheat" was published in *Everybody's Magazine* in 1902 before being incorporated into *A Deal in Wheat and Other Stories of the New and Old West* a year later, the title of the volume testifying to the instant popularity of the story. Virtually all of its artistic methods are congruent with Naturalistic aesthetics, including the use of an omniscient narrator who offers expository comment on the events, the portrayal of lower-class characters at the mercy of wealthy speculators in commodities, and a reformist theme railing against the pernicious effects of unbridled greed. Also typical of a literary tradition so devoted to social reform in accord with a populist ideology, the author has distorted history to emphasize personalized avarice as the prime cause of the misery and hopelessness of the protagonist, Sam Lewiston. This simple farmer is shown at the complete mercy of heartless men in Chicago who manipulate the market price of wheat by driving down the price so low that Lewiston is forced to sell his farm and then raising it, as a kind of game, which eliminates the bread that destitute men so dearly need on the mean streets of the windy city. Actually, international trade agreements with Europe had much more to do with the price of wheat in this era, and bad weather on the continent caused the normal balance between supply and demand to fluctuate wildly, resulting in price vacillations in the United States. Norris personalized both the origin of the variations in wheat prices and the effects on a single individual in the process of creating this powerful Naturalistic story.

The overall plot is rather simple. Sam Lewiston is forced to sell his farm when commodities speculators in far-off Chicago drive the price down. He does not know about these manipulations and does not understand

The American Short Story Handbook, First Edition. James Nagel.
© 2015 James Nagel. Published 2015 by John Wiley & Sons, Ltd.

the market, so he cannot narrate the story in first-person, necessitating the omniscient perspective to delineate the unreachable forces that cause his personal tragedy. He moves to Chicago to find work to support his family, but the price of wheat now has been driven so high that he cannot afford bread. These events in themselves would not have been enough to account for the immense popularity of Norris at the time, but the commentary by the narrator makes explicit the true theme behind the scene of the action. All of this is presented in five narrative sections, each of which serves its own unique function.

The first section opens in Kansas with the Lewistons still living on their farm. It is late summer, harvest time, and the crisis among the farmers in the area is that wheat prices are down to sixty-six, less than it costs to grow the crop. Brother Joe has a job waiting for them in Chicago, but Sam hates to give up, lose his property, and admit defeat. He drives the buckboard into town for one last try, but now the offer is only sixty-two a bushel based on the market in Chicago. The Lewistons admit failure and decide to move to the city. The point of the opening is that none of the farmers involved, Sam's family serving as a typical case, have done anything wrong. They have worked hard, produced an abundant harvest, and dealt honestly with everyone. The cause of their troubles lies elsewhere, in remote powers beyond their knowledge or control.

Part two shifts focus to the office of Hornung in Chicago, where he has just sold one hundred thousand bushels of wheat for export to Truslow at $1.10 a bushel, not the sixty-two cents a bushel Lewiston was offered in Kansas. Hornung and Truslow are competitors attempting to control the markets, but Hornung has the upper hand since he has monopolized supply. Part three continues this dynamic by shifting to the Chicago Board of Trade, where bidders are buying and selling and making fortunes without growing anything. The supply is strangely up, and Horning, wishing to continue his monopoly of available wheat, instructs his brokers to support the market.

Part four offers yet another shift of perspective by focusing on a detective named Cyrus Ryder who, investigating the mysterious new supply of wheat, pretended to be a hobo and stole a ride on the train hauling grain to market and discovered that rather than delivering anything it simply circled the city of Chicago and came back to be counted all over again. In effect, the wheat that Truslow bought from Hornung at $1.10 is sold back to him at $1.50. Hornung takes the maneuver in good humor, laughs it off as a joke, and promptly raises the price to $2.00. These sections on the manipulations of the market are reported with journalistic objectivity and detachment, as though there were no social implications involved, no people whose lives were impacted by the changes in price.

Section five shows the consequences of the game Truslow and Hornung were playing, its effect on the poor people living in the South Side of Chicago. Every night they lined up at the bakery for free bread, the only food they would have for the day, Sam Lewiston among them. He had worked for his brother Joe in his hat factory for a time, but then the federal government repealed the tariff on the importation of manufactured felt, and Belgian and French material flooded the market with cheap prices and Joe was forced out of business. Lewiston was left with nothing but the bread line to sustain him, but even that ended when wheat hit $2.00 a bushel in Hornung's manipulation to recover the money he had lost to Truslow. The bakery could no longer afford to give away bread, and the desperate men have no where to turn. The omniscient narrator, in typical Naturalistic fashion, explains all of these twists and turns in expository passages, drawing on the unlimited knowledge the narrative perspective possesses.

The end of the story is not typical of the movement, however, in that it ends not in tragedy but in hope for the future as Lewiston finds a job cleaning the streets and sends for his wife and children to join him in Chicago. The family has a new start, but, the narrator emphasizes, Lewiston never forgot that he had been "caught once in the cogs and wheels of a great and terrible engine," the metaphor stressing the unfeeling indifference of a machine to human tragedy. The narrator goes on to a didactic passage explaining that "the farmer—he who raised the wheat—was ruined upon the one hand; the working-man—he who consumed it—was ruined upon the other." The commodities manipulators, the investors, practiced their "tricks" and "deals" but finally were "reconciled in their differences and went on through their appointed way, jovial, contented, enthroned, and unassailable." This direct commentary on the meaning of the narrative is also indicative on the Naturalistic movement, which focused not on the integrity of art but on the reform of society.

What followed this story, and the series of novels Norris wrote in his "wheat trilogy," was revised legislation and greater government control on price manipulation in the markets. In this sense, Naturalism often had a direct impact on the society for which it was produced. By pointing out the human cost of destructive programs and policies, the movement often brought about changes in law and the regulation of businesses and banks. This story also had a dramatic effect on the readers of the day, all of whom could identify with Sam Lewiston and his hopeless plight, especially so because they had all lived through the depression in America of the 1890s, when bread lines in the cities and poverty on the farms were common occurrences. No one at the time dramatized the situation of the common man better than did Frank Norris in this historic short story.

Suggestions for Further Reading

Dillingham, William B. *Frank Norris, Instinct and Art*. Lincoln: University of Nebraska Press, 1969.

French, Warren G. *Frank Norris*. New York: Twayne, 1962.

Graham, Don. *The Fiction of Frank Norris: The Aesthetic Context*. Columbia: University of Missouri Press, 1978.

Graham, Don. *Critical Essays on Frank Norris*. Boston: G. K. Hall, 1980.

Marchand, Ernest. *Frank Norris*. Stanford: Stanford University Press, 1942.

Edith Wharton, "The Other Two"

Among the most perfectly crafted short stories in American Realism, Edith Wharton's "The Other Two" is also important for addressing a salient social issue of its time, the new domestic phenomenon of divorce. Published in *Collier's Weekly* in February of 1904 before its inclusion in *The Descent of Man and Other Stories* later that year, the story focuses on the awkward situation of the third husband of a twice divorced woman coming into close social contact with the first two. In fact, the structure of the plot begins with the innocuous suggestion that the first husband, the father of young Lily, who is confined to bed with typhoid fever, has asked to visit his daughter in her home. From that minor social engagement onward, the action moves toward greater involvement of the third husband, Waythorn, with the first (Haskett) and the second (Gus Varick), who is a client of Waythorn's financial firm, each encounter exacerbating the emotional tension. The artistry further heightens the intensity by employing a third-person narrative perspective limited to the mind and activities of Waythorn, a kindly man devoted to his wife who is nevertheless sensitive to the bewildering proprieties of a progressively more complex situation.

Nearly every formal aspect of the story is exquisite. The moment of the opening section is the first night Waythorn will spend at home with his wife. They have been summoned from their honeymoon by the illness of Lily, and Alice is upstairs seeing to the needs of her daughter. The girl carries the last name of her biological father, Haskett, a constant reminder of the multiplicity of marriages at issue. The identification of the third-person narrator with the mind of Waythorn provides an intimate look into the thoughts and feelings of a sensitive man in a delicate position, although New York society, ever eager to be at the forefront of modernism, has conveyed an "air of

The American Short Story Handbook, First Edition. James Nagel.
© 2015 James Nagel. Published 2015 by John Wiley & Sons, Ltd.

sanctity" upon Alice because of her two broken marriages. The assumption in each case was that the husband was a cad and she the virtuous spouse. Waythorn is aware of the general accounts, and he has the impression that Haskett had been a rude brute of some sort and Gus Varick, still a handsome man about town, had been at fault in the dissolution of their marriage.

Sitting in his drawing room, Waythorn expects a rather harried and concerned Alice to descend the stairs, but when she comes down from Lily's room she is composed in every sense, perfectly in "balance" emotionally. It is evident that she has considerable "presence" and is not to be shaken by commonplace events. She informs him that Haskett's lawyer has written regarding visitation rights and, since the girl is ill, he will have to call at the house in order to see her. She calls the situation "tiresome," and she further reveals that he is coming tomorrow while Waythorn will be at work. He is stunned at the prospect, but she seems unbothered by it, and they prepare to have dinner.

The second section involves both of the previous husbands, Haskett for his visit and Gus Varick for a chance encounter with Waythorn on a streetcar, during which he reveals that Waythorn's partner has the gout. He was handling an important transaction for Varick, and the duty eventually falls to Waythorn. In a car crowded with men on their way to the office, the two men are forced to sit close together. The narrator suggests that Waythorn thinks Varick may simply be making conversation to lessen the strain of their "propinquity," a rich term with two applicable meanings. The first is simply "closeness," their physical intimacy on a crowded seat. But another meaning is that they have "a close family tie," something they share in a certain awkward sense. Both meanings invest the situation with discomfort. Later, at lunch, Waythorn again sees Varick dining alone, and he later observes him pouring a bit of cognac into his coffee during dessert, an act with no particular meaning in that context. When he returns home that afternoon, Waythorn is somewhat surprised to find Alice perfectly serene despite Haskett's visit. After dinner, he marvels at her equanimity, in awe of her ability to handle complex emotional matters unflustered. When she pours coffee for him, however, she adds cognac to his cup, something he does not imbibe. It is clear, however, that she had performed the ritual for Varick throughout their marriage, and Alice blushes in embarrassment.

Section III takes place ten days later and contains further uncomfortable realizations for Waythorn. The first evolves out of his business interactions with Varick, who reveals himself to be handsome and "pleasant," but it is also clear that in recent years he has struggled financially, which suggests that his marriage dissolved not out of misbehavior, as Waythorn had assumed, but simply because Varick was not wealthy enough to please his wife. The possibility that she might be an economic opportunist makes Waythorn uneasy. He has a similar feeling as he grows to know Haskett better through the weekly visits to Lily. Rather than a brute, Waythorn sees him as a "small, effaced-looking man" with the appalling taste to wear a fake tie attached with a rubber band. He is polite, loving to his daughter, deferential to his host, and there is little to dislike about him. The narrator sums up the central awareness: "A man would rather think that his wife has been brutalized by her first husband than that the process has been reversed." These new realizations intensify as the events move toward a conclusion.

The penultimate section intensifies Waythorn's uneasy feeling that things are not as his wife has portrayed them. When Haskett visits his recovering daughter, the two men have another brief conversation during which it becomes clear that Alice lied about not talking to her first husband the first time he called, a realization that, in his mind, casts a "curious light on her character." He also realizes that Haskett loves Lily deeply and has sacrificed his career to be near her in the city. At the same time, Waythorn becomes even more intimately involved in Varick's business affairs, and they see each other frequently, sometimes in social settings. At one ball during this period, Waythorn discovers his wife engaged in lively conversation with Varick, and he reflects on their relationship: "Her pliancy was beginning to sicken him." Her ready affability, even with regard to previous husbands, makes it seem to Waythorn that she was "as easy as an old shoe" and, he further reflects, "a shoe that too many feet had worn."

This realization crystalizes in the concluding section in which Waythorn compared himself to a member of a "syndicate" in domestic matters, a good term for a man of high finance, but he concludes that he owns a third of a wife who can make him happy, and he settles into an acceptance of what the narrator calls "the newest social problem." Haskett continues to call, but his unobtrusive nature causes little concern in the life of the family. When Varick appears, however, the result is that all three husbands are in the house at the same time, a circumstance that could have been profoundly awkward had Alice not relieved the tension by ordering tea for four to be served in the library: "She swept aside their embarrassment with a charming gesture of hospitality." Her easy good nature relieves the moment of its "grotesqueness" as she offers each of her husbands a cup of tea.

Suggestions for Further Reading

Beer, Janet. *Kate Chopin, Edith Wharton, and Charlotte Perkins Gilman: Studies in Short Fiction.* New York: St. Martin's, 1998.

Caws, Mary Ann. "Framing in Two Opposite Modes: Ford and Wharton." *The Comparatist Journal of the Southern Comparative Literature Association* 10 (1986): 114–20.

Fedorko, Kathy A. *Gender and the Gothic in the Fiction of Edith Wharton.* Tuscaloosa: University of Alabama Press, 1995.

Sweeney, Gerard M. "Wharton's 'The Other Two'." *Explicator* 59.2 (2001): 88–91.

Totten, Gary. "Critical Reception and Cultural Capital: Edith Wharton as a Short Story Writer." *Pedagogy* 8.1 (2008): 115–33.

White, Barbara. *Edith Wharton: A Study of the Short Stories.* New York: Twayne, 1991.

Willa Cather, "A Wagner Matinée"

Celebrated widely as the foremost writer of the American plains, Willa Cather produced a rich legacy of stories and novels dealing with the austere life of the early years on the frontier. In *O Pioneers!* and *My Ántonia*, one of the finest novels in English, she achieved international recognition for her work portraying the financial and cultural deprivations of agrarian life in the late nineteenth century. "A Wagner Matinée" offers a variation on this intriguing theme by bringing back to the cultured East a woman who has been isolated on a Nebraska farm for three decades. First published in *Everybody's Magazine* in 1904, the story was later included in two important collections: *The Troll Garden* and then *Youth and the Bright Medusa*. The stories in these volumes deal with the centrality of the arts, particularly in the lives of people who, by circumstance, have little opportunity to enjoy them. The characters in these works need cultural enrichment to fulfill their humanity, to expand the parameters of their range of emotion, to move them in the way only the arts can do, especially music. A popular subject in European philosophy and literature of the age, the value of beauty became one of Cather's prime subjects, and nowhere did she portray its vital significance more grippingly than in the portrait of Aunt Georgiana in "A Wagner Matinée," one of her finest stories.

A great deal of the richness of this story derives from its seamless development of two parallel themes: the importance of music in the life of Aunt Georgiana, back in Boston from her restricted life on the Nebraska prairies, and the growth of insight and compassion on the part of her nephew, who also serves as narrator. This is the fictional expression of the musical tradition

The American Short Story Handbook, First Edition. James Nagel.
© 2015 James Nagel. Published 2015 by John Wiley & Sons, Ltd.

of counterpoint, and Cather used a similar narrative structure for *My Ánto-nia*, in which Jim Burden looks back on his early life and presents an account of the life of a girl he grew to love, a Bohemian immigrant named Ánto-nia Shimerda. In the process, he reveals as much of himself, his growth, his inner decency, as he does of her. Cather had worked out the central aesthetic strategy for this method in the earlier "A Wagner Matinée." Indeed, there is a genuine issue of who, in fact, serves as protagonist, Aunt Georgiana or Clark, the narrator, since both of them undergo psychological transformation and growth during the course of these events.

This dual focus is evident from the very beginning, when Clark receives a letter from his uncle Howard in Nebraska informing him that Aunt Georgiana is about to arrive in Boston for the settling of the estate of a relative. The news occasions a flood of memories for Clark, reminiscences of himself as a gangling farm boy, his hands cut and bruised from the endless husking of corn. His sharp recollections place him back in that world, a stranger to the refined environment of the city around him. At the same time he reflects on the hard prairie life endured by his aunt, who had grown up in Boston devoted to music, teaching at the Boston Conservatory. After her marriage, she left the East for a homestead on the plains, and there was only a parlor organ to provide the atmosphere she so dearly loved. Clark reviews her early life in Vermont, her courtship with a younger man, their elopement, and their rustic beginnings in a dugout house fifty miles from the closest town. Even before she arrives, Clark is aware of the contrast between her cultured early life and the rough deprivations of her move to Nebraska, raising six children under the comparatively primitive conditions of homesteading.

When she steps off the train, the reality of her poverty is evident in the dust and soot that cover her entire body: she has ridden all the way from Nebraska in a day coach, there being no money to pay for a sleeper car. Her years on the plains have transformed her appearance: her skin has grown yellow from the incessant wind; her false teeth fit her badly, suggesting that she could not afford proper dental care; and she has a perpetual facial twitch that Clark attributes to a "nervous disorder" caused by her decades of monotonous isolation on the farm. These are poignant observations, and he remembers the countless hours she spent with him when he was young, reviewing his lessons, teaching him music, seeing to his cultural education. As a young woman, she had traveled in Europe, attended the opera house in Paris, thrilled at the musical world before her. Now, he can see, she has resigned herself to a stoic hardness of expression, a wall of protection against daily life.

Clark has obviously succeeded financially, partly because of the home education and encouragement his aunt accorded him back in Nebraska. He now has an office on Newbury Street in Boston, the most elite area of the city, and it is clear he has tickets to the Boston Symphony Orchestra, which performs a short walk from his office. There are several subtle touches to his memories of his aunt, including her story of seeing Meyerbeer's *Huguenots* in Paris when she was young. The plot of the libretto focuses on the forbidden love between Valentine and Raoul. She becomes Protestant so that they can be wed, and they are both killed by the Catholics in 1572 as part of the St. Bartholomew's Day massacre. The romantic intensity of the plot parallels her own prohibited relationship with the much younger Howard. Her family and friends advised against the match, but she persisted, they eloped, and now she has spent thirty years on the wind-swept plains in a society devoid of cultural refinement. Aware of this background, Clark arranges for her to accompany him to a concert at Symphony Hall, and his attention is far more to her reaction to the music than to the performance itself.

His assumption is that Aunt Georgiana has become aesthetically inert over the years, that her hard exterior betrays a similarly insensitive emotional life, but he discovers he is totally wrong. The first number is the celebrated overture from Wagner's *Tannhäuser*, which prompts her to clutch at his sleeve. Meanwhile, he is thinking about the contrast between the "tall, naked house on the prairie" set amid the "rain-gullied clay about the naked house" and the elegance of the present moment, the opulence of the building, the beauty of the music, and he is sensitive to what it must mean to her after all these years. As the orchestra moves on to numbers from *Tristan and Isolde* and *The Flying Dutchman*, tears stream from her eyes, as well as from his, and he reflects "it never dies, then, the soul?" Even more pertinent is the following "Prize Song" from *Die Meistersinger von Nürnberg* since it alludes to Arthur Schopenhauer's theories about the supreme value of music in relieving the listener of the concerns of mundane life, in making life worth living. These ideas had influenced Richard Wagner, and he infused his work with them. It is a perfect allusion for Georgiana, fresh from the austere isolation of her prairie home, and the emotional response is nearly overwhelming. She weeps throughout the second half of the program, devoted to the *Ring* cycle, and Clark remembers that the only music she has heard for years would have been the hymns at Methodist church services. At the conclusion, she bursts into tears, pleading that she does not want to return to Nebraska, but he understands that she must, that the rude, unpainted house awaits her as do the turkeys pecking at the refuse thrown from the kitchen door. She has had her moment of transcendent aesthetic pleasure, and it has awakened an emotional dimension of her being long dormant. On the other hand, he has grown in his understanding of his aunt, in his appreciation of her sacrifices on his behalf, in his compassion for her situation, her restricted life. It is a moment of dual character transformation brought by a symphony orchestra, a topic Cather returned to throughout her life in novels and stories.

Suggestions for Further Reading

Arnold, Marilyn. *Willa Cather's Short Fiction*. Athens: Ohio University Press, 1984.

Gerber, Philip. *Willa Cather*. New York: Twayne, 1995.

Meyering, Sheryl L. *A Reader's Guide to the Short Stories of Willa Cather*. New York: G. K. Hall, 1994.

Murphy, John J. *Critical Essays on Willa Cather*. Boston: G. K. Hall, 1984.

O'Brien, Sharon. *Willa Cather: The Emerging Voice*. New York: Oxford University Press, 1987.

Sister Lucy Schneider, C. S. J. "Willa Cather's Early Stories in the Light of Her 'Land Philosophy'." *Midwest Quarterly* 9 (1967): 75–93.

Wasserman, Loretta. *Willa Cather: A Study of the Short Fiction*. Boston: Twayne, 1991.

Woodress, James. *Willa Cather: A Literary Life*. Lincoln: University of Nebraska Press, 1987.

Jack London, "To Build a Fire"

A prime example of Naturalism in fiction, Jack London's "To Build a Fire" reflects the tendencies in style, narrative method, characterization, and fundamental themes of the movement. Based to some extent on London's personal experiences in the frozen North, he set this story during the gold rush days when adventurers from warmer climates flooded into mining country seeking to get rich quick, and many of them found themselves in an environment they were little able to comprehend. That is the case in this piece of short fiction first published in *Youth's Companion* in 1902 in a rather different form. The protagonist was named Tom Vincent in that version, for example, and he was thus individualized as a unique character. He also survives his ordeal of traveling alone in the stormy cold, suffering only frozen toes as a result of his bad judgment. When the story next appeared in *The Century Magazine* in 1908, it was a good deal longer, the character was no longer named, and he dies at the end of exposure, leaving his dog to wander off in search of other food givers. These changes introduced a more standard Naturalistic aesthetic: that the man has no name makes him more of a representative figure rather than an individualized human being. This movement focused more on group identity than on unique persons, and its underlying philosophical underpinning was on pessimistic Determinism, an idea that portrays characters as victims driven to tragic destinies by forces beyond their control. From this point of view, Nature is a deadly and hostile force, and life is a struggle against it for survival, a Darwinian concept that influenced London's work a good deal.

Almost every aspect of this remarkable story exemplifies the tendencies of Naturalism, illustrating the logic of its themes and the congruence of its artistic methods with these ideas. The narrative perspective is omniscient,

The American Short Story Handbook, First Edition. James Nagel.
© 2015 James Nagel. Published 2015 by John Wiley & Sons, Ltd.

for example, reaching into the history of the Yukon, the geography of the area, and the dangers of extreme cold. Typical of fiction in the movement, much of what is offered is exposition, the narrator explaining things rather portraying action and revealing the thoughts of the protagonist. The point of view is also judgmental: "He was a new-comer in the land, a *chechaquo*, and this was his first winter. The trouble with him was that he was without imagination." The opening depicts him on a trail to a mining claim on Henderson Creek, and he is unaware of the danger of fifty degrees below zero, particularly for a man traveling alone. He persists despite the warnings, and he trudges into the snow and the cold.

The only other character is the man's dog, a husky related to the wolf, a meaningful alliance because animal instinct is a central issue, and it grows stronger as creatures move backward along the evolutionary chain. There is an irony in the situation, however: The dog's "instinct told it a truer tale than was told to the man by the man's judgment." When life becomes elemental, a matter of mere survival, primitive impulses prove superior to the rational faculties of human beings: "The dog did not know anything about thermometers. Possibly in its brain there was no sharp consciousness of a condition of very cold such as was in the man's brain. But the brute had its instinct." These judgments, made possible by omniscient access to the thinking of the dog as well as the man, present one of the central conflicts: the efficacy of reasoned intellect as opposed to brute instinct.

When the dog breaks through the thin ice covering a moving stream, it quickly leaps to off to the side to find firmer footing, flops down, and begins licking and biting out the ice that had formed on its paws. It thus quickly recovers from the accident, and the danger passes. When the man similarly breaks through to the water below, he builds a fire under a spruce tree, and as the snow on the branches above begins to melt, the snow load falls down, obliterating the fire. The narrator is characteristically judgmental, making sure the thematic point is clear: "He should not have built the fire under the spruce-tree." As he attempts to relight the fire, his fingers quickly freeze, and he is unable to sustain any kind of blaze. He decides to kill the dog and warm his hands in the dead body, but the instinctive fear of death urges the animal to move away from him. The man freezes and, after he dies, the dog senses death and trots off in search of the camp, where he will get food from other men.

This story has been widely anthologized and studied because it illustrates many of the basic principles of Naturalism. The emphasis is not on artistry, certainly not on style, but on the central ideas being promoted: that life is a struggle for survival in a Darwinian sense; that human life is linked to the animal world; that the basic instincts of that realm are sometimes better than the reasoning power people possess; that Nature is a power force inimical to human existence, and it stands ready to kill anyone subject to its power. The point of view is omniscient because only the narrator understands the ways of Nature and is in a position to explain them. The protagonist is a novice in the wilderness and could hardly serve as a guide to the meaning of the events. It is a harsh picture of life, as are all of London's stories of the Yukon, but it is also a gripping and poignant narrative of the fight for survival against overwhelming odds, a struggle the Naturalists felt accurately depicted life on earth.

Suggestions for Further Reading

Labor, Earle, and Jeanne Campbell Reesman. *Jack London*. Rev. Ed. New York: Twayne, 1994.

Labor, Earle, and King Hendrichs. "Jack London's Twice-Told Tale." *Studies in Short Fiction* 4. (Summer 1967): 334–37.

McClintock, James T. *White Logic: Jack London's Short Stories*. Cedar Springs: Wolf House Books, 1976.

Raskin, Jonah, ed. *The Radical Jack London: Writings on War and Revolution*. Berkeley: University of California Press, 2008.

Reesman, Jeanne Campbell. "'Never Travel Alone': Naturalism, Jack London, and the White Silence." *American Literary Realism* 29.2 (1997): 33–49.

Reesman, Jeanne Campbell. *Jack London: A Study of the Short Fiction*. New York: Twayne, 1999.

Jean Toomer, "Blood-Burning Moon"

Jean Toomer's celebrated short story "Blood-Burning Moon" first appeared in the *Cane*, a composite volume of fiction, poetry, and drama on the theme of race relations and African-American identity. Largely on the basis of this book, along with a series of highly-regarded poems, the author has been recognized as producing the most significant literary achievement of the Harlem Renaissance, a vitally important period in the history of American literature. Despite the heavy emphasis in *Cane* on poverty in the black community, Toomer himself grew up in wealthy white neighborhoods in Washington, D.C., and moved easily in all dimensions of society. He studied at the University of Chicago, New York University, and at City College, where he was exposed to a wide range of the major European and American writers, including Sherwood Anderson, whose *Winesburg, Ohio* is a clear influence. Set in a small Midwestern town, that volume is a story cycle that revolves around a central protagonist, and his psychological growth within the "village virus" is a major issue. *Cane*, despite its variety of genres, is also unified by the continuing emphasis on race relations, identity formation, and romance.

Always a poet, even when writing fiction, Toomer is skillful in handling the formal elements of his story, which is broken into three narrative units. The first focuses on Louisa, a young woman who works in the kitchen of the white Stone family, who apparently have lived in their Georgia house for generations. The first paragraph, indicating the stylistic nature of the language throughout, is a lyrical evocation of both scene and situation, with the moon rising and illuminating the main street in a small factory town.

The American Short Story Handbook, First Edition. James Nagel.
© 2015 James Nagel. Published 2015 by John Wiley & Sons, Ltd.

The image of the moon, and the sound of her singing create the mood of the opening, one dominated by Louisa's incipient sexuality: "Her breasts, firm and up-pointed like ripe acorns." Indeed, sex is central to the love triangle at the center of the plot, for she is involved with two men: Bob Stone, the white son of her employer, and Tom Burwell, a black man who works in the cotton factory. She is erotically attracted to both of them, and issues of race are foremost in her mind: "His black balanced, and pulled against, the white of Stone." Her song fills the evening air, illuminated by the recurring image of a dominating moon. The first section ends with a poetic refrain:

> Red nigger moon. Sinner!
> Blood-burning moon. Sinner!
> Come out that fact'ry door.

The first section thus sets up the conflict, the racial dimension of it, the sexual overtones behind it, and the evening mood in which it smolders. Tom and Bob are romantic rivals, but their social status is dramatically different. Tom, apparently uneducated, is a worker on the Stone cotton fields near a poor Southern town; the descendant of wealthy land owners, Bob assumes the legacy of sexual privilege his ancestors exercised in the days of slavery.

The second section focuses on Tom, fully ensconced in the local black community. The opening echoes the lyricism of the beginning of the story, and the poetic images of the rising moon and the odor of sugar cane invest the scene with tactile immediacy. Sitting around the fire, listening to the oral tales of Old David George, Tom first hears the rumors of the romance between Louisa and Bob Stone, and he fights another man for laughing at the situation. Foreshadowing the conclusion, he whips out a knife, but the scuffle ends without further violence. Tom ambles over to her house to tell her how much he loves her, but he is inarticulate, his emotions ineffable, and he makes a stumbling protestation of affection. He tells Louisa he has heard the rumors, and he threatens to kill Bob if they prove true: "Cut him jes like I cut a nigger." The haunting refrain at the end of the first section is repeated to conclude this part, with its imagistic suggestions linking the moon with race and sin.

The final part begins with Bob Stone, who thinks of the days of slavery when his family owned the black people who worked the land. He feels his ancestry, the blood of the old ones, and yet he loves a black woman and is jealous of her relationship with Tom. He finds her in the cane fields with Tom, whom he attacks, and in the ensuing fight Tom slashes Bob's throat. He staggers into town and, just before he dies, he tells a group of white men that it was Tom who cut him. The narrator catalogs the preparations for retribution: "Shotguns, revolvers, rope, kerosene, torches." The agent of revenge, the mob captures Tom and burns him over a well. The men shout in joy as he dies, and the yell echoes down the street of the town to Louisa, sitting on the steps of her house, looking at the full moon. The story ends with the haunting refrain that concludes all of its sections, an image that encapsulates love and desire, race and violence, and the pervasive smell of cane.

"Blood-Burning Moon" has been heralded for its inventive experimentation in style and method, an aesthetic which changed the nature of Modernism for both the white and black communities. Beyond this one story, the entire volume, utilizing fictional narratives, dramatic episodes, and lyrical poetic reveries, blended these various forms into an aesthetic whole that has never been duplicated with such consummate integrity. The images of nature blend with the evocation of black life in a Southern town, with pervasive poverty and violence imbedded in the red earth, and the rich sensory imagery of Toomer's prose brings to life the immediacy of the scene and the dramatic intensity of human tragedy. *Cane*, published in 1923, is still regarded as a classic book in American literature and an important statement about black culture at the time of the Harlem Renaissance.

Suggestions for Further Reading

Benson, Brian Joseph, and Mabel Mayle Dillard. *Jean Toomer*. Boston: Twayne, 1980.

Dorris, Ronald. *Race: Jean Toomer's Swan Song*. New Orleans: Xavier Review Press, 1997.

Durham, Frank, ed. *The Merrill Studies in Cane*. Columbus: Merrill, 1971.

Feith, Michael, and Genevieve Fabre, eds. *Jean Toomer and the Harlem Renaissance*. New Brunswick: Rutgers University Press, 2000.

McKay, Nellie. *Jean Toomer, Artist: A Study of His Life and Work, 1894-1936*. Chapel Hill: University of North Carolina Press, 1984.

Scruggs, Charles. *Jean Toomer and the Terrors of American History*. Philadelphia: University of Pennsylvania Press, 1998.

F. Scott Fitzgerald, "Babylon Revisited"

F. Scott Fitzgerald published "Babylon Revisited" in the *Saturday Evening Post* in 1931 in the midst of deep personal difficulties and domestic turmoil, factors that may account for the tone of hopeless resignation that concludes the action. He wrote it in Paris, the Babylon of the title, a place where a favorable exchange rate for American currency made living easy for writers and artists from the United States, and the relaxed French customs regarding sexual liberties and the consumption of alcohol provided an attractive alternative to the conservative attitudes back home. Scott and Zelda Fitzgerald reveled in the endless parties and careless lifestyle of the Lost Generation, especially after he became a world celebrity with the publication of *The Great Gatsby* in 1925. Five years later the fun was over: Scott was institutionalized for the treatment of alcoholism; Zelda was in a psychiatric hospital; and their daughter, Scottie, was no longer living with them. Most Americans were suffering from the stock market crash of 1929, but the Fitzgeralds had lost everything earlier during the boom, as the protagonist of this story indicates about his situation. The irony was that it all started and ended in Paris, which was truly Babylon revisited.

That is where the story begins, with masterful irony, in the city where the party went on so long that it consumed the revelers, long adrift in alcohol and debauchery. Charlie Wales must return to the scene of his ruin to retrieve his daughter, Honoria, who has been living with her aunt and her family. Charlie's wife, Helen, died one drunken night after an argument, and he spent months in a sanitarium for the treatment of alcoholism. Helen's sister, Marion, and her husband have absorbed the girl into their own family,

The American Short Story Handbook, First Edition. James Nagel.
© 2015 James Nagel. Published 2015 by John Wiley & Sons, Ltd.

sharing their modest means and quiet life. The first section of this highly structured plot deals with this circumstance, the return of Charlie to the scene of his downfall amid extravagant wealth, endless parties, and the careless life of American expatriates in the 1920s. The opening is thus rife with irony, for his return could not be more serious, a quest to be reunited with his daughter. Ironically, it opens in the American bar at the Ritz Hotel, the watering hole of the Lost Generation, where Charlie has gone to inquire about his friends, nearly all of whom have left Paris, often under unfortunate circumstances. The suggestion is that his former life was so shallow that the only common *locus* of activity he shared with the old gang was a bar. He leaves the address of his sister-in-law with the bartender in case someone inquires of him, a classic mistake that will cost him dearly. In this set-up scene, he reviews his Paris years, reveals that he is now in business in Prague, where he hopes to bring Honoria to live with him. Another irony is that that Marion and Lincoln Peters, the epitome of wholesome family life, live on the Left Bank, the Latin Quarter that featured the carefree excesses of the 1920s, even though they have only modest financial means. They resent the wasteful extravagance of Charlie's former life, especially so since it led directly to Helen's death. Charlie leaves the bar to go to their home, where Honoria greets him enthusiastically. Characteristically inept, he drops the comment that he has come from the bar, which prompts Marion's attention. He is off to a bad beginning. Marion has legal control of Honoria, and she is perpetually suspicious of Charlie's character, his drinking, his thoughtless profligacy. When he leaves that evening, he walks through the Left Bank in a recapitulation of the world he used to embrace: he watches Josephine Baker perform her "chocolate arabesques," observes the street walkers plying their trade, and looks in on some of his old haunts. Zelli's is closed, as are many of the hotels that catered to Americans, who are mostly gone now. Charlie is left alone amid the scene of his dissipation.

Section two belongs to Charlie and Honoria as they have lunch at Le Grand Vatel because he wishes to avoid the places that remind him of the destructive period of his life. He suggests that when they leave they will go to a toy store and then to a vaudeville show, but she objects, with astonishing maturity, that they are not rich any more and that she does not need any more toys. She is carrying a doll of her own. They launch a game of faux formality in which they both introduce themselves formally as two adults having met for the first time. He lists his home as Prague, she as "Honoria Wales, Rue Palatine, Paris." She treats her doll as a child, but she explains that her husband is dead, a concept exceedingly painful to Charlie, who moves on quickly to another subject. The game is fun, in other words, but there is a poignant past lurking behind it. On the way out of the restaurant, they encounter two friends from his former life, Duncan Schaeffer and Lorraine Quarles, who still embrace the revelry he is attempting to escape. After a quick exchange, Charlie and Honoria leave, and the section ends with her tender comment that she loves him better than anyone and wants to live with him. His intense desire to fulfill her wish dominates the rest of the action.

In the next section, Charlie visits Marion and Lincoln to ask for them to allow Honoria to live with him. They have legal custody, a control granted by the court when he was in a sanitarium. Marion revisits the death of her sister, which occurred after Charlie locked Helen out of the house in a storm. Charlie has planned carefully, and he controls his anger, not arguing to justify his actions but remaining contrite, keeping his eyes on the prize. Marion is hesitant, given his irresponsible past, but she finally relents, and the section ends on this positive note. All that remain, in effect, are the logistics of turning over the legal guardianship and arranging for the journey back to Prague.

All of these plans are ruined in the fourth section by the introduction of the past into the present, as Lorraine and Duncan appear at the worst possible time. Marion has decided to retain legal guardianship for a year even though Charlie will take Honoria to Prague when he leaves. He comes to the Peters apartment to make final arrangements, and Marion basically agrees to the entire plan for his parental control of his daughter. In the midst of these negotiations, the two drunken revelers appear, filled with hilarity and booze, and this graphic reminder of Charlie's past, with its tragic consequences, is enough to cause her to change her mind. Proclaiming she is ill, she retreats from the room. Charlie and Lincoln are left with Honoria, both knowing that the plans have all been changed, that father and daughter are not to be reunited. The past, ever lurking on the periphery, intrudes once again to destroy the protagonist's happiness, a frequent theme in Fitzgerald's work.

The conclusion takes place where the action began, in the Ritz bar, a locus resonant with the destructive Rabelaisian gaiety of three years ago, only now the American expatriates are nearly all gone, their parties gone stale, many of their lives ruined. The stock market has crashed, taking their lifestyle with it, and the bartender has heard countless stories of all that was lost in the financial collapse. Charlie has gained wisdom over the last few years, however, and he comments that he "lost everything I wanted in the boom." He knows he is still paying the price for the party, but separation from his daughter seems steep compensation. He consoles himself that he will get her back eventually, but for now there is only lonely resignation, the tone throughout the conclusion. "Babylon Revisited" is yet another iteration of the idea of surface celebration leading to tragic emptiness, one made all the more poignant by the parallels to Fitzgerald's own life.

This story has long been regarded as the most important work of fiction depicting the aftermath of the Lost Generation, that period in the 1920s when American and English expatriates, disillusioned by their war experiences, swarmed into Paris for the easy living, artistic excitement, and intellectual power of the Left Bank, the student section of the city filled with sidewalk cafés, bistros, and dancing clubs. "Babylon Revisited" depicts the human cost of a party that went on too long, with too much sex and drink and careless behavior, and it does so with impressive artistic care. The tone of hopeless resignation underscores the entire story, making the poignant failure at the end seem the inevitable consequence of things that happened before the opening scene. The narrative perspective, which is third person closely identified with Charlie's mind, allows a stance of objectivity at the same time it permits access to his thoughts and emotions as well as his action and dialogue. This device establishes his intense desire to win back his daughter, his tight control on what he says and does, and his willingness to endure humiliation without self-justification if it will result in his objective: bringing Honoria back to Prague to live with him. His old behavior haunts him, of course. His first stop is at the Ritz bar, where so many wild parties had originated, and that mistake indirectly costs him his daughter. The vestiges of the old days are personified in Duncan and Lorraine, and their appearance at the Peters during a delicate negotiation indicates that Charlie cannot escape his past. The sections of the story are carefully structured in the manner of scenes in a drama, one of Fitzgerald's favorite genres, and each has its own conflict and resolution, its own movement toward the final scene. The stylistic elegance of the prose, the skillfully plotted action, and the power of the underlying theme all testify to the fact that even after his breakdown, Scott Fitzgerald was a serious artist, one capable of producing some of the best prose fiction of the era.

Suggestions for Further Reading

Berman, Ronald. *Fitzgerald, Hemingway, and the Twenties*. Tuscaloosa: University of Alabama Press, 2001.

Bryer, Jackson. *The Short Stories of F. Scott Fitzgerald: New Approaches in Criticism*. Madison: University of Wisconsin Press, 1982.

Bryer, Jackson. *New Essays on F. Scott Fitzgerald's Neglected Stories*. Columbia: University of Missouri Press, 1996.

Curnutt, Kirk. "The Short Stories of F. Scott Fitzgerald: Structure, Narrative Technique, Style." *A Companion to the American Short Story*. Eds. Alfred Bendixen, and James Nagel. Chichester, England: Wiley-Blackwell, 2010, pp. 295–315.

Eble, Kenneth. *F. Scott Fitzgerald*. Boston: Twayne, 1977.

Glenday, Michael K. *F. Scott Fitzgerald*. New York: Palgrave Macmillan, 2012.

Higgins, John A. *F. Scott Fitzgerald: A Study of the Stories*. New York: St. John's University Press, 1971.

Kuehl, John. *F. Scott Fitzgerald: A Study of the Short Fiction*. Boston: Twayne, 1991.

Petry, Alice Hall. *Fitzgerald's Craft of Short Fiction: The Collected Stories, 1920-1935*. Tuscaloosa: University of Alabama Press, 1989.

Ernest Hemingway, "Indian Camp"

"Indian Camp" originally appeared in the *Transatlantic Review* in April of 1924, the first of Ernest Hemingway's short fiction to appear in a major magazine. It was later incorporated into *In Our Time* as the lead story in a volume that did much to change the direction of Modern literature, introducing a lean and vigorous style free of the florid British influence in prose that had predominated in the earlier century. This book also dealt with some of the harsh realities of pain and death that the western world had experienced in World War I with an emphasis on the psychological effect of violence. In "Indian Camp," it is significant that the protagonist is a child, a young boy exposed to tragedies he is too young to understand but still able to feel, and in the stories about him that follow he is never able to sleep well at night. In broad terms, Hemingway's presentation of the modern world proved to be deeply disturbing, but no one successfully argued that it was not an accurate portrait.

The story rewards interpretations from a multiplicity of perspectives, including a consideration of the biographical background. Hemingway's father was an obstetrician who saw his patients at home but delivered their babies in the hospital in Oak Park. However, the family also owned a summer home on Walloon Lake in Michigan, and the children spent all of their summers there hiking, fishing, and enjoying the lake and nearby streams. A short walk from their cottage, and on the same side of the lake, there was a historic settlement of Native Americans, part of the tribe spread throughout the upper region of the Midwest and known variously as the Chippewa, Ojibwa, or Odawa. The Hemingway and Indian children played

The American Short Story Handbook, First Edition. James Nagel.
© 2015 James Nagel. Published 2015 by John Wiley & Sons, Ltd.

and fished together, and Dr. Hemingway delivered the neighbors' babies and saw to their medical needs whenever he was on vacation at the lake, nearly always without charge. His brother George was a frequent guest, and the men fished together for trout. Through the generations, the Hemingways were devout Congregationalists deeply involved in humanitarian causes, and Dr. Hemingway saw his profession as a calling, not as a business. In any event, the practice of medicine was a frequent topic of conversation in the household, and traumatic complications in childbirth became a pervasive subject in Hemingway's early fiction.

In this story, the birth of a child is a particularly painful event, and it is followed by an even more gruesome discovery, one that the young protagonist, Nick Adams, finds deeply disturbing. The basic plot is rather simple, although the details are quite complex. Two Indians row young Nick and his father across a lake to an Indian camp, where a woman needs a Caesarian section to deliver her baby. Nick's Uncle George is already there, and they go inside a shanty to find the woman and her husband, who has been injured and is watching from a bed in the open room. Even this brief opening is rich in suggestions. Traditional Indian medicine has obviously failed, and the mother and baby will surely die without modern "white" intervention. The two rowers appear in rowboats, artifacts of the white world, since Native Americans used canoes. These are people in transition from one world to another. When they arrive at the camp, the economic disparities between the two worlds is apparent. The Indians live in "shanties," with little background in income-producing activities. Uncle George, on the other hand, smokes cigars and gives each of the rowers one when they arrive. There is a slight suggestion that he might be the father of the woman's child, although there are not enough supportive details to establish that idea as a viable interpretation, although it is interesting that he stays in the camp after the delivery of the baby.

As he scrubs up to begin the procedure, Dr. Adams is primarily concerned with Nick, not with the screaming mother. He speaks to his son as though educating him to become a physician, explaining that he must perform an operation without anesthetic and stressing that the screams of the woman are not the important thing. From his scientific point of view, the survival of both mother and baby are all that matter, but from Nick's perspective her agony is horrifying. She bites Uncle George on the arm when he attempts to hold her during the incision. As he extracts the baby, Dr. Adams asks Nick how he likes being an intern, but it is clear the boy does not like it at all. Dr. Adams takes some pride in having performed a Caesarian with a jack-knife and doing the stitches with a fishing leader. As they look into the bunk for the husband, however, they see that he has committed suicide by slitting his throat, presumably unable to stand his wife's agonizing screams.

Dr. Adams realizes that all of this has been more for Nick than was expected, and he says he is sorry he brought the boy along. Indeed, in the published story it is not clear why he has done so, although there is the imbedded suggestion that perhaps he saw this as an opportunity to instruct Nick in the practice of medicine, hoping he will follow in his footsteps. In the original manuscript, however, there is an explanation that was later discarded in revision. This section, later published separately under the title "Three Shots," reveals that Dr. Adams and his brother, George, go fishing earlier that evening, leaving Nick alone in the tent. He becomes afraid of the darkness and fires a rifle to signify an emergency. His father rushes in from the lake, and Nick lies to him, claiming that a wolf was trying to get into the tent. Dr. Adams realizes that his son is terrified to be alone, and that is why, in the manuscript, he brings him along to the Indian camp.

In the published story, on the way home from the incident, Nick asks why the husband killed himself, and the father responds "he couldn't stand things, I guess," a simple but philosophically profound observation. Interestingly, Uncle George remains in the Indian camp, further underscoring his ties to that community. It could be that the husband knows George is the father and killed himself out of humiliation, but more likely he simply empathized with her intense pain. In the boat heading home, Nick asks his father if dying is hard, and the father says no, although "it all depends." It is dawn over the lake, and Nick trails his hand in the water, a wonderful tactile image that further makes the situation real. In his immaturity, Nick feels certain he, himself, will never die. Biographically, this is poignantly ironic, since both Dr. Hemingway and Ernest committed suicide, probably for the same reason here given for the Indian father: they just could not stand things.

Suggestions for Further Reading

Benson, Jackson J. *The Short Stories of Ernest Hemingway: Critical Essays*. Durham: Duke University Press, 1975.

Berman, Ron. "Hemingway's Michigan Landscape." *Hemingway Review* 27.1 (2007): 39–54.

DeFalco, Joseph. *The Hero in Hemingway's Short Stories*. Pittsburgh: University of Pittsburgh Press, 1963.

Flora, Joseph M. *Hemingway's Nick Adams*. Baton Rouge: Louisiana State University Press, 1982.

Helstern, Linda Lizut. "Indians, Woodcraft, and the Construction of White Masculinity: The Boyhood of Nick Adams." *Hemingway Review* 20.1 (2000): 61–79.

Penner, Dick. "The First Nick Adams Story." *Fitzgerald/Hemingway Annual* (1975): 195–202.

Reynolds, Michael S. *Critical Essays on Ernest Hemingway's in Our Time.* Boston: G. K. Hall, 1983.

Smith, Paul. *A Reader's Guide to the Short Stories of Ernest Hemingway.* Boston: G. K. Hall, 1989.

Tanselle, G. Thomas. "Hemingway's 'Indian Camp'." *Explicator* 20 (1962): Item 53.

Young, Philip. "Big World Out There: The Nick Adams Stories." *Novel,* 6. (Fall 1972): 5–19.

John Steinbeck, "The Chrysanthemums"

Originally published in *Harper's* in 1937, the next year "The Chrysanthe-mums" became the opening story in John Steinbeck's popular collection entitled *The Long Valley*. The story marked a significant milestone in the author's fictional technique, and his substantial revisions in the manuscript demonstrate that he worked diligently on the art of his craft for the first time in his career. He restrained his tendency for authorial intrusions into the action, for example, and sustained a consistent point of view. In the various portrayals in this volume of the Salinas Valley in California, he infused meaning into the setting, relating the people of the area to their social and economic situation while developing the theme of hopeless resignation. A celebrated Naturalist, Steinbeck portrayed his characters as victims of an indifferent and often hostile environment made even worse by the economic determinism that controls their lives, leaving them with few alternatives. He marshaled his artistic creed in support of these ideas, infusing patterns of animalistic imagery, for example, to suggest the hostility of a Darwinian struggle for survival. The result was highly satisfying fiction in which the themes emerge from the action and dialogue rather than from direct state-ments from the narrator, which is common in Naturalistic tradition. It was these refinements of fictional technique that contributed to the success of his masterpiece, *The Grapes of Wrath*, the following year.

In "The Chrysanthemums," the protagonist is Elisa Allen, a farm wife in the Salinas Valley of California who leads a restricted life with limited financial and social resources. As the story opens, her husband, Henry, has just sold some cattle, and they are planning on going into town for dinner

The American Short Story Handbook, First Edition. James Nagel.
© 2015 James Nagel. Published 2015 by John Wiley & Sons, Ltd.

and a movie, apparently a rare treat for country people. Henry would prefer to watch the boxing, and Elisa likes rather more gentle entertainment, an early definition of the differences between them. Around them, the narrator describes the "grey-flannel fog of winter" as a persistent and unassailable fact of their existence, as are the other circumstances that control their lives. In Steinbeck's work, Nature is often an expression of the human situation. Indeed, one of the sustaining elements of Elisa's life is gardening, and she takes tender care of her flowers, digging in the fresh earth around the chrysanthemums with what are described as "terrier fingers," an image that links her to animal life, to a lower species on the evolutionary scale. It is clear that the Allens lead a hardscrabble existence with few refinements and that the wife longs for more, for adventure, new experiences, interesting people. That becomes particularly evident when two men in business suits come to buy some cattle, and Elisa watches them closely. They come from the outside world, from another stratum of economic activity, another dimension of social appeal. In contrast to their elegant appearance, Elisa "looked blocked and heavy in her gardening costume," and she wears a man's hat, "clodhopper shoes," and heavy gloves for working the soil. Beneath her clothing, however, there is the suggestion of inherent beauty, for her "face was eager and mature and handsome," and that suppressed grace of being becomes the central issue.

After the men leave, an itinerant peddler pulls into the yard in his horse-drawn wagon. He is a rough man with soiled clothes and calloused hands, but he seems to awaken something in Elisa, who straightens her hair. He is clearly looking for a way to make money at each stop, sharpening tools and mending pots, and he has perfected a social manner that is disarming for her, especially when he admires her gardens. He knows her weakness, and he tells her about another woman who gardens who has a wide variety of flowers but no chrysanthemums, and she has asked him to bring her some seeds. To any skilled gardener, this comment is an obvious ruse in that these flowers are not normally grown from seeds but from cuttings, and she offers to make a pot of them for her. Her eyes shine in response to his interest, and as she instructs him how best to grow them, the imagery reveals a sexual dimension to their interaction as her breasts swell and her innate beauty emerges. She presents him with a pot of them, and he feigns deep satisfaction in the gift, placing them on the seat of his wagon. As part of his sales stratagem, he has established a bond between them. His compassionate comment that it must be lonely there on the ranch touches her deeply, and it is clear that she longs to go with him on his journey north to Seattle. She hires him to fix some aluminum saucepans, and watching him work, she tells him that she can sharpen tools, but he does not respond. In her desperation, she nearly seizes him by the leg, crouching on the ground in front of him "like a fawning dog" demonstrating sub-servience. As he leaves, she says "goodbye—goodbye" to herself, knowing that a rare opportunity for a richer, more varied life goes with him.

The second half of the plot contains an even more devastating disillusion-ment. At first Elisa is transformed by even this paltry hope of a richer, more varied life, a change her husband refers to when he says "you look differ-ent, strong and happy." Her response seems to indicate she is aware of her sudden psychological growth when she says "I'm strong.... I never knew before how strong." In preparation for the evening in town, she scrubs her-self hard and examines her body in the mirror, stressing her sexual appeal. She puts on her best clothes and does her makeup carefully, expressing her newfound self-respect. As they drive into town, they follow the same road as the tinsmith's wagon, and she sees a dark spot ahead in the road. She knows it is the chrysanthemums she gave the peddler and that he has discarded them, keeping the pot for sale. It is a harsh realization, that his interest in her gardening, in her, was only a ruse in his sales technique, a lie meant to create a false bond between them that would inspire her to pay him for fixing something around the house. It also had a secondary impact on her sense of self, a revitalization that was transformative if tragically brief. In the context of this harsh new situation, she realizes not only that she was duped but that she is trapped in a life with few satisfactions and no promise of a more sat-isfying future. Her husband also notices this change in her. Her resignation to this limited life is evident when she expresses her view that having wine with dinner will be enough for her, and then she cries "weakly–like an old woman."

Although the artistry of this fine story is more complex than in most Naturalism, which tends to press home a single theme of pessimistic deter-minism, the basic ideas are consistent with that movement. Elisa is trapped by socio-economic circumstances that are too powerful for her to contest, and she is left with no alternative but resignation to an unsatisfying life. That idea was particularly widespread in America in the 1930s, when the Depression hit the country hard and the dustbowl years destroyed nearly all the agriculture in the western half of the country. The reading public could relate to Elisa's fate since the vast majority of the population had seen or experienced similar deprivations. Unlike most Naturalistic fiction, however, Steinbeck's skill in rendering "Chrysanthemums" rests to some extent in his ideological restraint and his deft artistic touch. When Elisa first responds to the peddler, for example, she holds her posture in the manner of a "fawning dog," signifying not only her willing subservience but her link to a subordi-nate species, an enduring Naturalistic motif. Human beings are animals in this intellectual tradition, and they are driven by instincts and passions as are the beasts. They make few decisions in life, since they lack sovereignty, and bereft of effective agency, they can only fool themselves by thinking they can determine their own futures through an expression of will. In this regard, this story is classic American Naturalism, a movement in literature and intellectual life that flourished in the first half of the twentieth century.

Suggestions for Further Reading

Hayashi, Tetsumaro, ed. *A Study Guide to Steinbeck's* The Long Valley. Ann Arbor: Pierian Press, 1976.

Hughes, R. S. *Beyond the Red Pony: A Reader's Companion to Steinbeck's Complete Short Stories*. Metuchen: Scarecrow Press, 1987.

Hughes, R. S. *John Steinbeck: A Study of the Short Stories*. Boston: Twayne, 1989.

Osborne, William R. "The Texts of Steinbeck's 'The Chrysanthemums'." *Modern Fiction Studies* 12 (1966–1967): 479–84.

Simmonds, Roy S. "The Original Manuscripts of 'The Chrysanthemums'." *Steinbeck Quarterly* 7 (Summer-Fall 1974): 102–11.

Timmerman, John H. *The Dramatic Landscape of Steinbeck's Short Stories*. Norman: University of Oklahoma Press, 1990.

Eudora Welty, "Petrified Man"

One of the most famous stories in Southern fiction, Eudora Welty's "Petrified Man" appeared in *The Southern Review* in 1939 in the heart of the Great Depression. In terms of literary history, it draws from the American traditions of Local Color in its portrayal of regional characters and dialects, but it also derives from the nineteenth-century English genre of Dramatic Monologue, a poetic method that emphasizes self-revelation for the speaker, often negative in its implications. Robert Browning's "My Last Duchess" is such a poem, as is T. S. Eliot's "The Love Song of J. Alfred Prufrock." Robert Frost modified the form to involve a dialogue in which both speakers unwittingly suggest aspects of their character and personality, and Eudora Welty used this method for this celebrated work of short fiction. It involves two characters in a beauty shop who, in two separate sessions, reveal the most appalling things about themselves while discussing recent events in town and in their personal lives.

The story is primarily dialogue, in fitting with its artistic heritage. It involves a hairdresser named Leota who, after a torrid courtship, married Fred, who is dominated by her. Her customer is Mrs. Fletcher, several months pregnant, who has been hiding that fact and contemplating an abortion. She controls her husband with passive aggression, staging one of her "sick headaches" whenever he edges out of her domination. From the beginning of their conversation they reveal a desire to present a false representation to the world about them. Mrs. Fletcher has hidden her pregnancy; Leota appears to be blonde but has black hair evident in the part. Beyond appearance, they regard themselves as benevolent members of local society despite the fact that they have vicious things to say about virtually everyone they know. Leota has rented out rooms to Mr. and Mrs. Pike, for example, but she stresses that

The American Short Story Handbook, First Edition. James Nagel.
© 2015 James Nagel. Published 2015 by John Wiley & Sons, Ltd.

not only is the woman attractive but "she has her a good time," suggesting extramarital affairs. Mrs. Pike's young son, Billy Boy, is playing on the floor of the shop, listening to the conversation despite his youth, and he intervenes with telling comments at several points in the action. Mrs. Fletcher displays a curious attitude for a pregnant woman, saying that she does not like children "much," and that she is tempted to terminate the pregnancy, an ironic thought given the proximity of Billy Boy. Leota says that someone speculated that Mrs. Fletcher is pregnant, and it turns out that Mrs. Pike made the remark.

The lexicon of the two women suggests that they are toward the bottom of the middle-class spectrum since their speech is replete with grammatical lapses and their topical references are to rustic events and tawdry relationships. Using the linguistic techniques of the Local Color movement, they identify themselves as uneducated, common, and highly regional in their attitudes. Leota's language is humorous and ironically self-revealing: "Honey, me and Fred, we met in a rumble seat eight months ago and we was practically what you might call on the way to the altar inside of a half an hour." She touches on a carnival sideshow playing in town, especially Lady Evangeline, a fortune teller from New Orleans, a hotbed of Voodoo and superstition perfect for someone who purports to read palms. Mrs. Pike asks Lady Evangeline for information about Leota's former beau, whom the hairdresser contends married a woman for money. The fortune teller obligingly reports that the man is unhappily married and the union will not survive three years, precisely what Leota wanted to hear.

The dominant themes evident in this desultory conversation are manipulation and false presentation. The first half of the story establishes all of the women as coldly calculating, insensitive, domineering forces in their marriages, which are based on superficial emotional commitments. That motif is further emphasized in the second half, which takes place in the same beauty shop a week later. Leota recounts how Mrs. Montjoy had her hair done the same day she delivered a baby, and her husband waited outside in the car, bags packed: "Her husband kep' comin' in here, scared like, but couldn't do nothin' with her a course." Rather ironically, for a woman who so clearly controls her husband, Mrs. Fletcher observes that Mr. Montjoy "ought to put his foot down." This conversation goes on to establish that Mrs. Fletcher dominates her husband as totally as Leota does hers. When Leota recounts how Mrs. Pike, her former tenant, recognized the photograph of the petrified man from the "freak show" as Mr. Petrie, who lived near her on Toulouse Street in New Orleans, Mr. Pike realized that she could receive $500 if she notified the police, who were looking for him on a charge of rape. Mr. Pike was reluctant to harm someone he had come to know, but Mrs. Pike insists, telling her husband "he could just go to hell." The thematic implications of these conversations is startling. Marriage is revealed to be not a loving, pro-creative, familial commitment but a locus of power crudely exercised, and in each case the woman is the dominant force. The second half of the story began with Mrs. Fletcher bemoaning the fact that now that Mrs. Pike has told the community about the pregnancy, Mrs. Fletcher is denied the option of an abortion, as though social reputation is the only value involved. A child is an odious prospect for her.

Another motif throughout the conversation is money, even when it is only tangentially involved in the situation. More directly, Leota obviously runs her hairdressing business to earn a living, a key point because the action takes place during the Depression and jobs are scare. Both Fred, Leota's husband, and Mr. Pike are unemployed, for example, giving their wives leverage in the battle for control. Fred and Leota rent out rooms in their home, where Sal and Joe Fentress lived until they were evicted for pilfering beer; Mr. and Mrs. Pike then moved in. Mrs. Pike apparently works, for there is reference to her bringing the petrified man his breakfast. That they had seen each other in New Orleans does not occur to her until she sees his photograph in a magazine in the beauty parlor. Leota is outraged that it was her parlor, her magazine, that occasioned Mrs. Pike's windfall of $500, and she cries all night about it. She takes out her anger on Mrs. Pike's small son, Billy Boy, who plays about on the floor. When he eats some peanuts out of her purse, she paddles him with a brush, inspiring his retort "if you're so smart, why ain't you rich?" The story thus ends on the financial theme, uttered by a child, tying together the pregnancy motif with that of money.

What is significant is that in what appears to be a simple regional story about women discussing local affairs in a beauty shop, nearly every com-ment diminishes the speaker of it. In accord with the dramatic monologue technique, the self-revealing conversation between these two women exposes their jealousy, envy, and deflating small-mindedness. Far from benevolent neighborhood news, their speech unmasks their inner characters, their fun-damental values, and what can be seen there is disconcerting. Romantic love has been corrupted into domination; none of the women speak of the men in their lives as someone deserving of respect and affection, and marriage is little more than an inconvenience. That it produces children deepens the theme, since Mrs. Fletcher contemplates abortion, and Billy Boy, Mrs. Pike's son, is a constant annoyance. The women seek virtue in the external beauty of a coiffure, meanwhile demonstrating the most demeaning of human feel-ings. Their lack of sensitivity for the people exhibited in what they call the "freak show" further underscores their superficial humanity. They live in a world of false appearances, of callous disregard of the misfortune of others, and of envy of the people about them. The artistic skill of the story is that the characters establish all of this information through what they say; they are not the victims of external gossip. In this fictional adaptation of the poetic monologue technique, Welty allows her characters to diminish themselves, and despite the charm of their conversations, they are without redeeming virtues.

Suggestions for Further Reading

Johnston, Carol Ann. *Eudora Welty: A Study of the Short Fiction*. New York: Twayne, 1997.

Prenshaw, Peggy Whitman. *Conversations with Eudora Welty*. Oxford: University Press of Mississippi, 1984.

Richmond, Lee J. "Symbol and Theme in Eudora Welty's 'Petrified Man'." *English Journal* 60 (1971): 201–03.

Schmidt, Peter. *The Heart of the Story: Eudora Welty's Short Fiction*. Jackson: University of Mississippi Press, 1991.

Turner, W. Craig, and Lee Emling Harding. *Critical Essays on Eudora Welty*. Boston: G. K. Hall, 1989.

Kieft, Vande, and M. Ruth. *Eudora Welty*. Boston: Twayne, 1962.

William Faulkner, "Barn Burning"

Part of William Faulkner's intriguing fictional history of the South, "Barn Burning" was placed first in his volume of collected short stories. Originally published in *Harper's Magazine* in 1939, it was chosen to be included in the O. *Henry Memorial Award Prize Stories of 1939*, and it has been continuously anthologized ever since. Part of its appeal is that it represents, in miniature, one aspect of what has become known as Faulkner's myth of the South, the intersecting trajectories of a descending aristocracy in the wake of the Civil War and a rising lower class that moves out of the hill country to take advantage of new opportunities in a changing economy. The plantation owners no longer have slaves to work their fields, and they turn much of the cultivation over to sharecroppers, who live in the former slave quarters. For their part, the "poor white trash," ably represented by the Snopes family in three novels and numerous short stories, seize the chance to earn a better living on the bottom land and in the small agricultural towns. They have on their side a powerful weapon: they are almost totally without moral principles, and thus they recognize no restraints on their behavior. They emulate the pride of the aristocracy but not the substance, and thus they retaliate vastly out of proportion in response to the smallest slight. Since there are no limits to what they will do to defend their "honor," they resort to the most outrageous means of revenge, the key events at the heart of "Barn Burning."

The story is told from the point of view of a boy, Sarty Snopes, son of Abner, a sharecropper. The narrator uses Sarty as a center of consciousness, recording what he can experience, what he thinks, what he conceals.

The American Short Story Handbook, First Edition. James Nagel.
© 2015 James Nagel. Published 2015 by John Wiley & Sons, Ltd.

His name, Colonel Sartoris Snopes, is a reference to Colonel John Sartoris, who organized a Confederate regiment from Yoknapatawpha County during the Civil War and later brought the railroad to the area. His name might also suggest Abner's vain attempt to somehow get money from a wealthy man by providing him with a namesake, a strategy that reveals how little the Snopes clan understands the aristocracy.

The opening scene is rife with tension. A drumhead court has convened in a general store hearing a case against Sarty's father, and the boy's thoughts confirm that his first allegiance is to his family, not to abstract concepts of justice or decency. Mr. Harris is testifying against Abner, his tenant, who allowed a pig to run loose in the cornfield. Harris explains that he gave Snopes enough wire to repair his fence, but the roll remained untouched, Abner's pride not allowing him to mend anything when ordered to do so. When Harris again captured the pig and, this time, charged a dollar to return it, Abner sent the message that "wood and hay kin burn," and that night the barn was destroyed in a fire.

Sarty is next called to testify, and walking to the front of the room he thinks "he aims for me to lie," referring to his father, "and I will have to do hit." But before he is able to give his account, Mr. Harris allows the boy to leave, and the judge dismisses the case with the admonition that Abner move his family out of the area. Sarty clearly understands what kind of a man his father represents, but there is little he can do about it. Abner is called a barn burner as they leave the store, and he fights with someone, losing the confrontation. The family wagon is waiting outside with all of their possessions already packed, anticipating the outcome, and they leave for yet another sharecrop arrangement. The background situation is that after the war, with the slaves gone from the huge plantations, the owners had to turn to the poor white class for labor. That brought a genteel segment of the population, with its European codes of honor and noblesse oblige, into contact with poor people who resented wealth and privilege and were willing to resort to nefarious means to even the score. Abner now moves from his dispute with Harris to a new one with Major de Spain, who derived his rank from his position in the Civil War and came home to become sheriff and to expand his extensive holdings in land.

The journey to the new cabin is revelatory of the character of human relations within the Snopes family. Riding in the wagon, Abner strikes his son savagely on the side of the head because he fears Sarty would have told the truth, saying "you got to learn to stick to your own blood." As they arrive at the unpainted shack they are to live in, one of his sisters says "likely hit ain't fitten for hawgs," and her father responds "fit it will and you'll hog it and like it." This is a family at the bottom of society, condescended to by even the black population, and they have few skills and little knowledge on which to build a better life.

Abner's relationship with Major de Spain replicates what he experienced with Mr. Harris: his perverse pride prevents him from making even the slightest accommodation with his employer for fear of showing deference. Hence, as he approaches Major de Spain's mansion, he refuses to alter his stride to avoid stepping in some fresh horse droppings. He enters the house with his soiled boots and stains a new carpet in the foyer. Learning that the major is not at home, he leaves and returns to his shack. When the major learns what has happened, he brings the carpet to the Snopes to be cleaned, a process Abner performs with lye and a piece of field stone, ripping the wool into scoriations. Major de Spain, seeing the rug, charges Abner for ruining it against his crop for the season, and Abner sues him.

The narrative emphasis throughout the conflict is not so much on the principles to the dispute but on the boy, Sarty, who has two disparate values systems played out before him. His internal struggle is intense: emotional in its immediacy, profound in what it reveals about his character. When the judge finds against Abner, Sarty knows that his father's retribution will be to burn de Spain's barn, killing the horses. His anticipation is borne out when his father fills a kerosene can in preparation. Sarty yells at his father that he had at least given warning to Mr. Harris, and Abner orders his wife to hold the boy so he cannot alert the major. When Abner leaves, the boy breaks free and runs to the de Spain mansion. Hearing the shouting, the major gets his gun, and Sarty heads off down the road, fleeing the scene of this confrontation. He hears shots in the distance but does not know what they mean or whether his father has been killed. As he runs, he tries to convince himself that Abner was a brave man, serving in the Confederate army, but the boy does not know that his father disgraced himself by stealing and selling horses. He treated the conflict as an economic opportunity, not as a confrontation between two different visions of national society. Despite his misunderstanding, Sarty does not come back and never reappears in Faulkner's work, one of the few important characters who totally vanishes.

Sarty's decision to warn Major de Spain carries profound thematic implications for the myth of the South. The first dramatic transitional event in Faulkner's coverage of the region is the Civil War, which began the process of the multifaceted decline of the aristocracy, the beginning of new opportunities for lower-class whites, and the freedom of the slaves, many of whom move North to take the jobs wrought by the industrial revolution. All of these transformations involve significant psychological changes as well, of course, and different social patterns and economic roles. In general, the Snopes family enjoys considerable financial success in the course of two generations, Sarty's older brother Flem eventually becoming a vice-president of a bank and moving into Major de Spain's mansion in Jefferson. But unlike Sarty, Flem never internalizes the genteel codes of the class he aspires to join; even in the home of the major, he is still the man he was born to, cheating whenever possible, and using his wife's sexual allure to gain promotions and power. Of all the Snopes clan, it is Sarty who best understands the nature of the difference between his people and de Spain, and he overcomes a lifetime of the inculcation of Snopesian traditions to endorse the values the major represents. That is perhaps why he does not appear again in Faulkner's work: there would be no place for him in the society of Yoknapatawpha County. He has brought yet another change to the region, demonstrating that even the lower classes are not frozen in place, that they can aspire, grow, and create a new life for themselves, free of the heavy tradition and constraining legacy that doomed many of their ancestors. It is an optimistic and liberating thematic conclusion to one of the finest stories in American literature.

Suggestions for Further Reading

Carothers, James B. *William Faulkner's Short Stories*. Ann Arbor: UMI Research Press, 1985.

Ferguson, James. *Faulkner's Short Fiction*. Knoxville: University of Tennessee Press, 1991.

Howell, Elmo. "Colonel Sartoris Snopes and Faulkner's Aristocracy: A Note on 'Barn Burning'." *The Carolina Quarterly* 11 (1959): 13–19.

Ruppersburg, Hugh. "William Faulkner's Short Stories." *A Companion to The American Short Story*. Eds. Alfred Bendixen, and James Nagel. Oxford (England): Wiley Blackwell, 2010, pp. 244–55.

Skei, Hans. *William Faulkner: The Novelist as Short Story Writer*. Oslo: Universitetsforlaget As, 1985.

Skei, Hans, ed. *William Faulkner's Short Fiction: An International Symposium*. Oslo: Solum Forlag, 1997.

Flannery O'Connor, "The River"

Despite the fact that she died when she was only thirty-nine, Flannery
O'Connor established herself among the most important American writers
of fiction. Indeed, her work in the genre is important in that her volumes
of stories have attracted a great deal more attention than did her two
novels, *Wise Blood* and *The Violent Bear It Away*. Throughout the tales
collected in *A Good Man is Hard to Find*, *Everything That Rises Must
Converge*, and *The Complete Stories of Flannery O'Connor*, which won
the National Book Award, her rich depiction of Southern folk is startling
in its grotesque evocation of Christian mythology amid what are often
devastating circumstances of poverty and religious confusion. Even the
basic situations she presents are original, unusual, and sometimes grimly
humorous, as in "Good Country People" when a woman has her artificial
leg stolen by a Bible salesman. In "The Life You Save May Be Your Own,"
a mother pays a one-armed man to marry her daughter, and he runs away
on the honeymoon. One story features a serial killer, and many others
present examples of greed, cruelty, ignorance, and exploitation. The plots
are often violent and destructive, and deformity and death are common.
Nearly always, however, the central themes have a basis in Roman Catholic
theology and involve spiritual growth and transformation. Most of her
best stories deal with the absurd and the mysterious, and these dramas
frequently feature solitary Southern women caught in violent conflicts and
the search for the redemption and grace promised by religious salvation.

These themes are pertinent to "The River," originally published in the
Sewanee Review in 1953 before it was included in *A Good Man is Hard to
Find and Other Stories*. In this story, which features a young boy as pro-
tagonist, the mysterious promises of a Christian ritual, baptism, leads to

The American Short Story Handbook, First Edition. James Nagel.
© 2015 James Nagel. Published 2015 by John Wiley & Sons, Ltd.

a devastating conclusion, one appreciated most profoundly by a religious skeptic. Central to the impact of this event are modulations of narrative point of view, as events unfold largely from the perspective of the boy but shift at crucial times to an adult point of view with a greater understanding of the meaning of the situation. O'Connor is also subtle with structural principles, especially parallelism and juxtaposition, and the images in her fiction often underscore the progressive thematic development as the plot unfolds.

All of these matters hold true in "The River," one of her finest works. It opens with a scene in an urban apartment where young Harry Ashfield has just awakened and is being dressed, carelessly, by his father. The details of the room stress the secular dissipation of the family, with the residue of a drinking party still evident and the smell of ashtrays filled with cigarette butts filling the air. Harry's mother lingers in bed with a hangover. Clearly Harry's parents care little about him, and neither of them embraces him before he leaves. He is going to spend the day with Mrs. Connin, an obviously lower-class woman who has children of her own to attend, but she plays a maternal role with him. She has worked all night and falls asleep during their long ride on a street car to the periphery of the city, where she lives in a ramshackle house a mile from the end of the car line, a "paper brick" structure with a barn and a pig-pen just outside. She made it clear that she is taking the boy to a healing at the river this Sunday and that the minister's name is Bevel Summers.

The second section demonstrates O'Connor's deft use of juxtaposition. Harry mattered little in the opening, an inconvenience for his inebriated parents. In the Connin home he is the center of attention, the focus of concern for Mrs. Connin, especially after the boy says his name is "Bevel," the same as the minister about to do the baptizing in the river. She is impressed, saying it is a "coincident," and the fabrication also underscores the sub-theme of identity, as the boy creates a new persona for himself. He does not count at home, where he is "Harry"; here, in a rustic setting, the name "Bevel" means something, and it gives him a momentary stature. The home is humble, only two rooms and two porches, but religious pictures line the walls, the suggestion being that there is something marvelous about the pictures of Jesus. The Connin children play a childhood prank on Bevel, luring him into a direct confrontation with a young pig, which frightens him terribly, but Mrs. Connin holds him and comforts him, and the terror passes.

The third section magnifies the religious theme at the center of the plot, and in preparation for the baptism, Mrs. Connin reads him a book about the life of Jesus. Things become even more mysterious for Bevel when they reach the service and find a preacher in the water proclaiming loudly that he is standing in the River of Life made out of the blood of Jesus. Bevel, who has probably never before witnessed a religious proceeding, is in awe of the man who talks about the river having the power to make the blind see, the leper clear, the dead come back to life. To the young boy, somehow the Kingdom of Christ is in the river, the locus of reverence, mysterious powers, and something good the adults call salvation. The minister baptizes him, ducking him under and then lifting him up and telling him that "you count now .... You didn't even count before." In counterpoint, an old religious skeptic, Mr. Paradise, is observing the proceedings, and he scoffs at the pious language, the melodramatic submerging of sinners in the river to be reborn, the hosannas of the newly transformed.

The conclusion begins with Harry back in his apartment, where his parents receive him with indifference, focusing their attention on a party. The boy needs adult attention, with his running nose and eye swollen shut, but receives none. His father offers Mrs. Connin money for attending Harry for the day, but she is offended by the parents mockery of her report of the baptism and their ridicule of the biography of Jesus, and she leaves without payment. The shift in name from Bevel back to Harry indicates the boy's loss of stature: After the river incident, he counted; now, back home with insensitive and self-absorbed parents, he is nothing, an inconvenience at best. So the next morning he leaves his home before his parents are awake and retraces his route to the river, where the Kingdom of Christ calls to him under the water, where someone will care about him. Ironically, the only person who observes him and understands the boy's objective is the skeptical Mr. Paradise. As the boy dashes into the water, he does so as "Bevel" once more, seeking Christian grace through redemption in the river. Mr. Paradise dives in after him, and he risks his own life in the swift currents, attempting to lure the boy with a peppermint stick, but he is too late. The boy is swept downstream, and Mr. Paradise comes out of the river "like some ancient water monster" and stares down the river, still searching for some sign of Bevel.

It is significant that the only person who cares about the boy enough to risk his own life for him is the religious skeptic, the man described as a "monster" and whom Bevel, sinking in the water, sees as a "pig," linking this final episode to the earlier experience with the Bonnin children and the animals in the religious picture book. The true monstrosity in the story exists not with a kindly old man who scoffs at religion, but with parents who care nothing about their own son. Surely some responsibility for the death of the boy is a fundamentalist religious cult enthralled by mystical superstitions about salvation in the water, an abstraction beyond the comprehension of a young boy. These people imagine a deity who is impressed by someone's submersion in a river, by sanctimonious proclamations and pious bromides rather than by dedication to a life of love and decency, of respect for others and acts of kindness. That is the final implication of the mysteries in "The River," as Bevel finds only death in his search for redemptive life, a grotesque irony typical of the mysterious thematic complexity in the fiction of Flannery O'Connor. The popular fundamentalist reading of the story is that it is an allegory that presents the central Christian mystery that eternal life with Christ is available only through death and redemption. The humanistic alternative interpretation is that the death of Bevel is a tragedy, an unnecessary one that results from a child's need for human connection and affection, a desire to count. His family has failed him, as has his community, and in the end it is only Mr. Paradise who cares, who witnesses his death in the river.

Suggestions for Further Reading

Coles, Robert. *Flannery O'Connor's South*. Baton Rouge: Louisiana State University Press, 1980.

Eggenschwiler, David. *The Christian Humanism of Flannery O'Connor*. Detroit: Wayne State University Press, 1972.

Elie, Paul. *The Life You Save May Be Your Own: An American Pilgrimage*. New York: Farrar, Straus & Giroux, 2003.

Friedman, Melvin J, and Beverly Lyon Clark. *Critical Essays on Flannery O'Connor*. Boston: G. K. Hall, 1985.

Gentry, Marshall. *Flannery O'Connor's Religion of the Grotesque*. Jackson: University of Mississippi Press, 1986.

Paulson, Suzanne Morrow. *Flannery O'Connor: A Study of the Short Fiction*. Boston: Twayne, 1988.

Whit, Margaret E. *Understanding Flannery O'Connor*. Columbia: University of South Carolina Press, 1995.

Tillie Olsen, "Help Her to Believe" ["I Stand Here Ironing"]

Tillie Olsen's first short story, now known as "I Stand Here Ironing," was published in the *Pacific Spectator* in 1956 as "Help Her to Believe." The alterative titles have rather different thematic suggestions for a monologue by a mother who is ironing and thinking about the life of her daughter. The original title puts the emphasis on a mother's concern for her daughter, whom she feels needs assistance to be able to lead a fulfilling life. The revised one shifts the focus from daughter to mother, to her preoccupation with herself, her problems, her inability to guide her daughter toward a successful career and personal relationship. A full reading of the story necessarily involves both considerations, but the degree of emphasis given to each plays a major role in interpretation.

The underlying issue of the mother's plight is poverty. She is obviously a lower-class woman of limited education and restricted prerogatives, a theme consistent with Tillie Olsen's participation in the Communist Party in the 1930s. The fact that the woman is ironing throughout her monologue presents her on the most mundane level of domestic activities, yet her maternal pain, her thoughts about herself and her children, and her introspection portray a humane level of concern that a wide audience could appreciate. The mother's thoughts seem in response to a teacher or other official at school who has indicated that her daughter Emily requires assistance, someone to help her believe in herself, as the original title of the story suggested. The first sentence establishes the dynamic: "I stand here ironing,

The American Short Story Handbook, First Edition. James Nagel.
© 2015 James Nagel. Published 2015 by John Wiley & Sons, Ltd.

and what you asked of me moves tormented back and forth with the iron." There is motion throughout the narrative, but it is energy that does not go anywhere. The narrator is still in place at the end of her monologue, the problems unsolved, her situation unchanged. The "you" seems to have asked her to help her daughter, a "youngster" who needs assistance, as designated in a note, presumably from a teacher. However, the narrator soon reveals the daughter is nineteen years old, hardly a "youngster," especially in the 1930s when few students went to school beyond the eighth grade and most people her age were working or seeking employment. The mother feels impotent, unable to offer much guidance. She seems to reason that she has never had time to "remember, to sift, to weigh, to estimate, to total," although it would seem that she has had countless hours at the ironing board when she could have done so. She decides that she will have to search her memories again and determine, for her own sense of self-justification or guilt, why she did not help her daughter, why she has failed a maternal duty.

Her musings about Emily occasion a progression of self-revelations. She has had five children, although her preoccupation is with her oldest daughter, who was a beautiful baby but was regarded as plain as she grew older. The mother raised her child by the book, nursing her on a prescribed schedule until the father left the family, leaving mother and child in poverty and, in effect, separating them when the mother went to work every day. Life was hard during the Depression, and eventually the mother was forced to bring her daughter to the father's family to live. It took the mother two years to acquire enough money to get the child back, and when she did the girl was not a baby any more and they had lost some of the bonding they should have experienced. The mother worked during the day and, having no other option, left her daughter in a shoddy day-care facility. Both mother and child are, in a sense, victims of poverty.

The narrator remembers how good the girl was, and she stops ironing: "What in me demanded that goodness in her? And what was the cost, the cost to her of such goodness?" It is an odd question suggesting an element of strangeness in the mother, a perspective that assumes that rather than acquiring an element of discipline that would serve her well in life, her daughter paid a price for not misbehaving. But the mother also reflects on the fact that she sent Emily away a second time and called her back only when she had a new father to greet her. Unfortunately, the girl later contracted the measles just as the mother's baby was due, and Emily spent time alone when she was delirious. Her convalescence lingered, and she did not return to health for some time.

The last section of the story moves on to more positive concerns, as Emily's talent on stage begins to be recognized. She is invited to perform at various high schools, a rather old student at nineteen, but the mother perceives her success in negative terms, that her daughter is "as imprisoned in her difference as in her anonymity." The mother attends a play and seems shocked at her daughter's "control" and "command" of the audience, and that moment betokens a transition in their relationship. Emily becomes more assertive, more critical of her mother's long stints ironing, for example. The mother seems resentful that officials suggest that Emily should be given more opportunity to develop her talent, but poverty limits what can be done for her.

The concluding paragraphs contain the mother's justification for not having done more for her daughter, that Emily's father left before her first birthday, that the mother was young and distracted by the other children, and that, in a sense, it seems unfair to expect that she should have done anything beyond what she did, which was very little. The mother's final thoughts are to "let her be" even though it means Emily will never realize her full potential and will have to accept a diminished life, a tormented existence such as the mother has lived. The final wish is that her daughter will "believe that she is more than this dress on the ironing board, helpless before the iron."

There are decided Naturalistic overtones in this recitation of helplessness against overwhelming social and economic circumstances. The mother is powerless to alter her situation to any significant degree, and she has accepted the idea that she is without moral agency, that she is unable to do anything to change her daughter's life, that the situation is hopeless. What is apparent on another level, however, is that the mother has denied simple compassion to her daughter, has not extended a warm embrace, a kind word, guiding advice. Confined within a swirl of self-justification, the mother accepts the view that there was nothing she could do, even now, when her daughter is nineteen and has exhibited extraordinary talent on the stage. Many famous actors came from impoverished circumstances, even in the era of the Depression, and they worked their way up from menial jobs within the theater to an opportunity to display their thespian ability. Certainly the mother could encourage her daughter psychologically if not financially. Those thoughts do not occur to her, however, for she is locked intellectually into a circumscribed vortex of limitation, hopelessness, and despair, and she has embraced the emotional void of pessimistic determinism, a hallmark of Naturalistic fiction of the Great Depression.

Suggestions for Further Reading

Burstein, Janet. *Writing Mothers, Writing Daughters: Tracing the Stories by American Jewish Women.* Urbana: University of Illinois, Press, 1996.

Faulkner, Mara. *Protest and Possibility in the Writing of Tillie Olsen*. Charlottesville: University Press of Virginia, 1993.

Frye, Joanne S. *Tillie Olsen: A Study of the Short Fiction*. New York: Twayne, 1995.

Martin, Abigail. *Tillie Olsen*. Boise: Boise State University Western Writers Series, No. 65, 1984.

Nelson, Kay Hoyle, and Nancy Huse, eds. *The Critical Response to Tillie Olsen*. New York: Greenwood Press, 1994.

O'Connor, William Van. "The Short Stories of Tillie Olsen." *Studies in Short Fiction* 1 (1963): 21–25.

Orr, Elaine Neil. *Tillie Olsen and a Feminist Spiritual Vision*. Jackson: University Press of Mississippi, 1987.

Pearlman, Mickey, and Abby H. P. Werlock. *Tillie Olsen*. Boston: Twayne, 1991.

Raymond Carver, "Cathedral"

Despite the fact that his publishing career covered just over a single decade, Raymond Carver quickly established himself at the forefront of contemporary American fiction, largely on the basis of his short stories. His subjects normally deal with the everyday lives of blue-collar workers, the working poor, who feel left out of the progression toward social and economic advancement, caught in a world of family obligations, insecure relationships, and unfulfilling romantic entanglements. His approach to writing about such characters is essentially Minimalistic, a sparse prose in the manner of Ernest Hemingway: direct, unadorned, unpretentious. Carver's stories are not abstract allegories, nor do they develop meaning through metaphor or allusion. They derive their power through the establishment of the immediate context of characters and situations drawn from the world of common experience.

For example, in "Fat" a waitress reflects on one of her customers, the heaviest person she has ever seen, who eats a gigantic meal. Later, she is troubled by his politeness and courtesy, and she struggles to understand why she is preoccupied with him, although she suspects it is because there is something missing from her life. The protagonist in "Why Don't You Dance" is similarly perplexed at not being able to articulate the meaning of what has happened. Carver often confounded the endings of his stories in this way, offering not so much a clarifying revelation as a reluctant admission that some events in life are too complex, some outcomes too perplexing, to be comfortably understood.

The situation is somewhat more reassuring in "Cathedral," Carver's most famous story. Originally published in the *Atlantic Monthly* in 1982, it was reprinted later that year in *Best American Stories*. Told in first person by

The American Short Story Handbook, First Edition. James Nagel.
© 2015 James Nagel. Published 2015 by John Wiley & Sons, Ltd.

a narrator who is also the protagonist, it is a subtle narrative that shows human weaknesses and character flaws in the speaker, who thinks all he is revealing is a blind man named Robert who is visiting for the night. The unnamed speaker begins by setting up the situation: many years before, his wife was once employed for a summer by blind man in Seattle, reading to him and assisting him with household matters. Subsequently, he married and enjoyed a period of happiness that has now ended with her death from cancer. Now, in the narrative present, he is visiting the people he has cared about over the years, and the speaker's wife has invited him to spend the night at their house, much to the irritation of the narrator. He has no sympathy for the blind man, no insight into his limitations, no capacity to imagine what it is might be like emotionally to have to depend on others for daily needs. He is filled with contempt, not compassion, resentful for even a small intrusion into his routine. The speaker admits that his only insights into the condition of being without sight derive from the stereotypes in movies, yet he lives in accord with them.

The second section is a flashback to his understanding of his wife's life in Seattle a decade earlier, which provides the background for how she became close to Robert. It is also another occasion for self-revelatory admissions by the narrator, whose comments suggest a superficial mind, a person who lives in a world of surfaces. In relating what his wife has told him, he reports that she responded to an ad in the newspaper and took a job reading "stuff" to Robert through which they became close friends. On her last day of work for him, he asked if he could touch her face, and what follows is an intimate, tactile, and, in a sense, loving memory of how he traced the contours of her face with his fingertips. She later wrote a poem about the experience, lines of verse the obtuse narrator could not understand and did not like. As he admits, he does not appreciate poetry.

The narrator then goes on to discuss his wife's first husband, who was an Air Force officer, a rather more sophisticated man than the speaker, and they began a peripatetic marriage, moving from base to base. During this period, she began sending Robert audio tapes instead of letters, and their correspondence in this manner continued over the years. She felt isolated in her marriage, with no close emotional bonds except with Robert, and in despair she attempted suicide but only vomited the poison, something she described in a tape sent to the blind man. The narrator, her present husband, is oblivious to the depth of her anguish at that time, insensitive about the fact that the only person she had to confide in was Robert, whom she had not seen for years. She then went on to a divorce and, in time, a relationship with the narrator, who became her second husband. Meanwhile, Robert married his next assistant, Beulah, and he had a period of happiness until his wife developed cancer and, only recently, died. He is still grieving at the time of his visit. The narrator seems not to possess any insight into the feelings of either his wife or the blind man but to revel in the superficiality of his own experience: "I don't have any blind friends," he says. At one point he injects that he feels sorry for Robert, but then he rejects those sentiments by thinking about how difficult Beulah's life must have been having to live with him. That is the emotional context for Robert's arrival.

The evening with Robert proves transformative for the narrator, which becomes the central emotional issue of the plot. At first he is rather annoyed by the guest, who wears a beard, speaks loudly, and possesses a strong handshake. The narrator is especially attentive to how his wife regards Robert, with admiration and affection. She looks at the blind man and then at him, and the narrator says "I had the feeling she didn't like what she saw." He shrugs it off. The narrator describes Robert in detail, his clothing all in brown, the lack of a cane or sunglasses. After dinner the narrator turns on the television, which irritates his wife, but it provides a transitional moment. A travel program comes on, showing a number of cathedrals, including one in Paris, probably Notre Dame, and the narrator attempts to describe the architecture of such a structure. Robert has no idea what one would look like, but he asks for clarification. The narrator is inept at verbal description, but he gets the idea that he will draw the outline of a cathedral and Robert can hold his fingers and grasp at least the shape of such a huge building. The blind man holds the back of the narrator's hand while he draws, and there is a communication between them, a sense of common experience, an intimacy that is emotionally transformative for the speaker, who says "it was like nothing else in my life up to now." He closes his eyes to approximate what blindness must be like, and he sustains the experience longer than necessary: "It's really something," he says.

For what is apparently the first time in his life, the narrator has empathized with someone, come to feel what it must be like to be that person, in this case a blind man living with extraordinary limitations and yet someone who is fully human. It suggests that even the speaker's relationship with his wife is comparatively superficial, that he has never entered into her emotional construct, never sensed what she must feel, never understood another person. The simple experience of attempting to describe a cathedral to a man who cannot see has led to a new level of awareness for him. The only true conflict in the story is thus within the narrator, his revelation of his superficial relationships with other people leading up to this moment of connection, an epiphany that is not fully explained but is suggested by his startled reaction to the intimacy established in the drawing episode, a moment of emotional modification that enlarges his world and leaves him a different person.

That this transformative process is still somewhat inchoate at the end of the story is typical of Carver's fiction, which often withholds final conclusions, total resolutions of conflicts, direct explanations of how the protagonist has been changed in the course of the action. Nonetheless, it is clear that the simple intimacy of having a blind man hold his hand while he was drawing proves expansive for the narrator. It also seems to come as a surprise to a man who did not know another person well until that moment. The remarkable shock of that experience would seem to be the motivation for the telling of the narrative, which is not essentially complimentary of the speaker but reveals how a pathetically insensitive man achieved a moment of connection to someone else when an unwelcome guest, a blind man, came for a visit. That is when a moment of insight into Robert also gave the narrator a new, and fundamentally enriching, understanding of himself.

Suggestions for Further Reading

Campbell, Ewing. *Raymond Carver: A Study of the Short Fiction*. New York: Twayne, 1993.

Gentry, Marshall Bruce, and William L Stull. *Conversations with Raymond Carver*. Jackson: University of Mississippi Press, 1990.

Meyer, Adam. *Raymond Carver*. New York: Twayne, 1995.

Nesset, Kirk. *The Stories of Raymond Carver: A Critical Study*. Athens: Ohio University Press, 1995.

Klepe, Sandra Lee, and Robert Mittner, eds. *New Paths to Raymond Carver: Critical Essays on His Life, Fiction, and Poetry*. Columbia: University of South Carolina Press, 2008.

Salzman, Arthur. *Understanding Raymond Carver*. Columbia: University of South Carolina Press, 1988.

Skelicka, Carol. *Raymond Carver: A Writer's Life*. New York: Scribners, 2009.

Louise Erdrich,
"The Red Convertible"

Now one of Louise Erdrich's best known works of short fiction, "The Red Convertible" was first published in the *Mississippi Valley Review* in 1982 before being incorporated, in a different version, into *Love Medicine*. That volume of fourteen interrelated stories won the National Book Award for 1984. In the magazine text, the narrator is a character named "Marty" who has an intense relationship with an older brother, Stephen, just home from the Vietnam War. Since this was only the second of the *Love Medicine* selections to appear in print, the indications are that the author had not yet worked out the basic concept for her story cycle about the Lamartine family and a small circle of other characters near a Chippewa reservation in North Dakota. When "The Red Convertible" became one part of the larger volume, the characters were now Lyman Lamartine as narrator and Henry Jr. as his older brother. In both cases, however, the central plot concerns Henry's return home from the war after a period in a POW camp, and he is suffering from post-traumatic stress disorder. Lyman desperately tries to find some method to give his brother a purpose to live, but ultimately he fails and Henry drowns himself in the flooded Red River of the North.

Lyman's ironic tone and indirect approach to telling the sequence of events gives the narrative an increment of interest in the gradual discovery of the meaning of what he says. The opening demonstrates his basic method: "I owned that car along with my brother Henry Junior. We owned it together until his boots filled with water on a windy night and he bought out my share. Now Henry owns the whole car, and his younger brother Lyman (that's myself), Lyman walks everywhere he goes." All of these

The American Short Story Handbook, First Edition. James Nagel.
© 2015 James Nagel. Published 2015 by John Wiley & Sons, Ltd.

remarks require clarification, and the events that follow provide it. When he jumped into the river and drowned, Henry's last words before he went under were that his boots were filling. Lyman saw him go down but could not reach him in the swift current of the spring flood. Henry thus purchased Lyman's half-share of the car with his life, since there was no way a loving brother could continue to drive an automobile his dead brother had restored so faithfully. Lyman then drives it into the river, giving the entire car to his brother in the sense that they have both vanished into the same water. Thereafter, Lyman walks out of despondency, tortured by the death of the brother who was his closest friend. He could easily purchase another one because he has a gift for making money, but an automobile would remind him constantly of Henry and what has happened, and he has not yet recovered when the story ends.

Much of Lyman's narration is about himself, how he has a gift for making money, a rare skill among the Chippewa on the reservation, who often live in poverty dependent upon a monthly check from the government. Lyman works in the outside world, however, and he succeeds at a very early age, becoming the manager and owner of a restaurant when he was only sixteen. His older brother, Henry, also succeeds financially before the war, and together they buy a red convertible and drive into Canada, where they pick up a hitchhiker named Susy, who convinces them to take her home to Alaska. There the brothers live in a tent (an Indian dwelling) next to her family house. The family comments that the two boys look so unlike one another, a remark that has little meaning in this individual story but complex resonance in *Love Medicine* where it is clear that neither boy is the child of their putative "father," the senior "Henry," nor are any of the other of the mother's children. Perhaps for that reason, Henry Sr. commits suicide by jumping in front of a train. Henry Jr. is actually his uncle's son; the mother, Lulu Lamartine, is the archetypal girl who cannot say no. All of the children deal with the uncomfortable knowledge of their sexual origin and the fact that they do not resemble one another.

When the boys return home, Henry is reminded that he has enlisted in the army, and he is called to service. Just before he leaves he throws the keys to the car to Lyman, saying that it is his now, a statement that becomes significant later in the action. Lyman here states that the army was so happy to have Henry that they made him a marine, which does not make sense. The Marine Corps grew out of the Navy, not the Army, and in no way could one service elevate a recruit to another branch of the military, something Lyman apparently does not understand. Henry's profile is decidedly Native American, and Lyman says that they used his likeness for the image of the man who killed Sitting Bull, Red Tomahawk, whose image is iconic on road signs in North Dakota. Henry enters the war in 1970 just as the conflict is escalating to its most vicious level, and he is taken prisoner and does not return home for three years.

When he comes back he has changed, the issue for the rest of the story. Henry clearly suffers from posttraumatic stress disorder, a term that did not exist in 1970, and it goes without effective treatment. He has internalized deep psychological pain, and rather than striking out he inflicts punishment on himself, biting through his lip while watching television, for example. Lyman worries that Henry will hurt himself in some way, and he devises a strategy to give him an alternative focus for his pain. Lyman purposely damages the red convertible, and Henry spends some months restoring it to pristine condition just in time for the spring floods. The Red River of the North floods every year because it flows directly northward into lakes and streams that are still covered with ice, so there is no room for the excess water, which then backs up the entire length of the river, flooding vast fields and towns along its path. Henry finishes restoring the car while the river is high but still rising, and once again he informs Lyman that he is giving it to him. He then jumps into the river fully clothed, and just before sinking looks at Lyman and says "my boots are filling." Lyman jumps into the river but is unable to find his brother. In his grief, he runs the car into the river, giving it back to the brother he loves, which is why Lyman now says at the beginning that he walks everywhere he goes.

The story is thus told in retrospect, all of the events having happened before Lyman tells the beginning of it. His narrative is a kind of eulogy for his brother, a lament, a sorting out of what happened. He does not assess responsibility, nor does he suggest ways in which the tragedy could have been avoided. His voice has the tone of cold rationality, although emotion is suggested indirectly. For example, when Henry vanishes under water, and Lyman drives the car into the river, his sense of loss is expressed in terms of the automobile and the flood: "The headlights reach in as they go down, searching, still lighted even after the water swirls over the back end. I wait. The wires short out. It is all finally dark. And then there is only the water, the sound of it going and running and going and running and running." The death of the red convertible is described with poetic misdirection since the true emotion is about Henry's suicide, a sober fact that now has temporal permanency, something "running and running" forever. Lyman cannot reverse it, but it changes him forever, something that is evident in *Love Medicine* but not in the story alone.

Indeed, "The Red Convertible" is thematically and psychologically richer in the content of the other thirteen stories than it is in isolation. For example, in "A Bridge," Henry is shown in Fargo, North Dakota, on his way home from the war, before the action of "The Red Convertible." He meets young Albertine Johnson in the city in 1973, out on her own for the first time, and they have a brief romance, spending the night together in a hotel. She finds him emotionally unstable, violent without cause one moment, and weeping uncontrollably the next. He has been psychologically wounded by the war, by his treatment during imprisonment, and that is the most important fact about him. This emotional construct is what he brings home to Lyman, and it explains his biting through his lip, his preoccupation, and his ultimate suicide. Other stories in the volume reveal that Henry is the product of a tryst between his mother and his uncle, Beverley, on the very day of the funeral for Henry Senior, and Lulu's unbridled sexual craving is clearly evident. Lyman is finally left to tell about the events in "The Red Convertible," and in context it is clear that his telling is a painful attempt to absorb the death of his brother into some kind of meaningful pattern of events making it possible for him to accept what has happened, to get on with his life. In the context of Erdrich's later work, it is clear that he is finally able to do so, for he eventually becomes a wealthy man in the era of casino gambling on the reservation.

Suggestions for Further Reading

Castillo, Susan Pérez. "Postmodernism: Native American Literature and the Real: The Silko-Erdrich Controversy." *Massachusetts Review* 32.2 (1991): 285–94.

Chavkin, Allan Richard. *The Chippewa Landscape of Louise Erdrich*. Tuscaloosa: University of Alabama Press, 1999.

Erdrich, Louise. "The Red Convertible." *Mississippi Valley Review* 11.2 (1982): 10–17.

Hafen, PJane. *Reading Louise Erdrich's Love Medicine*. Boise: Boise State University, 2003.

Nagel, James. *The Contemporary American Short-Story Cycle*. Baton Rouge: Louisiana State University Press, 2001.

Stirrup, David. *Louise Erdrich*. Manchester: Manchester University Press, 2010.

Stookey, Lorena Laura. *Louise Erdrich: A Critical Companion*. Westport: Greenwood Press, 1999.

Wong, Hertha D. Sweet. *Louise Erdrich's Love Medicine: A Casebook*. Oxford: Oxford University Press, 2000.

Susan Minot, "Hiding"

"Hiding," which begins Susan Minot's brilliant short-story cycle *Monkeys*, was first published in 1983 in *Grand Street*. The nine stories in this volume cover several years in the lives of the Vincent family living in a suburb north of Boston. The short narratives are drawn together by the same central characters functioning in a consistent setting and, more importantly, by a coalition of common themes introduced in the opening story: emotional pain, isolation, socioeconomic conflict, religious differences, and a dysfunctional family. "Hiding" is typical of the entire book in that it essentially minimalistic, functioning through suggestion, implication, and subtle dramatic rendering, all of which are presented in the mind of ten-year-old Sophie. In her innocence, she observes more than she understands, and her descriptions of events reveal conflicts and issues much deeper than she can articulate directly.

The story is more about character and emotion than it is about plot, which lends itself to brief summary. On a Sunday morning in winter, Mum dresses her six children and takes them to mass, leaving the father, a protestant, at home. That afternoon, the family goes ice skating at a local rink. When they all return home, Dad goes off on a brief shopping trip, and Mum hides the children in a linen closet, expecting that their father will search frantically for them and they can all leap out in surprise. Instead, he calls out for his family and sits down to watch professional football on television, leaving Mum and the children humiliated by his lack of concern. Within this sequence of events, Sophie, the narrator, alludes to other family experiences, each with a significance to the central family issue, the emotional distance between the parents, something the girl feels deeply.

Inherent in these simple events are implications suggested in this story and further developed in others throughout *Monkeys*. For example, Dad,

The American Short Story Handbook, First Edition. James Nagel.
© 2015 James Nagel. Published 2015 by John Wiley & Sons, Ltd.

a proper Episcopalian from a wealthy family, went to Harvard, as did his father. A family of privilege, they live in a fine home in an upscale neighborhood, the attic filled with memorabilia of African safaris, photographs, and other artifacts of wealth. On the other hand, Mum grew up in the poor Irish neighborhood of South Boston and went to Boston College, a bastion of Catholicism in a city with Puritan origins. Mum and Dad are obviously separated by religion, social class, education, family legacy, and social custom. They have six children because a Catholic wife will not practice birth control. Mum is warm and loving, while her husband is self-absorbed and distant from her and the children, an issue that is a source of conflict and tragedy in the course of the volume.

The personality and insight of the narrator, Sophie, gives the story both innocent charm and dramatic tension, since much is implied in rather simple statements. For example, the first line begins "our father doesn't go to church with us" without further explanation, but through indirection and implication the multifaceted gulf between the parents becomes apparent, here simply the religious differences. Mum singlehandedly prepares the children for mass while Dad stands apart from his family, waiting outside for them to leave. It is Mum who calls the children "monkeys," her loving playfulness evident in everything she does and says. Sophie recalls that during the collection in church Mum will take back change for a five-dollar bill, suggesting her background of limited financial resources. Sophie understands little of the service, reflecting simply that there is a lot of kneeling near the end of mass, a child's view of a solemn proceeding. After the service, Mum picks up lollipops for the children and they drive home.

That juncture in the narrative leads Sophie to intrude with a flashback to how sometimes on weekends the family will go to Castle Hill in Ipswich even in the fall, when everything is closed but the long beach and the outdoor gardens. Sophie recalls that the area has a legend about a maiden who came to a garden to meet her lover, who never arrived. The young woman was distraught with her jilting and jumped off a cliff to her death. This recollection is of enormous significance for the entire volume of stories because Mum, trapped in an unfulfilling marriage, has an affair with a wealthy man who jilts her after fathering her youngest child. Mum sees him with another woman and commits suicide by driving onto a crossing in front of a speeding train. Some of the children maintain it was an accident, but, artistically, the telling of this local legend of a suicide in the opening episode foreshadows the parallel death of Mum in a subsequent story.

Small details mean a great deal in Minot's minimalist fiction. Sophie recounts how playing in the woods the children hid in a pile of leaves and jumped out when their parents walked by, getting leaves and brush on everyone. Dad had a pine needle on his collar, and Mum brushed it off, showing affection and attention. Dad jerked his head, thinking it was an insect, paying no attention to the meaning of the gesture. That incident establishes the paradigm for his relationship with his wife and family. Sophie then tells about an ice skating expedition and how that, too, reveals distance between the parents. A former hockey player, Dad uses his old skates and focuses on speed and power; Mum prefers figure skates and lyrical movement, spinning and swirling gracefully, handling herself like a dancer. Characteristically, Dad does not watch his wife skate, does not see the residual artistry of her flowing form. Later, watching television, the children imitate the singers and dancers they see perform, and Mum does a spirited tap dance right in front of Dad, who keeps his eyes on his book, ignoring the family activity directly before him.

In another incident, Dad brings the children home from an outing and announces he will run back to the grocery store. Sophie wonders why he did not stop there when they went by it a few moments ago. What becomes clear later is that Dad wants to buy liquor secretly, so he always purchases some innocuous item to cover for it. While Dad is gone, Mum organizes a surprise for his return, hiding with the children in a linen closet, ready to jump out when Dad searches for them. The children hold their breath, listening for the return of the car, the sound of Dad coming in, his footsteps as he comes up the stairs to find them. Instead, Dad comes in, pays no attention to their absence, and turns on the television to the Sunday football game. His lack of concern humiliates all of them, and the children are sensitive to the tension between their parents. Sophie pays attention to the hurt her mother feels, the wince on her face as she folds the towels the children have knocked down in the closet. Emotionally alienated from their father, the children focus on Mum, always sensitive to her pain, her longing, her rejection.

"Hiding" is thus not only an important work in its own right but a brilliant introduction of the issues central to the Vincent family in all nine stories in *Monkeys*. The conflicting religions between Mum and Dad are only the surface of a fundamental value struggle based on social class, financial resources, education, family background, and nationality, matters that mean a great deal in traditional Bostonian culture. Even more pertinent is the contrasting emotional construct that separates the warmth and loving nature of Mum and her husband's more stolid demeanor, an issue that resonates throughout a volume that traces her emotional humiliation in the beginning and goes on to portray her desperate search for affection in an affair, her suicide when she discovers even that relationship is based on betrayal, and the final scattering of her ashes at sea. Minot is a master of minimalism not only in style but in subject as well, taking routine family events and infusing them with powerful emotions revealed in the thoughts and conversations of children.

Suggestions for Further Reading

Nagel, James. *The Contemporary American Short-Story Cycle: The Ethnic Resonance of Genre*. Baton Rouge: Louisiana State University Press, 2001, pp. 80–103.

Pryor, Kelli. "The Story of Her Life." *New York* 12 (1989): 52–55.

Thiebaux, Marcelle. "Susan Minot." *Publishers Weekly* 16 (1992): 42–43.

Tyler, Anne. "The Art of Omission." *New Republic* 23 (1986): 34–36.

Wilson, Robley. "Interview with Susan Minot." *Short Story* 2. Spring (1994): 112–18.

Amy Tan, "The Joy Luck Club"

Amy Tan's "The Joy Luck Club" first appeared in the *Ladies Home Journal* in March of 1989. This early version of the text was without several key sections that were added later in preparation for a tightly structured volume under the same title. Inspired by Louise Erdrich's story cycle *Love Medicine* in 1984, Tan designed her book in accord with the conventions of Chinese Mah Jong, which features four players on each side of a small table. Tan thus constructed a book about four families that gather monthly to play the game and share a traditional dinner. Each family is the focal point for four of the stories, two about the mothers, two dealing with the daughters. In general, the mothers all tell of their lives in China, the decision to come to America, the difficulties with assimilation, and their deep desire that their daughters retain the language and customs of their ancient land. The young women all have a rather different agenda, seeking immediate acceptance into American culture and participation in the contemporary life of San Francisco. This generational conflict is one of the elements that unites the sixteen units that comprise the volume, along with the hidden lives the mothers left behind when they came to the United States, their hopes for their daughters, and the conflicting ambitions the families attempt to resolve.

In the version of "The Joy Luck Club" that appears in the book, it is the most complex of the sixteen stories in that it must introduce the characters, establish the situation, and define the conflicts that unify the collection thematically and give it artistic and psychological cohesion. In the narrational logic of the book, the first four stories are to be told by the mothers, which presents a problem because Suyuan Woo, who should be speaking, has been dead for two months when the volume begins. Instead, her daughter Jing-Mei, known as "June," takes her seat at the mah jong table and her

The American Short Story Handbook, First Edition. James Nagel.
© 2015 James Nagel. Published 2015 by John Wiley & Sons, Ltd.

place in the storytelling, a substitution that is psychologically ironic because mother and daughter never understood each other. June feels deeply that she has failed to meet her mother's expectations and is a disappointment even to herself, adrift in the new world, alienated from the old, living without a sense of identity. She finds herself in the emerging account of her mother's earlier life in China, a saga she knew only in fragments but that, in the wake of her death, begins to take shape and explains much about their lives in San Francisco.

Suyuan founded the Joy Luck Club in 1949 and was its most important member. It was at these monthly gatherings that the daughters formed a bond of common experience and the mothers shared their tales of life in China, holding their families together with an awareness of community and ethnic loyalty. They are such close friends that the daughters call the parents of the other girls "auntie" and "uncle," indicating the role of surrogate family that the group has assumed. The same basic issues pertain to all four families: a desire on the part of the mothers to pass on to their daughters a knowledge of their former lives through the tales they tell, an understanding of what life was like in China, a deeper sense of the anguish and loss that led them to come to America. The daughters resist the attempts to tie them to the past even though that history could do much to clarify their own issues in the present. Thus two threads of narrative form this opening story: the mother's tale about her earlier marriage to a Kuomintang officer during the Japanese invasion when she was forced to flee Kweilin pushing her two young daughters in a wheelbarrow. When the wheel broke, and she was totally exhausted, she placed the two girls by the side of the road and left them there, never knowing what became of them. It is a powerful narrative, one June pieces together over a number of years, and it invests her life with the feeling that somewhere in this account of unthinkable loss rests the possibility for comprehension of who her mother truly was, why it was crucial that June succeed in some notable way, and why mother and daughter were never able to understand each other. One of the last things her mother says to her before she dies is "you don't even know little percent of me."

This opening narrative focuses on Suyuan, not on June, so it is the mother's history that predominates and results in two significant journeys for her daughter: a trip back to China to find the two abandoned sisters she has never known, and a psychological journey into herself to integrate this new knowledge of her mother into her sense of self, into her capacity to understand and empathize with the woman she has never really known. The Joy Luck Club plays an important role in all of this for the Jong and Hsu families have both been to China and have found the missing daughters. The club members also contribute the money for June to make the trip along with her father, Canning Woo. Not much is done with the men, the stress being on two generations of women in each case, but Canning proves to be a sensitive and insightful companion for her in the last story in the book, the one in which June and her lost sisters are finally united.

Imbedded in the drama of Suyuan's dramatic tale is another narrative line about June, one that emerges obliquely in what she tells about her mother. June lacks a strong sense of identity and purpose, and she has internalized her mother's view of her as a failure. When Suyuan died, the club did not meet for two months since the next occasion was to be at the Woo home. June apparently feels inadequate to handle even such a simple social event, so she relinquished the hosting duties to Auntie An-Mei Hsu. But she feels a failure in other ways as well: She did not prove to be the prodigy her mother expected; she could not compete with Waverley Jong in chess; she was not a brilliant student, nor a marvel on the piano, nor a great success in any of the jobs she attempted. She is socially awkward, perpetually tardy, and the subject of humor within the club. She remembers her mother saying that her daughter was a "college drop-off" and has failed at everything. However, within the sensitive narrative she weaves together of her mother's life, June reveals her inherent virtues, especially her sensitivity to the needs of others. She is perceptive about the emotional states of the people around her, their desires, their fears, their vulnerabilities. Perhaps most important of all, she realizes that she needs to understand her mother, and she can do so only by fully comprehending the meaning of the story she tells.

Tan strengthened the story when it became the opening episode for the collected cycle, a position giving it a function it lacked when it appeared alone in the magazine. She added substance to Suyuan's reflections on the Kweilin episode of the abandoned daughters, a matter with intriguing biographical significance. Tan's own mother left three children by the roadside, not two, and it was during the Communist Revolution, not the Japanese invasion. Indeed, the Japanese came into China a decade earlier and the timeline would have required extensive revision. Tan simply changed the event but kept the chronology the same, perhaps not wishing to anger the powerful communist regime on the mainland. This complex narrative line comes directly from her mother's experience, however, and it became even more central in the final revision of the story. She also strengthened the background of the founding of the Joy Luck Club, perhaps because those meetings would become the central unifying principle of the entire collection, providing the occasion for all the women to relate the history of their families. When they do so, there is a more negative portrait of the suffering in China than in the original text and a stronger emphasis on the need to be "lucky," the purpose of the club itself. June's final good fortune is revealed in the conclusion of the volume,

"A Pair of Tickets," in which she and her father fly back to China for a union with the missing daughters. June thus meets her older sisters, from whom she learns much. Her mother's name means "long-cherished wish," a reference perhaps to the reunification of the family with the two abandoned girls, a desire fulfilled by June in her mother's place. She also learned the meaning of her own name, "Jing-mei," which translates as "best quality little sister," an indication of her role from her mother's perspective. It is on this trip that June finally hears the full account of the Kweilin event, why the babies were abandoned, how Suyuan longed to find them, how they were adopted by a peasant family, and how her deepest wish was to return to China and embrace them. This is the deepest wish, one that June fulfills, finding not only her lost sisters but herself in the process, the Chinese part of her identity.

Suggestions for Further Reading

Beard, Carla J. *Amy Tan's The Joy Luck Club*. Research and Education Association: Piscataway, 1996.

Braendlin, Bonnie. "Mother/Daughter Dialog(ic)s In, Around, and About Amy Tan's *The Joy Luck Club*." *Private Voices, Public Lives: Women Speak on the Literary Life*. Ed. Nancy Owen Nelson. Denton: University of North Texas Press, 1995, pp. 111–24.

Ho, Wendy Ann. "Swan-Feather Mothers and Coca-Cola Daughters: Teaching Tan's *The Joy Luck Club*." *Teaching American Ethnic Literatures: Nineteen Essays*. Ed. John R. Maitino, and David R. Peck. Albuquerque: University of New Mexico Press, 1996, pp. 327–45.

Huntley, E. D. *Amy Tan: A Critical Companion*. Westport: Greenwood Press, 1998.

Nagel, James. "Generational Identity and Form: Amy Tan's *The Joy Luck Club*." *The Contemporary American Short-Story Cycle: The Ethnic Resonance of Genre*. Baton Rouge: Louisiana State University Press, 2001, pp. 188–222.

Shear, Walter. "Generation Differences and the Diaspora in *The Joy Luck Club*." *Critique* 34.3 (1993): 193–99.

Shen, Gloria. "Born of a Stranger: Mother-Daughter Relationships and Storytelling in Amy Tan's *The Joy Luck Club*." *International Women's Writing: New Landscapes of Identity*. Eds. Anne E. Brown, and Marjanne E. Gooze. Westport: Greenwood Press, 1995, pp. 233–44.

Souris, Stephen. "'Only Two Kinds of Daughters': Inter-Monologue Dialogicity in *The Joy Luck Club*." *MELUS* 19.2 (1994): 99–123.

Tim O'Brien, "Sweetheart of the Song Tra Bong"

The first publication of "Sweetheart of the Song Tra Bong" was in *Esquire* in 1987, three years before it was included in Tim O'Brien's volume of short fiction, *The Things They Carried*. Among the best known of these stories about Americans during the Vietnam War, it has been widely interpreted as a metaphoric account of the corruption of innocence, tracing, as it does, the transformation of a pure young woman into a vicious killer in a matter of a few months. It is also an engaging account of how to tell a war narrative, a subject of interest throughout the book. In this case, however, it is of particular moment because of a persistently unreliable point of view, as a fictional character named Tim O'Brien tells what he heard from Rat Kiley, a medic in his outfit, who observed some of the action and was told the rest by people who had heard about it second hand. The truth is difficult to ascertain since it is deeply imbedded in multiple accounts of doubtful veracity, and yet there seems to be something real in the general theme of Mary Anne's transformation once she arrives in country to be with her boyfriend. Psychological reality in the telling of a war story may be more important than the historical facts, a point O'Brien has made elsewhere in his numerous accounts of the horrors of war.

This issue of the method of telling a story is emphasized from the very beginning as the character Tim O'Brien serves as narrator relating what was told to him. He has personally observed none of the events. Rather, he heard about Mary Anne from Rat Kiley, who was known to exaggerate and overstate things and could not be trusted: "He wanted to heat up the truth, to make it burn so hot that you would feel exactly what he felt." Much of Rat's

The American Short Story Handbook, First Edition. James Nagel.
© 2015 James Nagel. Published 2015 by John Wiley & Sons, Ltd.

narration was heard by O'Brien in the company of Mitchell Sanders, who is skeptical about the truth of it and often interrupts to question various points. This technique of dramatic narration lends a tone of authenticity to extraordinary events because of the uncertainty in Rat's tale and the plausible realism in the method of the relating of it. For example, Rat tells about Mark Fossie's high school sweetheart arriving at a remote base on a helicopter and getting out wearing white culottes and a pink sweater. Mitchell does not buy it. Rat says "no lie … Culottes." At other points, Rat pauses to reflect on what he is saying and Mitchell objects, wanting to get on to the end, and they argue about how stories work. When Mary Anne disappears for a few days, Mitchell guesses she went out with the Green Berets because their small hutch on the edge of the base has to be in the story for a reason. Details have to pull together. Mitchell turns out to be right about that, but he objects to the digressions: "What you have to do, Sanders said, is trust your own story. Get the hell out of the way and let it tell itself." Rat continues commenting on his narration instead of continuing with it. Mitchell says "all these digressions, they just screw up your story's *sound*. Stick to what happened." Rat does so until the ending. Because he was not present to observe any of the final action involving Mary Anne, he can only relate what he heard about it, sometimes third hand.

The narrative line is thus incomplete with gaps in the action and an uncertain conclusion when Mary Anne simply vanishes, an unlikely event that nonetheless is perfect metaphorically: many of the young people who went to Southeast Asia to fight in the war were so transformed that the person who left home was not the one who came back. They, too, vanished in an important sense, losing their innocence, their optimism, their sense of themselves. That conclusion is not predictable from the beginning, however, for when she alights from the helicopter she is American youth personified, innocent, naive, optimistic, and in love. As Rat remembers it, "she had long white legs and blue eyes and a complexion like strawberry ice cream." She and Mark Fossie have planned to be married and live the archetypal middle-class life with three children, a "gingerbread" house near Lake Erie, and a long and idyllic life together. Vietnam takes that dream away from them. She comes to a grisly post, a medical station behind the front that processes freshly wounded grunts, amputating legs and feet blown apart by the mines and booby traps that surround the area. After initial treatment, these men were shipped out to hospitals in Chu Lai or Danang. During the down time the men play volleyball and lounge about smoking and getting drunk. Mary Anne wants to understand it all, see everything, talk to everybody. She becomes fascinated by the Green Berets, who never speak, and who disappear into the jungle for long periods and then slip silently back into their hootch. Their mood is suspicious, their tone dangerous, and they live with death all around them. At first she watches them, their movements, their attitude, starts dressing like them, and finally she goes off on missions with them. It changes her: "There was a new confidence in her voice, a new authority in the way she carried herself." She goes out on ambush with the six greenies, not returning for days, no longer interested in Mark or their dream: "She wore a bush hat and filthy green fatigues; she carried the standard M-16 automatic assault rifle; her face was black with charcoal." Rat tells Fossie that Mary Anne will make a "sweet" bride, "combat ready."

Rat is sensitive to what is happening to Mary Anne, and he comments that "it was nearly three weeks before she returned. But in a sense she never returned. Not entirely, not all of her." She now lives in the hootch with the greenies, where Rat and Eddie Diamond go to search for her one night. They hear what they assume to be her singing coming out of the jungle, a sound "like the noise of nature," and Mark Fossie has heard it too. Inside the hootch there is tribal music playing and in the back they find the decayed head of a leopard beneath decaying strips of skin hanging from the rafters. Against the wall rests a stack of bones and a sign that reads "assemble your own gook!! Free sample kit!!" This is the psychic world Mary Anne has blended into, something confirmed when she arrives wearing a necklace comprised of human tongues. Mark says he cannot let her go like that. Rat's comment is perceptive: "Man, you must be deaf. She's already gone."

At this juncture Rat is transferred to another base, so he is not present for the end of Mary Anne's story. Months later he hears bits and pieces of news from some of the greenies, and all they know is that she disappeared on a mission and never came back. She is out there, somewhere. Rat reflects that the same thing awaited everyone: "You come over clean and you get dirty and then afterward it's never the same." Mary Anne Bell went to Vietnam, became absorbed in the horror of it, the blood and death and danger it posed. She loved the adrenaline, the mystery of it, Rat speculates. He thinks she is still out there somewhere: "She was dangerous. She was ready for the kill." She was what could have happened to countless young American soldiers.

Rat Kiley told all of this to the character Tim O'Brien, who is not to be confused with the author of the same name. As is clear throughout *The Things They Carried*, the fictional O'Brien is distinct from the actual person in several respects. For one thing, the "real" person does not have a daughter. The O'Brien in the book does, and she scolds him for his obsession with writing about the war. That character has not published a book, while the real author can claim *If I Die in a Combat Zone*, a personal memoir of the Vietnam war that covers many of the gritty and horrifying scenes that appear in his stories. It was these experiences that allowed O'Brien to create "Sweetheart of the Song Tra Bong," a powerful, nightmare story of degradation and dehumanization that provides focus on the ethical and psychological reality of America's most disputed military conflict.

Suggestions for Further Reading

Vernon, Alex, and Catherine Calloway, eds. *Approaches to Teaching the Works of Tim O'Brien*. New York: Modern Language Association, 2010.

Baughman, Ronald. "Interview with Tim O'Brien." *Dictionary of Literary Biography Documentary Series*. Ed. Ronald Baughman. Vol. 9. Detroit: Bruccoli-Clark-Layman-Gale, 1991, pp. 204–14.

Coffey, Michael. "Tim O'Brien." *Publisher's Weekly* 237 (1990): 60–61.

Farrell, Susan Elizabeth. *Critical Companion to Tim O'Brien: A Literary Reference to His Life and Work*. New York: Facts on File, 2011.

Heberle, Mark A. *A Trauma Artist: Tim O'Brien and the Fiction of Vietnam*. Iowa City: University of Iowa Press, 2001.

Kaplan, Steven. *Understanding Tim O'Brien*. Columbia: University of South Carolina Press, 1995.

McNerney, Brian C. "Responsibly Inventing History: An Interview with Tim O'Brien." *War, Literature, & the Arts* 6.2 (1994): 1–26.

Nagel, James. "The Nightmare of Resonance: Tim O'Brien's *The Things They Carried*." *The Contemporary American Short-Story Cycle*. Baton Rouge: Louisiana State University Press, 2001, pp. 128–52.

Vernon, Alex. *Soldiers Once and Still: Ernest Hemingway, James Salter, & Tim O'Brien*. Iowa City: University of Iowa Press, 2004.

Jamaica Kincaid, "Columbus in Chains"

Jamaica Kincaid's celebrated "Columbus in Chains" is a difficult story to discuss because it exists as two quite distinct texts, the one that appeared in *The New Yorker* in 1983 and a longer and more political version that was included in *Annie John*, a story-cycle that constitutes a *Bildungsroman* for the titular protagonist. That book traces the growth of a young girl from childhood in Antigua to her final departure from the island in the concluding episode. The emphasis throughout the eight short works is on her loving parents, who care for her every need with extraordinary tenderness, and her rebellion against her mother, her society, and the cultural traditions she was expected to maintain. For the most part, Annie's struggle throughout is a domestic one, as she resists the constraints her adoring parents place on her and embraces friends who are disobedient and defiant, sometimes with regard to childish issues such as playing marbles. In "Columbus in Chains," however, Annie gains a new level of awareness as she first realizes what the journey of Columbus meant to African people, how they were brought to the West Indies as slaves living in a culture dominated by British history and tradition. It is a crucial epiphany for Annie, and it lends an important political and social dimension to her personal saga of growth toward individuality and maturity.

These are the central ideas that Kincaid gave special emphasis in her revision from the magazine text to the one in the volume. As a general matter, she is a stronger character in the book, more rebellious, more aware, more determined. Reading a history of the settling of the islands, she discovers that on one of his missions Columbus was brought back to Spain in chains

The American Short Story Handbook, First Edition. James Nagel.
© 2015 James Nagel. Published 2015 by John Wiley & Sons, Ltd.

for his treatment of the slaves. In the magazine, Annie rather simply remarks that she has always loved the picture of him so constrained. In the book version, however, her comment is more pointed: "How I loved this picture—to see the usually triumphant Columbus, brought so low, seated at the bottom of a boat just watching things go by." Here there is a stronger statement of outrage, more satisfaction in the revenge the picture of Columbus provides, greater pleasure in seeing the great man in the position the slaves occupied during the passage to the West Indies: helpless and totally at the mercy of superior power. As this small change indicates, the general direction of the revisions in the story is from purely family rebellion to her confrontation with the history of her world, the exploitation of her people during slavery and later under British colonialism, and the racial implications of the expeditions of Christopher Columbus.

Although Columbus discovered the islands for the Western world, the Caribbean area was largely a slave colony for Great Britain. Antigua was colonized in 1632 and from that date always had a numerically black population. When England abolished slavery in 1834, the people were given immediate freedom but still educated in British schools teaching European history and swearing allegiance to the English crown. A key experience is when Annie reads *A History of the West Indies* and learns about the voyages of Columbus and the ensuing enslavement of Africans to work on the island. She has been unaware of this background until this moment, and it causes her to think about her classmates, some of whom descend from an English background and others who have slaves in their ancestry. These reflections cause her to feel contempt for Columbus and to write under the picture of him "so the great man can no longer just get up and go." At age twelve, Annie becomes aware of another dimension of her personal conflicts, and her outrage and rebellion become part of her growth as she moves into her teenage years.

Those developmental themes constitute the majority of attention in the story, rather than the more weighty issues of ethnicity and political history. Annie is twelve, and the language, tone, and focus of the narration reflects the mindset of her age. She begins her narrative with an emphasis on childish rebellion and the irony that as the worst behaved child in her class she has been named prefect and is given *Roman Britain* as a prize, underscoring the extent to which Annie's identity is formed by the culture of the United Kingdom. She attends the Anglican Church, for example, studies English history, and pays homage to Queen Victoria on her birthday decades after her death. Her misbehavior is of a charming sort, a preference for Ruth, the dunce in the class, rather than the dutiful and studious Hilarene. But she particularly treasures her friendship with Gwen, with whom she shares walks home. On evenings with a full moon, they lie in the pasture and expose their bosoms to the light hoping that their breasts will grow larger. These kinds of longings for maturity have many manifestations, all of them harmless enough. More significant, however, is her engrossing conflict with her mother. On one occasion, since Annie refuses to eat breadfruit, her mother runs it through a masher to look like rice, and the daughter eats it. When Annie discovers the deception, her view of the betrayal changes her view of her mother: standing in the sunlight, she appears to have "big, shiny, sharp white teeth. It was as if my mother had suddenly turned into a crocodile." Annie's Narcissistic obsession does not allow for even the slightest deviation from constant devotion to her every whim.

Her most important rebellion, however, is not within the domestic realm but with regard to the historical context of her region. While the rest of her history class is focusing on a chapter in the book, she is far ahead on the section covering the third voyage of Columbus, the one on which he was taken prisoner. Annie does not fully integrate this historical scene with her family history, but it is significant. Columbus originally landed in Dominica, which eventually became a French colony, which is where Annie's mother grew up. Although the adventures of the Italian Columbus were financed by the Spanish throne, France came to dominate a section of the Caribbean comprising Guadeloupe, Martinique, as well as Dominica until the island was annexed by the British in 1783. Annie's mother has apparently gone through a rebellion of her own, since she resents the authority of her father, Pa Chess, and when he becomes ill she says, with pleasure, "so the great man can no longer just get up and go," which Annie writes under the picture of Columbus in her textbook. Personal and national issues are thus entwined in Annie's life, and her rebellion in one area is mirrored in her growing quest for independence in another.

Those are the two main issues at the heart of "Columbus in Chains" and the seminal contribution to the sequence of eight stories that comprise *Annie John*. In previous scenes Annie has resented the control her mother's loving protection afforded her, but this time she makes an emotional break from the mother, seeing her as a crocodile. In another dimension, it is here, at age twelve, that Annie first realizes the meaning of the history of her race in the West Indies and its connection to the historic exploits of Christopher Columbus. Race has meant little to her thus far in her life, and her best friends have been white and English. From this point forward she is much more conscious of the ancestral backgrounds of the people around her, and she seems to feel that the sins of one generation descend through the years to rest on the shoulders of another. It is of interest, therefore, that when, at the age of seventeen, Annie flees her parents and her island, intending never to return, never to see her mother and father again, she sails to England, not to Africa, not to another Caribbean island. It is in England that she records her memories of growing up in Antigua, and she writes in English, not in an African language. Her fundamental sense of identity is tied to her British colonial childhood, and she carries these values into adult life. It is this Annie who narrates all of the stories in the book, and she does so in retrospect, an act of reflection that requires that she now synthesize her heritage, emotions, and experience into the person she is still forming, the human being she wishes to become.

Suggestions for Further Reading

Cudjoe, Selwyn R. "Jamaica Kincaid and the Modernist Project: An Interview." *Caribbean Women Writers: Essays from the First International Conference.* Ed. Selwyn R Cudjoe. Wellesley: Calaloux, 1990, pp. 215–32.

Dutton, Wendy. "Merge and Separate: Jamaica Kincaid's Fiction." *World Literature Today* 63.3 (1989): 406–10.

Edwards, Justin D. *Understanding Jamaica Kincaid.* Columbia: South Carolina University Press, 2007.

Ferguson, Moira. *Jamaica Kincaid: Where the Land Meets the Body.* Charlottesville: University Press of Virginia, 1994.

Ismond, Patricia. "Jamaica Kincaid's 'First They Must Be Children'." *World Literature in English* 28.2 (1988): 336–41.

Nagel, James. "Desperate Hopes, Desperate Lives: Depression and Self-Realization in Jamaica Kincaid's *Annie John* and *Lucy*." *Tradition, Voices, and Dreams: The American Novel Since the 1960s.* Ed. Melvin J. Friedman, and Ben Siegel. Newark: University of Delaware Press, 1995, pp. 237–53.

Nagel, James. "Jamaica Kincaid's *Annie John*: Genre and Cultural Duality." *The Contemporary American Short Story Cycle.* Baton Rouge: Louisiana State University Press, 2001, pp. 56–79.

Paravisini-Gebert, Lisabeth. *Jamaica Kincaid: A Critical Companion.* Westport: Greenwood Press, 1999.

Simmons, Diane. *Jamaica Kincaid.* New York: Twayne, 1994.

Snodgrass, Mary Ellen. *Jamaica Kincaid: A Literary Companion.* Jefferson: McFarland, 2008.

Judith Cofer, "Nada"

Judith Cofer has established herself as one of the most productive and impor-
tant Latina writers to emerge the last half of the twentieth century. Her first
short story, "Nada," was highly celebrated when it appeared in *The Georgia
Review* in 1992, and she went on to win an O. Henry award, a Rockefeller
Grant, a Pushcart Prize, and recognition as the Georgia Author of the Year.
"Nada" is based on her personal experience of immigration from Puerto
Rico and living in a tenement in Patterson, New Jersey. An advocate of what
is called "creative non-fiction," which blends elements of true experience
into imaginative situations, she has used her childhood on the island and
life in the United States as a rich source for the portrayal of ethnic identity,
emotional conflict, and deeply personal tragedy. This story blends these elements with consummate skill in showing women living in "El Building" who
respond to the devastating consequences of a woman's loss of a husband and
a son in the course of one year.

Much of the artistic complexity of "Nada" derives from the fact that it is
told by a first-person narrator who is not the protagonist but another Puerto
Rican woman living in the same building. She can present her own knowledge of the events but must also draw on the gossip and speculation that the
other women share during their frequent conversations in "El Basement,"
where they gather to wash clothes and talk about their lives. The initial point
of view is expressed in plural terms, what "we" did not understand, what
Doña Ernestina finally told "us" about the death of her son Tony in Vietnam,
and the passing of her husband a year before. Ernestina spends most of her
time alone in her apartment, however, and most of what can be told concerns the observers and the issues in their lives, their domestic conflicts and
personal aspirations.

The American Short Story Handbook, First Edition. James Nagel.
© 2015 James Nagel. Published 2015 by John Wiley & Sons, Ltd.

For example, the narrator is separated from her husband, who is still tied to his mother's apron strings, although he frequently returns asking for a hot meal and "something more," the sex they celebrated when they were first married. The narrator reflects on how intense their erotic couplings quickly became: "I would walk around thinking: Do not light cigarettes around me. No open flames. Highly combustible materials being transported." But when her husband's mother came on the scene, the tone of their relationship quickly changed. He became ineffectual, and their marriage dissolved.

Other residents are preoccupied with their own concerns. Lydia and Roberto are newlyweds, and they are trying very hard to have a baby, trying so hard that the sound of their exertions reverberates through the walls into the other apartments: "They were just kids who thought they had invented sex." But Roberto has received his draft notice and will soon leave for military service, and Lydia knows that she, too, could receive a dreaded telegram. The priest who comes to console Ernestina is bereft of personality and even normal social skills, and the narrator describes him as "pitiful." In the context of these horrifying events, she reflects on the efficacy of religion in general: "I am not convinced that priests are truly necessary—or even much help—in times of crisis." Religion will not assuage the anguish of Doña Ernestina, and the narrator finds it impossible to take it seriously.

The major concern of the narrator throughout the story is the meaning of what happened to Doña Ernestina when she learned about the death of her son, Tony. Everyone in the building understands that "here was a woman deep into her pain" and that there is little they can do about it, so they decide to give her some "space." It quickly becomes evident that Ernestina is withdrawing, pulling back from everything that has had meaning for her. When the ineffectual priest Padre Alvaro comes to comfort her, she tells him to go away. She returns to the government the medal and flag the military had sent, and she marks the package "*Y a no vive aqui*, does not live here anymore." She begins giving away her most prized possessions, and she works deep into the night preparing to empty her apartment. When she finally invites the other women to visit her, her home has become a temporary shrine to her husband and son, with photographs of both of them surrounded by candles on a table. She announces that in the wake of her loss she has nothing, *nada*, and she forces her prized possessions onto her friends. The narrator prays for her friends that evening, and the following week she follows the sounds that indicate things are being thrown out the window to the street below. The women of the building discuss the implications of what Ernestina is doing: "It is due to the shock of her son's death." They decide to go as a group to visit her only to find her naked body curled up in the corner, empty bottles of pain pills nearby, clearly implying a suicide. The women dress her in their own best clothes to preserve her dignity, and their collective thinking is that "asi es la vida," "that is the way life is."

The narrator has been brought to a profound realization of tragedy and the catastrophic emotional damage possible for even the most innocent and vulnerable of people. A woman who at one point had a rich family life, with a husband, a handsome son, a vibrant household, now has nothing, "Nada." In a sense, this is the important transformation in the story. Ernestina is already dead at the time of the telling of the story, when the narrator can look back on events and select the most meaningful, portraying them in the order in which the women in El Building became aware of them. There is no internal revelation of what Ernestina thought or felt, only a description of what she did. The narrator, on the other hand, can reveal as much as she wishes about herself, her personal feelings, her reaction to what happened. She is circumspect about showing her own feelings, but the sparse language used to express the responses of the women reflects the surface of deep emotion and realizations of what it means to confront "nada."

Suggestions for Further Reading

Acasta-Belén, Edna. "A *MELUS* Interview: Judith Ortiz Cofer." *MELUS* 18.3 (1993): 83–97.

Bruce-Novoa, Juan. "Judith Ortiz Cofer's Rituals of Movement." *The Americas Review* 19. Winter (1991): 88–99.

Chick, Nancy L. "Judith Ortiz Cofer." *The Facts on File Companion to the American Short Story.*, Vol. 1 Ed. Abby H. P. Werlock. New York: Facts on File, 2019, pp. 145–46.

Jago, Carol. *Judith Ortiz Cofer in the Classroom: A Woman in Front of the Sun.* Urbana: National Council of Teachers of English, 2006.

Nagel, James. *Anthology of the American Short Story.* Boston: Houghton, Mifflin, 2008.

López, Lorraine M, and Molly Crumpton Winter, eds. *Rituals of Movement in the Writing of Judith Ortiz Cofer.* Pompano Beach: Caribbean Studies Press, 2012.

A Glossary for the Study of the American Short Story

Allegory A traditional form of literature establishing multiple levels of interpretation. The first level is always literal, as though things are to be taken on face level. On the second level, the characters, places, and events take on symbolic, or abstract, significance. Nathaniel Hawthorne's "Young Goodman Brown," for example, can be read as a simple tale of a young man who journeys into a forest and sees a strange ceremony. On the symbolic level his wife is not simply a woman named "Faith" but is that quality of belief, so that when he leaves home he leaves his religious system behind. "Goodman" is not only a man but stands for all of innocent humanity encountering the potential evil in everyone, and he cannot bring himself to accept that reality and it destroys him. As an abstraction, the old man is the embodiment of evil, the Devil, whose kindly manner and knowledge of the village tempt Goodman to join in the ceremony. Allegories can have multiple symbolic or abstract level meanings.

Anecdote A brief narrative presenting dialogue or an incident, often something that has actually happened. Anecdotes can be used to describe a character trait, or an ironic event, but often they are humorous, unexpected events.

Antagonist Traditionally the person with whom the main character, or protagonist, has a conflict. On occasion the actions of the antagonist have a positive effect in bringing the protagonist to a new realization, but most often there is a simple animosity between the two.

The American Short Story Handbook, First Edition. James Nagel.
© 2015 James Nagel. Published 2015 by John Wiley & Sons, Ltd.

Anthropomorphism The presentation of animals with human traits, such as the ability to speak. Sometimes the animal wears human clothing and lives in a house. A basic trait of the Beastial Fable, which that features anthropomorphic characters.

Apocalyptic fiction Stories that depict the end of the world and the final judgment day. Based on biblical sources. A good deal of American Puritan literature, especially sermons, feature such cataclysmic events.

Authorial intrusion A moment when the author appears to be speaking directly to the reader without the intervention of a narrator. In early stories the conclusion was sometimes a didactic passage in which the author pointed out the moral of the story. Intrusions of this type are extremely rare in Modern stories.

Autobiographical stories Stories based on the author's own life. Often biographers can point to incidents in the writer's life that directly parallel what happens to a character in a story. Some of Ernest Hemingway's early fiction is essentially autobiographical as is Hamlin Garland's "The Return of a Private."

Avant-Garde stories Experimental fiction that deviates from the prevailing mode of writing. In the early twentieth century, those stories that employed stream-of-consciousness narration were considered avant-garde as were William Faulkner's shifts in point of view. Gertrude Stein's use of repetitions in *Three Lives* was considered experimental. Some recent fiction purports to be about itself, fiction about the writing of fiction, and would be considered avant-garde.

Bildungsroman Fiction, most often a novel but sometimes a long story, that depicts the growth of a character to maturity. German term made popular by the fiction of Goethe. Most often used in a story cycle in short fiction, as in the growth of George Willard in Sherwood Anderson's *Winesburg, Ohio*.

Burlesque A comic form of story based on mockery.

Catharsis A concept that derives from Aristotle that holds that one virtue of literature is that it allows the reader, or viewer of a play, to suffer with the character and to find a psychological cleansing from the process. The process depends upon the capacity for "empathy," for feeling that the tragedy involves not just the character but the readers themselves.

Collection of stories A group of stories by the same author. The stories have little relation to one another other than a common writer. Virtually all of the important story writers in America have had their short fiction appear in a collection.

Climax The highpoint of action in a story at which the conflict reaches its most dramatic moment. It can be physical, as in the gunfight at the corral, or psychological, when the protagonist experiences an epiphany, a new realization.

Collection of stories A group of stories by the same author. The stories have little relation to one another other than a common writer. Virtually all of the important story writers in America have had their short fiction appear in a collection.

Conflict Most stories are based on a central conflict that finds resolution in the climax of the action. The conflict can be physical, between two characters, or psychological, as the protagonist decides on a course of action. In ancient literature, conflicts sometimes involved entire civilizations. Contemporary fiction has come to favor struggles within the mind of the main character.

Cycle Ancient form of literature that continues to have an influence on the writers of contemporary stories. A cycle consists of independent stories that gain significance through their relationship with the other short fiction in the same volume. Boccaccio's *The Decameron* and Chaucer's *Canterbury Tales* are examples of the medieval cycle. Amy Tan's *The Joy Luck Club,* Susan Minot's *Monkeys,* and Louise Erdrich's *Love Medicine* are contemporary examples of story cycles.

Denouement French term for the part of the story that follows the climax, often used to tie up loose ends. With the artistic development of the Modern story, the use of denouement went out of favor, and many elements are left hanging, unexplained, at the end.

Dialect The representation of the speech of a character, most often one from a particular region or ethnic group. The dialect of a character can be used to denote social class, national background, or educational level, among other traits. The presentation of dialect was crucial for writers in the Local Color tradition.

Dialogue The representation of a conversation between two or more characters. Much can be revealed about the values of the characters from what they say or, in more subtle fiction, from what they leave unsaid. Ernest Hemingway was a master of the meaningful pause or the unspoken crucial point of a scene, so his fiction needs to be read closely. Some early stories of the eighteenth century were entirely dialogues.

Didactic story A work of short fiction that is designed to teach a moral lesson. In the Bible, the parables are essentially didactic. Early American stories often ended with a direct statement of the point. Only the most simplistic Modern stories are regarded as being didactic. However, many stories are instructive in more subtle ways, by making the reader aware of the feelings of a character or the significance of a common event, a young person leaving home, for example.

Diegesis The speech and actions of characters as described by the narrator. Scholars who emphasize this theoretical point stress their awareness that the narrative point of view filters and shapes the meaning of events.

Doppelgänger A secondary character who seems to be the psychological double of the protagonist, often paving the way for changes within him. Joseph Conrad's "The Secret Sharer" contains such a situation as does, in a more mysterious form, Henry James' "The Jolly Corner." Robert Louis Stevenson's pairing of Dr. Jekyll and Mr. Hyde is another such instance.

Epic In most cases an epic is a very long novel written in elevated language and featuring a protagonist whose fate is tied to that of a nation or culture. Homer's *Odyssey* is a classic example and Leo Tolstoy's *War and Peace* a more recent one. Very few short stories could properly be called an epic.

Epilogue An afterword or concluding statement at the end of a novel or story that ties up loose ends or continues the action after the climax. William Faulkner provided an epilogue to *The Sound and the Fury* to account for the characters after the formal novel had ended. Epilogues are rare in short stories.

Epiphany A sudden instant of insight in which the protagonist has a new awareness that changes the course of the plot. Normally an epiphany will serve as the climax to a psychological story or novel. In William Faulkner's "Barn Burning," Sarty Snopes has an epiphany in which he realizes that his father intends to burn the barn of Major De Spain.

Epistolary story A short story that is in part or whole composed of a letter or a series of such epistles. Some early stories were entirely a letter. By the late nineteenth century, stories often contained a letter that was crucial for the plot. Theodore Dreiser's "The Second Choice" has a key letter that causes the protagonist to realize that she has been sexually manipulated and that her lover has rejected her. Some novels are entirely made up of letters, hence the term "epistolary novel."

Exposition Explanatory comments made by the narrator, often establishing the scene at the beginning of a story. The descriptive function of exposition differs from the role of narrative, which describes action, and dialogue, which records speech.

Fable A short narrative featuring anthropomorphic animals as characters, fables were most often used in didactic tales to teach a moral lesson.

Sometimes these are called the "Beastial Fable." The Greek writer Aesop brought together a volume of early fables that have had influence for more than two thousand years. Chaucer's "The Nun's Priest's Tale" is a famous medieval fable.

First-person narration   Fiction told by narrators who make reference to themselves, as in "As I turned the corner I could see the crowd gathering in front of the bank." In many such cases the first-person narrator will also serve as the protagonist. Occasionally, writers will use first-person plural to show how things looked to a family or entire community, as in William Faulkner's "A Rose for Emily."

Flashback   The temporal movement back to prior action that helps explain the motivation of the scene in the present. Sometimes the narrator summarizes such a scene, but most often the flashback is presented dramatically with both action and dialogue.

Flat character   A character who does not change or grow in the course of the story. Most often a secondary figure, sometimes the antagonist.

Foreshadowing   A predictive event or comment that precedes some notable development later in the story. In general, major events do not happen in fiction without some kind of earlier hint of what is possible, especially with tragic action. In drama the understanding is that if a shotgun is on stage in Act 1, it must go off before the end of Act 3. In serious fiction, no major action occurs without foreshadowing.

Frame story   Sometimes called an "envelope story," a frame narrative contains a beginning and an ending involving a certain situation and internal sections that describe action in another location with other characters. Stephen Crane's "The Clan of No-Name" is such a story. The frame device gives a definite structure to the design of the story.

Gothic story   A narrative normally set in an ancient location such as a castle or mansion with action that is mysterious and suggests the supernatural. Edgar Allan Poe's "The Fall of the House of Usher" is regarded as the prime example in American fiction.

Grotesque   A term made popular by Sherwood Anderson, a "grotesque" character is one that is physically or psychologically deformed, often driven by an obsession. The American Naturalists, especially Frank Norris, used the concept for some of the protagonists of their stories.

Image   A sensory picture created by a word or passage describing an external scene. Most images are visual but they may be auditory or even tactile. Imagery can be used to draw the reader into the fiction, creating the feeling of actual participation in the scene. Joseph Conrad advocated such a methodology, and it was used brilliantly by Stephen Crane and Ernest Hemingway.

Impressionism   The description of reality as perceived in an instant of sensory experience, what the painters called a "vistazo." It is an "objective" form in that it begins with the external reality and records the character's, or the narrator's, sensation provoked by it. In "Expressionism," the subjective images begin internally and description is used to express an emotional state. Impressionism records an encounter with reality; Expressionism need not obey the laws of physics.

In medias res   A story that begins "in the middle" of the action or scene, as in the first line "At that, George turned around and looked at Emily." No explanation is given of the previous action that caused George to turn about. Sometimes the narrator will present a flashback later in the story that helps explain the meaning of the opening scene.

Intentional fallacy   The attempt to judge the worth of a work of literature based on how well it fulfilled the intentions of the author. Since New Criticism, the assumption has been that a reader's assessment of the intentions of the author is at best a guess and is not a reliable basis for interpretation. Blatantly polemical fiction often seems to present an obvious indication of intention, but even then it is sometimes the opposite meaning that is the intention, as in Jonathan Swift's "A Modest Proposal" or in some of Ring Lardner's short stories.

Interior monologue   A method of narration that records the thoughts of the protagonist but nonetheless presents a coherent plot. Stream of consciousness often includes random or fleeting thoughts. An interior monologue normally reveals a coherent plot, as in Katherine Anne Porter's "The Jilting of Granny Weatherall."

Irony   Normally implies distance, a discrepancy between what is said and what is meant, as when a character says "Yeah, he is a great guy" about someone he hates. Irony of action deals with the difference between what is expected and what actually happens, as when the bucket of water falls on the head of the person who put it over the door rather than on the intended victim. Some of the best dialogue contains ironic comments that need to be read carefully to be understood.

Legend   A traditional narrative, told in verse or prose, about real people and events in the past. The stories have become more heroic, more dramatic, more notable than when first recounted, and that enlargement has made them all the more enjoyable, as in the many legends of Daniel Boone and Davy Crockett.

Local Colorism Primarily a mode of fiction, although a few poets contributed to the movement, Local Color stories captured the characters, language, customs, and regional issues of a particular setting in the United States. Of special interest is the use of the vernacular, the everyday language of common folk, for the purposes of literary art. These stories were extremely popular from 1865 till to the turn of the century.

Minimalism A movement of the early twentieth century, largely in fiction, that stripped language down to a spare, unobtrusive style with direct description and an emphasis on action and speech. The style grew out of the poetic movement of Imagism and was championed by Ernest Hemingway in the 1920s. Since then, Raymond Carver and Susan Minot have used the technique for remarkable fiction.

Modernism An American movement generally thought to have begun at the end of World War I and ending sometime after World War II, perhaps as late as 1961, when Joseph Heller's *Catch-22* appeared. The Modernists experimented with narrative methods such as stream of consciousness and with fragmentation in plot and action, but their frank presentation of the psychological states of the characters, especially those recovering from the war, shocked the reading public of the day. William Faulkner's narrative methods reflected the achievements of experimentation in point of view as well as subject.

Multiple narrators A method of telling the story through different narrators, often characters in the action. The use of "parallax" suggests that reality appears to change when viewed from different perspectives. Another implication of the method is that reality is difficult to ascertain, and people see things from their own point of view. The result is that if several characters observe an event, they will all describe it differently. The play *Rashoman* demonstrated the principle brilliantly.

Myth A story that has the function of explaining the origin of a people, the cause of natural phenomenon, or the heroic exploits of national leaders. Myths often exceed what is realistically possible, sometimes involving supernatural entities, but they often unite a culture in a system of shared belief.

Narration The description of events and conversations that constitute the story itself, that is, the "telling" of the story, whether from an all-knowing perspective, the omniscient method, in first person, or from multiple points of view. All of these strategies can present the description of the action that comprises the narration.

Naturalism A mode of fiction, popular from 1890 to 1940 in America, that dealt with the downtrodden caught in a hopeless situation. The central mood of Naturalism is pessimistic determinism, the concept that the lives of the characters are driven by forces beyond their control, and therefore they are not responsible for what happens to them. Among the great Naturalistic novels are *The Grapes of Wrath, Native Son,* and *An American Tragedy.*

Novel A long work of fiction that shows a character, or a group of characters, involved in a conflict that is normally resolved by the conclusion. There is greater development of secondary characters in the novel than in the story, and the greater length allows for the construction of subplots in which action takes place over a length of time. Stories usually focus on the development of a single character involved in one central issue.

Novella A French form of long short story containing more episodes and subplots than are common in the story. There is room for multiple characters to be developed and for more than one conflict to be resolved. Two of the great novellas in American literature are Herman Melville's "Benito Cereno" and William Faulkner's "The Bear."

Omniscient narrator The god-like voice that knows everything and can thus relate all aspects of a story, including events in the past and in the future, and the thinking of multiple characters. Common in Romantic and Naturalistic stories; rare in Modernism and Contemporary fiction.

Parable An ancient form of narrative, the parable is a didactic story meant to teach a moral lesson, as in the numerous parables in the scripture. Often directed at children, the parable entertains as well as instructs. Early American fiction sometimes offered parables about civic virtues.

Personification The use of abstract qualities as characters in fiction, as in the portrayal of Faith in Hawthorne's "Young Goodman Brown." Often used to set human virtues (Faith, Constancy, Prudence) against the temptations of weakness (Sloth, Greed, Lust). Early fiction often used the device, but only stories for children employ them in modern times.

Picaresque novel A narrative form that features a rascal as protagonist (a picaro) who normally goes on an episodic journey, as in *Don Quixote.* Mark Twain's *Adventures of Huckleberry Finn* is a picaresque novel. The techniques of the picaresque are not often employed in the short story.

Plot The arrangement of the events of a story, most often centered on a conflict. In a story with a tight plot, everything that happens is related to that key problem, and the conclusion is its final resolution. A loose plot might contain digressive episodes.

Point of view The narrative method of the story, the vantage point from which things are observed and described for the reader. A first-person point of view would simply relate a series of personal events, as in "after I left the party I drove Susan home, stopping for pizza at the Hitchin Post." An omniscient perspective could reveal the thoughts of many characters in the story as well as events in the past and the future: "As they ate their pizza they did not know that the son they would have four years later would one day own the Hitchin Post."

Protagonist The main character in a story, usually presented in a positive manner. In earlier periods the protagonist was sometimes called the "hero" of the story, but the inception of Modern fiction introduced the concept of the antihero, an unlikeable character with few desirable traits who nonetheless is the central figure. The conflict of the protagonist often involves an "antagonist," the subject of the struggle at the center of the plot.

Realism A movement in literature thought to have begun at the end of the Civil War in 1865. Its tendencies were to portray ordinary characters in everyday situations who spoke in the vernacular, the language of common folk. The plots did not involve outlandish quests for eternal Truth but more mundane issues of personal growth, making wise ethical choices, treating other people fairly. Realism involves plausible characters and actions and seems true to life. The assumption is that people are free moral entities, able to make their own decisions, and are thus responsible for what they do, unlike the characters in Naturalism.

Round characters Characters who are capable of change and growth in response to events and conversations. Normally the central character is "round," the secondary ones "flat," unable to alter their basic nature. Most stories about adolescents show round characters in the process of forming themselves.

Setting The location of the action, usually described by the narrator. Settings often carry values far beyond the physical topography. A religious story set in Puritan New England would have a very different social climate than the one in liberal New York. A story about race set in the deep South would have values quite distinct from those in the Midwest. Setting was a crucial element in Local Color fiction and became important in Realism as well.

Story As defined by Edgar Allan Poe, among other writers, a story is a short narrative that can be read at one sitting. It features a central character who encounters some form of conflict, which could be physical, moral, or psychological, and the resolution of the struggle provides the plot. Stories normally do not develop important subplots or secondary characters.

Stream of consciousness   A method of narrating a story that records the thoughts of a character unmediated by a narrative intelligence. As a result, these thoughts might be random and disorganized, might include dream elements, and could be fanciful or dramatic. Conrad Aiken's celebrated story "Silent Snow, Secret Snow" is a demonstration of the technique, as is the last section of Ambrose Bierce's "An Occurrence at Owl Creek Bridge."

Symbol   An object in fiction that has a significance associated with it that has been established by an entire culture over an extended period of time. Symbols tend to be static and change very slowly, unlike metaphors, which can be given a new significance in each story. The Cross is a religious symbol for Christians of the sacrifice of Christ, and it would be difficult to cause it to have a meaning distinct from that value. Every research library will have dictionaries of symbols showing what values are historically associated with each symbol.

Tale   A story of adventure, usually one that stretches the truth, as in the "tall tale." In American literature, tales were immensely popular as part of the oral tradition and folk literature in the mid-nineteenth century. Mark Twain was known for his tales, with an emphasis on the manner of telling, and his were often fanciful accounts of adventures hunting in the wild woods or mining for gold. Normally a tale will have an unbelievable plot and a protagonist of exaggerated strength or athletic agility, as in the tales of Mike Fink.

Theme   The main values or ideas at the center of the story. The subject of a story might be war, for example, but the theme could be heroism in war, the mindless destruction of war, or the psychological damage war can bring to the human mind. Subjects can thus have many possible themes. Normally all of the elements of a well-crafted story will contribute in some way to the enriching of the theme.

Unreliable narrator   A teller of a story who cannot be believed totally. The narrator may be concealing some unpleasant fact, exaggerating the nature of events, or guessing about what happened, but the reader has cause to doubt that the narrator can be trusted. A good deal of Modern and Contemporary fiction employs an unreliable narrator.

Yarn   Normally a narrative, derived from the oral tradition, that stretches credulity. The manner of telling implies that the teller is seated in a room speaking to a group gathered about listening to the story, and sometimes there are intrusions as the audience members ask questions. Yarns are usually entertaining, often humorous, and are told in the dialect of a specific region of the country. Basically a nineteenth-century form.

Selected Books for Further Study of the American Short Story

Allen, Walter. *The Short Story in English*. Oxford: Clarendon, 1981.

Ammons, Elizabeth. *Conflicting Stories: American Women Writers at the Turn into the Twentieth Century*. Oxford: New York, 1991.

Aycock, Wendell M. *The Teller and the Tale: Aspects of the Short Story*. Lubbock: Texas Tech University Press, 1982.

Bendixen, Alfred, and James Nagel, eds. *A Companion to The American Short Story*. Oxford: Wiley-Blackwell, 2010.

Bone, Robert. *Down Home: Origin of the Afro-American Short Story*. New York: Columbia University Press, 1988.

Bonheim, Helmut. *The Narrative Modes: Techniques of the Short Story*. Cambridge: Cambridge University Press, 1982.

Brown, Julie, ed. *Ethnicity and the American Short Story*. New York: Garland, 1997.

Canby, Henry S. *The Short Story in English*. New York: Holt, 1932.

Coltelli, Laura. *Winged Words: American Indian Writers Speak*. Lincoln: University of Nebraska Press, 1990.

Crow, Charles L. *The Regional Literatures of America*. Oxford: Blackwell Publishing, 2003.

Crowley, Donald. *The American Short Story, 1850-1900*. Boston: Twayne, 1982.

Curnutt, Kirk. *Wise Economies: Brevity and Storytelling in American Short Stories*. Moscow: University of Idaho Press, 1997.

Current-Garcia, Eugene. *The American Short Story Before 1850*. Boston: Twayne, 1985.

Engler, Bernd, and Oliver Scheiding, eds. *Re-envisioning the Past: Historical Self-Reflexivity in American Short Fiction*. Trier: Wissenschaftlicher Verlag, 1998.

Foster, David William. *Studies in the Contemporary Spanish-American Short Story*. Columbia: University of Missouri Press, 1979.

Fusco, Richard. *Maupassant and the American Short Story*. University Park: Pennsylvania State University Press, 1994.

Gelfant, Blanche H, ed. *The Columbia Companion to the Twentieth-Century American Short Story*. New York: Columbia University Press, 2000.

Gerlach, John. *Toward the End: Closure and Structure in the American Short Story*. Tuscaloosa: University of Alabama Press, 1985.

Herrera-Sobek, Maria, and Helena Maria Viramontes, eds. *Chicana Creativity & Criticism: New Frontiers in American Literature*. Albuquerque: University of New Mexico Press, 1996.

Ingram, Forrest L. *Representative Short Story Cycles of the Twentieth Century*. The Hague: Mouton, 1971.

Kennedy, J. Gerald. *Modern American Short Story Sequences: Composite Fictions and Fictive Communities*. Cambridge: Cambridge University Press, 1995.

Kim, Elaine. *Asian American Literature: An Introduction to the Writings and Their Social Context*. Philadelphia: Temple University Press, 1982.

Levy, Andrew. *The Culture and Commerce of the American Short Story*. Cambridge: Cambridge University Press, 1993.

Lohafer, Susan. *Coming to Terms with the Short Story*. Baton Rouge: Louisiana State University Press, 1983.

Lohafer, Susan, and Jo Ellyn Clarey, eds. *Short Story Theory at a Crossroads*. Baton Rouge: Louisiana State University Press, 1989.

Lubbers, Klaus. *Typologie der Short Story*. Darmstadt: Wissenschaftliche Büchgesellschaft, 1977.

Lundén, Rolf. *The United Stories of America: Studies in the Short Story Composite*. Amsterdam: Rodopi, 1999.

Mann, Susan Garland. *The Short Story Cycle: A Genre Companion and Reference Guide*. Westport: Greenwood, 1989.

Matthews, Brander. *The Philosophy of the Short Story*. New York: Longmans, 1901.

Nagel, James. *Anthology of the American Short Story*. Boston: Houghton Mifflin, 2008.

Nagel, James. *Race and Culture in New Orleans Stories: Kate Chopin, Grace King, Alice Dunbar-Nelson, George Washington Cable*. Tuscalosa: University of Alabama Press, 2014.

Nagel, James. *The Contemporary American Short-Story Cycle: The Ethnic Resonance of Genre*. Baton Rouge: Louisiana State University Press, 2001.

O'Brien, Edward J. *The Advance of the American Short Story*. New York: Dodd, 1931.

O'Connor, Frank. *The Lonely Voice: A Study of the Short Story*. Cleveland: World, 1963.

Pattee, Fred Lewis. *A History of American Literature Since 1870*. New York: Century, 1915.

Pattee, Fred Lewis. *The Development of the American Short Story: An Historical Survey*. New York: Harper, 1923.

Peden, William. *The American Short Story: Front Line in the National Defense of Literature*. Boston: Houghton Mifflin, 1964.

Reynolds, Margaret, ed. *The Penguin Book of Lesbian Short Stories*. New York: Penguin, 1994.

Rhode, Robert D. *Setting in the American Short Story of Local Color: 1865-1900*. The Hague: Mouton, 1975.

Sollors, Werner, ed. *Multilingual America: Transnationalism, Ethnicity, and the Languages of American Literature*. New York: New York University Press, 1998.

Stevick, Philip, ed. *The American Short Story, 1900-1945*. Boston: Twayne, 1984.

Voss, Arthur. *The American Short Story: A Critical Survey*. Norman: University of Oklahoma Press, 1973.

Walker, Warren S. *Twentieth-Century Short Story Explication, 1900-1975*. 3rd ed. Hamden: Shoe String, 1977.

Ward, Alfred C. *Aspects of the Modern Short Story: English and American*. London: University of London Press, 1924.

Weaver, Gordon, ed. *The American Short Story, 1945-1980: A Critical History*. Boston: Twayne, 1983.

Weixlmann, Joe. *American Short-Fiction Criticism and Scholarship, 1959-1977*. Chicago: Swallow, 1982.

West, Ray B. *The Short Story in America: 1900-1955*. Chicago: Regnery, 1952.

Winther, Per, Jakob Lothe, and Hans H Skei, eds. *The Art of Brevity: Excursions in Short Fiction Theory and Analysis*. Columbia: University of South Carolina Press, 2005.

Wright, Austin. *The American Short Story in the Twenties*. Chicago: University of Chicago Press, 1961.

Yin, Xiao-huang. *Chinese American Literature Since the 1850s*. Carbondale: Southern Illinois University Press, 2000.

Zyla, Wolodymyr T, and Wendell M Aycock, eds. *Ethnic Literature Since 1776: The Many Voices of America*. Lubbock: Texas Tech University Press, 1978.

Index